# LEISURE AND TOURISM

## Intermediate GNVQ

# LEISURE AND TOURISM

## Intermediate GNVQ
## Updated edition

Katherine Kemp
Stephen Pearson
Sandra Nichol

*An imprint of* **Pearson Education**

Harlow, England · London · New York · Reading, Massachusetts · San Francisco · Toronto · Don Mills, Ontario · Sydney
Tokyo · Singapore · Hong Kong · Seoul · Taipei · Cape Town · Madrid · Mexico City · Amsterdam · Munich · Paris · Milan

**Pearson Education Limited**
Edinburgh Gate, Harlow
Essex CM20 2JE, England
*and Associated Companies throughout the world*

First published 1997
Updated edition 2000

**British Library Cataloguing in Publication Data**
A catalogue entry for this title is available from the British Library

ISBN 0-582-38162-2

Set by 30 in Palatino 10/12 and Helvetica
Printed in Great Britain by Henry Ling Ltd,
at the Dorset Press, Dorchester, Dorset

# Contents

## Unit 4 Contributing to the running of an event

# Acknowledgements

We would especially like to thank the following organisations and people for the support and advice they have provided while we have been researching the information for this book:

Manchester Evening News Arena, Manchester (**David Davies**, Executive Director) Cottons Hotel, Knutsford (**Jason Carruthers**, Manager) Vale Royal Borough Council (**Andrea Peattie**, Tourism Officer) Eureka!, Halifax (**Peter Clinker**, Operations Director) Causeway College (**Lowell Courtenay**) Forest Enterprise at Delamere Forest Park, Youth Hostel Association, North West Tourist Board, English Tourism Council, BAA plc, Civil Aviation Authority.

The following people may be contacted for further information and advice on educational visits and resources for use in teaching GNVQ Leisure and Tourism:

| | |
|---|---|
| **Sarah Hotter** | Education Officer, Salt Museum, Northwich 01606 41331 |
| **Theresa Chiltern** | Education Officer, Jodrell Bank, Macclesfield 01477 571339 |
| **Christine Chadwick** | Education Officer, Quarry Bank Mill, Styal 01625 527468 |

Finally, thanks to our long-suffering families, Margaret, Stuart, Rachel, Les, Sarah and Lindsay, for their support and understanding while we have been writing this book.

*Katherine Kemp*
*Stephen Pearson*
*Sandra Nichol*

The authors and publishers are grateful to the following organisations for permission to reproduce copyright material:

North West Tourist Board for our Fig. 1.2; Manchester United Football Club for our Figs 1.9 & 3.33; the Forestry Commission for our Figs 1.19 & 1.22 (© Crown copyright. Published with the permission of the Controller of Her Majesty's Stationery Office. The views expressed are those of the authors and do not necessarily reflect the views or policy of the Forestry Commission or any other government department.); Chester City Council for our Fig. 1.13 (brochure designed and produced by Shawn Stipling); GMPTE for our Fig. 1.15; Shire Inns Ltd for our Figs 1.16, 1.17, 1.18, 1.37, 1.38 & 1.39; Goodwood Travel Ltd for our Fig. 1.29; Bolton College of Further Education for our Fig. 1.56; Cheshire County Council Museums Service for our Fig. 2.6; Birmingham International Airport Ltd for our Fig. 3.38; McDonald's Restaurants Ltd for our Fig. 3.39.

While every effort has been made to trace the owners of copyright material, in some cases this has proved impossible and we take this opportunity to offer our apologies to any copyright holders whose rights we have unwittingly infringed.

# Unit 1

# INVESTIGATING LEISURE AND TOURISM

**Investigate the leisure and recreation industry nationally and locally**

**Investigate the travel and tourism industry nationally and locally**

**Prepare for employment in the leisure and tourism industries**

The purpose of this unit is to help develop your awareness and understanding of what is generally considered to be the leisure and tourism industry. The business of leisure and tourism can generally be subdivided into two interrelated parts:

- The **leisure and recreation** industry.
- The **travel and tourism** industry.

Leisure and tourism is the world's fastest growing industry and is one of the UK's biggest employers. It is important that students are aware of the importance of the industry in order to prepare themselves for the wide range of employment opportunities which it offers.

# What is leisure and recreation?

Leisure time is the free time we have left over after working, sleeping, eating and carrying out domestic duties. This is the time when we have the freedom to enjoy quality leisure time.

During free time we may take part in a range of recreational activities such as walking, playing football or watching television.

In the UK there has been a steady increase in the amount of individual leisure time over the past forty years. The growth in leisure time and the increasing participation in recreational activities is due to:

- A reduction in the average working week.
- Rising disposable incomes – this is the amount of money left after your wages have been used to pay for basic necessities such as food, heating, clothing and rent.
- People living longer – life expectancy has increased as medical standards and standards of living have risen.
- Technological developments in the home mean that people (especially women) now spend less time carrying out domestic chores.

# Investigate the leisure and recreation industry nationally and locally

A common misunderstanding is that the leisure and recreation industry is limited to leisure centres and sports stadia. It is a very complex and diverse industry. To help with our understanding of what the industry comprises and the activities they offer, and to appreciate its breadth, we can divide leisure and recreation into a number of 'component areas' or headings (Fig. 1.1).

The boundaries between each of the component areas are not always distinct and you will find that some leisure and recreation facilities will overlap across several component areas.

For example, a motorway service station will offer **catering and accommodation services** for motorists and their families with **play** areas for children and **entertainment** in the form of video games.

Leisure centres provide facilities for **sport and physical recreation** and may at the same time offer **catering** facilities in the form of cafés or licensed bars. If we include leisure centres which have climbing walls we may also be considering **outdoor pursuit** activities within a setting which would normally be considered to be purely a provider of **sports and physical activities**.

Figure 1.2 shows the covers of the North West Tourist Board's Guide to the North West

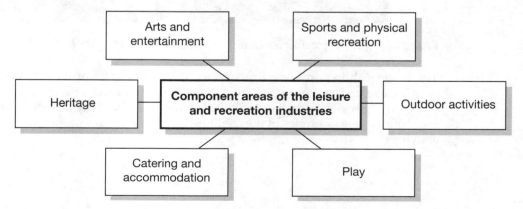

**Fig. 1.1** *The components areas of the leisure and recreation industries*

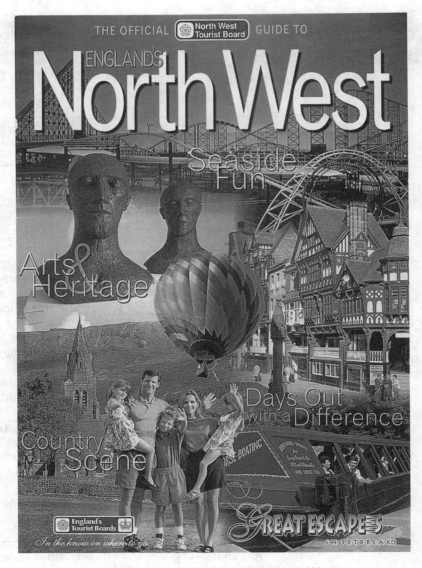

***Fig. 1.2*** *North West Tourist Board's* Guide to the North West

The images shown in these brochures reflects the range of recreational activities which make up the component areas of the leisure and recreation industry.

We will now define each of the component areas under the six headings shown in Fig. 1.1 and give examples of the facilities, locations and venues which provide these activities.

# Arts and entertainment

Included within the arts and entertainment component area will be:

| Type of facility/venue | Examples of facilities/venues |
| --- | --- |
| Art galleries | Tate Gallery, Liverpool |
| Ballet and opera | Covent Garden Opera House |
| Concert halls and venues (classical/rock/contemporary) | Royal Albert Hall, London |
| | Roundhay Park, Leeds |
| | Milton Keynes Bowl |
| Libraries | National Library, London |
| Discos and nightclubs | Cream, Liverpool |
| | Stringfellows, London |
| Amusement and theme parks | Blackpool Pleasure Beach |
| | Alton Towers |
| | Camelot, Preston |
| Television | Satellite and cable TV has dramatically increased the range and choice of programmes available to viewers |

# Sports and physical recreation

People can take part in sport either as a participant (player) or as a spectator.

Sports and physical recreation includes sports such as football, cricket and tennis which generally take place at specially constructed venues which may be indoor or outdoor.

| Type of facility/venue | Examples of facilities/venues |
| --- | --- |
| Leisure centres | Many leisure centres are locally based facilities, however the Sports Council operate national centres of excellence for specific sports |
| National centres of excellence | Lilleshall, Shropshire – football, cricket, gymnastics |
| | Bisham Abbey, Bucks – tennis, hockey, rugby |
| | Plas y Brenin, Gwynedd – mountain activities |

| Type of facility/venue | Examples of facilities/venues |
|---|---|
| National centres of excellence | Holme Pierrepoint, Nottingham – water sports<br>Crystal Palace, London – swimming, athletics |

The Sports Council for Scotland, Wales and Northern Ireland also have their own National Sports Centres.

The following list gives examples of some well known sporting venues.

| Type of facility/venue | Examples of facilities/venues |
|---|---|
| Athletics tracks | Crystal Palace, London<br>Gateshead Stadium<br>Cosford International Arena |
| Golf courses | Wentworth, Surrey<br>St Andrews, Scotland |
| Motor racing circuits | Oulton Park, Cheshire<br>Donnington Park, Leicestershire |
| Cycle tracks | Manchester Velodrome |
| Football grounds/stadia | Villa Park, Birmingham<br>Riverside Stadium, Middlesbrough<br>Pittodrie, Aberdeen |
| Cricket grounds | Lords<br>The Oval<br>New Road, Worcester |
| Tennis | The All England Tennis Club, Wimbledon<br>Queens Club, London |

# Heritage

These facilities may range from ancient monuments to stately homes or the display of artefacts in museums.

| Type of facility/venue | Examples of facilities/venues |
|---|---|
| Ancient monuments | Stonehenge, Wiltshire<br>Hadrian's Wall |
| Stately homes | Blenheim Palace<br>Chatsworth Hall, Derbyshire |

| Type of facility/venue | Examples of facilities/venues |
|---|---|
| Religious buildings | Westminster Abbey<br>Canterbury Cathedral |
| Buildings associated with famous characters | Anne Hathaway's Cottage, Stratford upon Avon<br>Dove Cottage, Grasmere (where William Wordsworth lived) |
| Museums | Natural History Museum, London<br>Museum of Science and Industry, Manchester |
| Industrial heritage | Wigan Pier<br>Ironbridge Gorge, Shropshire |
| Military relics/sites | HMS Victory, Portsmouth<br>Bovington Tank Museum, Dorset<br>Battlefield of Culloden, Scotland<br>Imperial War Museum, London |

Heritage is one of the fastest growing sectors of the leisure and recreation industry. This is reflected in Table 1.1 which lists the number of visitors to attractions paying admission and shows that heritage attractions are amongst the most popular visitor attractions in the UK.

**Table 1.1 Top twenty attractions charging admission – the importance of attractions with a heritage theme**

| Rank | Attraction | 1997 visits | 1998 visits |
|---|---|---|---|
| 1 | Alton Towers, Staffordshire | 2,701,945 | 2,782,000 |
| 2 | Madame Tussaud's, London | 2,798,801 | 2,772,500 |
| 3 | Tower of London | 2,615,170 | 2,551,459 |
| 4 | Natural History Museum, London | 1,793,400 | 1,904,539 |
| 5 | Chessington World of Adventures | 1,750,000 | 1,650,000 |
| 6 | Legoland, Windsor | 1,414,621 | 1,646,296 |
| 7 | Science Museum, London | 1,537,151 | 1,599,817 |
| 8 | Canterbury Cathedral | 1,613,000 | 1,500,000 |
| 9 | Windsor Castle, Berkshire | 1,129,629 | 1,495,465 |
| 10 | Edinburgh Castle | 1,238,140 | 1,219,055 |
| 11 | Victoria and Albert Museum, London | 1,040,750 | 1,110,000 |
| 12 | Flamingo Land Theme Park, North Yorkshire | 1,103,000 | 1,105,000 |
| 13 | St Paul's Cathedral, London | 964,737 | 1,095,299 |
| 14 | Windermere Lake Cruises, Cumbria | 1,131,932 | 1,060,600 |
| 15 | London Zoo | 1,097,637 | 1,053,000 |
| 16 | Drayton Manor Park, Staffordshire | 1,002,100 | 1,003,802 |
| 17 | Kew Gardens, London | 937,017 | 1,000,000 |
| 18 | Chester Zoo | 829,800 | 920,000 |
| 19 | Royal Academy, London | 858,854 | 912,714 |
| 20 | Roman Baths and Pump Room, Bath | 933,489 | 905,426 |

*Adapted from:* English Tourist Board Statistics Digest

# Outdoor activities

These tend to take place in the natural environment and may involve physical or mental challenge. Although many of these activities take place in the countryside/open air rather than within a traditional sport venue there are centres which are devoted purely to the provision of such activities.

| Type of facility/venue | Examples of facilities/venues | |
| --- | --- | --- |
| | **Man-made venues** | **Natural venues** |
| **Land-based activities** | | |
| Skiing | Rossendale Ski | Aviemore |
| | Snowdome, Tamworth | Fort William |
| Climbing | Keswick Climbing Wall | Lake District |
| | Plas y Brenin | Snowdonia |
| Hiking/orienteering | Tollymore Outdoor Centre, N Ireland | Chilterns |
| | | Cairngorms |
| Pony trekking | National bridleways | Nationwide activity |
| **Air-based activities** | | |
| Gliding | North Wales Gliding Club | |
| Hang gliding | | Peak District National Park |
| | | Yorkshire Dales |
| **Water-based activities** | | |
| Water skiing | Trafford Water Park | Lakes, e.g. Lake Windermere |
| | | Sea, e.g. North Wales coast |
| Wind surfing | Marine Lake, West Kirby | Menai Straits, Anglesey |
| Sailing | Kielder Water, Northumberland | Cowes, Isle of Wight |

# Play

Play includes facilities and schemes which encourage children to play and will include parks, playgrounds, play schemes and play groups. Most play facilities are provided on a local basis to suit the needs of the community. Parks will include facilities such as play areas, sports pitches, tennis courts, planted areas and open spaces.

| Type of facility/venue | Examples of facilities/venues |
|---|---|
| Parks | Hyde Park, London |
| | Trentham Gardens, Stoke on Trent |
| | Lyme Park, near Stockport |
| Playgroups | Tumbletots – a national organisation with locally based groups |
| Play schemes | Locally organised – usually by the local council within the area |
| Summer camps/adventure | Camp Beaumont |
| Holidays for children | PGL Holidays |

# Catering and accommodation

This component area covers a wide range of facilities from bed and breakfast guest houses to five-star luxury hotels, from fast food outlets to gourmet restaurants.

| Component area | Examples of facilities/venues |
|---|---|
| International-standard hotels | Savoy, Ritz and Hilton – London |
| | Piccadilly, Ramada – Manchester |

A large percentage of hotels are owned by multinational chains and it is not uncommon to see a Hilton hotel in London, Manchester or Huddersfield.

| Component area | Examples of facilities/venues |
|---|---|
| Motor lodges | Forte Motorlodge – such as Haydock, Merseyside Wrexham, Clwyd |
| Fast food outlets | McDonalds    Wimpy |
| | Burger King    Harry Ramsdens |
| Ethnic restaurants | Indian    Italian |
| | Thai    Cantonese |
| | Chinese    French |
| | Mexican |
| Gourmet restaurants | Langans Brasserie |
| | The Waterside – Michel Roux |
| | La Garolle – Albert Roux |
| | Quatre Saisons – Raymond Blanc |
| Hostels | Youth Hostel Association (YHA) |
| | YMCA |

## Activity

**'Describe the main components of the leisure and recreation industry'**

The examples which we have given are national facilities and show the breadth of the industry.

1. Construct a table similar to the one shown above and complete it using other examples of national facilities.

2. Write a brief description of each of the component areas.

3. Working in pairs, present your findings to the rest of the group. Try to be imaginative in your presentation. For example, use a range of visual aids rather than reading out lists of facilities – this can be very tedious for the listener!

Word process your findings for tasks 1 and 2.

**Key skills satisfied:** *Communication* **2.2**
*Information Technology* **2.3**

---

Compare the characteristics of the public, private and voluntary sectors

---

The leisure and recreation industry can be broken down into three main economic sectors:

● Public Sector
● Private Sector
● Voluntary Sector

This classification is based upon the ways the various organisations are funded and managed.

# Public sector

Public sector facilities are those which are organised, managed and funded largely by national or local government. On a local scale, local county and borough councils provide a range of leisure services which will include leisure centres, museums, libraries, civic halls, community centres and parks and gardens.

Public sector facilities are staffed by paid employees and their main objective is to provide a service to the community.

The public sector has recently had a change of emphasis so that it now works towards principles which might be considered as private sector such as profit making. Facilities now have to be more cost conscious than they might have been previously.

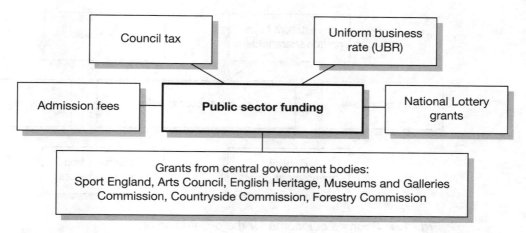

**Fig. 1.3** *Sources of income for the public sector*

Examples of public sector leisure and recreation facilities which are of national significance include:

- Crystal Palace Athletics Stadium.
- Museum of Science and Industry, Manchester.
- National Parks, e.g. the Lake District.

## Funding in the public sector

Local authority leisure facilities receive much of their funding from local taxation (council tax) and through grants from central government bodies such as Sport England and the Arts Council. The range of sources of funding and income is shown in Fig. 1.3.

# Private sector

Facilities in the private sector exist to provide a service to the public whilst at the same time generating a financial profit for their owners or shareholders. Such facilities are staffed by paid employees.

Private sector facilities are very conscious of their position in the market place and will work hard to be seen as the market leader.

Examples of private sector leisure and recreation facilities of national importance include:

- David Lloyd Tennis Centres
- Waterworld, Hanley (part of Rank Leisure)
- Thorpe Park, Surrey

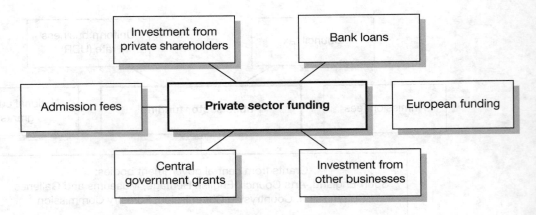

**Fig. 1.4** *Sources of income for the private sector*

## Funding in the private sector

Most of the funding requirements of private sector organisations will be met by other large businesses and lending organisations such as the banks who have large amounts of capital (money) to invest. Private individuals may also wish to invest in order to obtain a financial return. An investor will only make a profit on the investment if the facility performs well. It is also possible for private sector facilities to apply for grants from central government and they may also bid for funding from the European Union (EU) if they can prove that the project will benefit the community, i.e. create jobs (see Fig. 1.4).

# Voluntary sector

Voluntary sector organisations exist to provide a service which may not otherwise be provided by the public or private sectors.

The voluntary sector depends very heavily on the work of unpaid volunteers but does use paid employees to run the headquarters and branches of national voluntary bodies such as the National Trust and the Youth Hostel Association.

Examples of voluntary sector leisure and recreation facilities and organisations of national significance include:

- National Trust Properties, e.g. Tatton Park, Cheshire
- Youth Hostel Association (YHA)
- Environmental groups, e.g. Royal Society for the Protection of Birds (RSPB)
- Ramblers Association

# Funding in the voluntary sector

Funds are usually generated via a variety of sources including membership sub-scriptions, donations, government grants, fund raising activities, trust funds and the sale of souvenirs and refreshments. Voluntary bodies usually have charitable status. Sometimes private sector organisations will sponsor the activities of voluntary organisations (see Fig. 1.5).

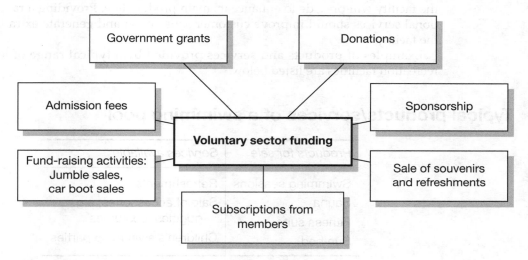

**Fig. 1.5** *Sources of income for the voluntary sector*

## Activity

**'Compare the characteristics of public, private and voluntary sectors'**

Choose three leisure and recreation facilities, one from each of the economic sectors. Write a report in which you make comparisons between the three sectors on the following basis:

1. Methods of funding.

2. The staff structure – is the facility staffed by paid employees, part-time staff or unpaid volunteers?

3. The organisational structure – e.g. is the facility a branch of a large organisation, where is the head office?

Your report should be word processed.

When preparing this report you will find it useful to refer to the three case studies: Cottons Leisure Club, Delamere Forest and the Youth Hostel Association.

**Key skills satisfied:** *Communication* **2.1b**, **2.2**
*Information Technology* **2.3**

A leisure and recreation product or service can be defined as the saleable product or service to customers which is provided by a venue.

A product is the main function of the facility. Services are the extra features which the facility will provide to enhance its main product line. Providing a range of additional services should improve customer satisfaction and generate extra income for the facility.

Examples of products and services provided by a typical range of leisure and recreation facilities are listed below.

## Typical products/services of a swimming pool

| Products for sale | Services available |
|---|---|
| Swimming sessions | Refreshments |
| Sauna | Sale of accessories, e.g. goggles, costumes |
| Fitness suite | |
| Sun bed | Children's swimming parties |

## Typical products/services of a theme park

| Products for sale | Services available |
|---|---|
| White knuckle rides | Sale of refreshments and souvenirs |
| Amusements | |
| | Car parking |

## Activity

Complete the following table with examples of the products and services which can be obtained for each of the component areas. The facilities which you choose should be of national importance.

| Component area | Name of facility | Products for sale | Services available |
|---|---|---|---|
| Arts and entertainment | | | |
| Sports participation | | | |
| Sports spectating | | | |
| Outdoor activities | | | |
| Heritage sites | | | |
| Play schemes | | | |
| Catering | | | |
| Accommodation | | | |

Give examples of leisure and recreation facilities of *national significance*

A facility of national significance can be regarded as one which is known to the general public and is used and visited by visitors from all over the UK.

A facility acquires national significance if it is unique or different in some way. Uniqueness could be measured in the following ways:

- Natural landscape features
- Unique facilities in terms of size
- Historical/cultural significance

# Natural landscape features

The natural landscape may be unique in a number of ways. For example, National Parks, such as Snowdonia or Dartmoor, are countryside areas which are designated by the Countryside Commission as areas of outstanding scenic beauty and also for their recreational opportunities. Figure 1.6 shows the National Parks of England and Wales.

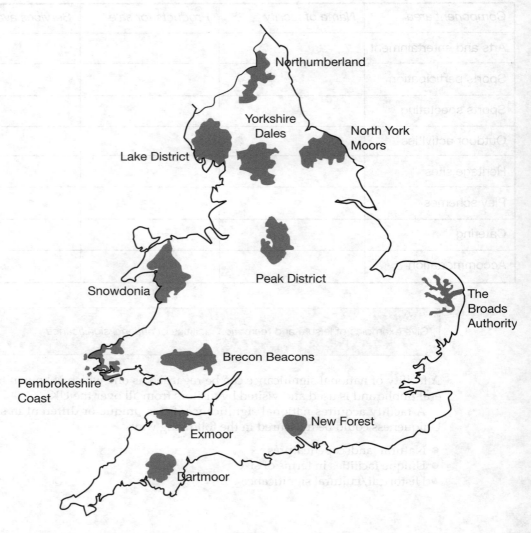

**Fig. 1.6** *The National Parks of England and Wales*

There also exists a number of unusual geomorphological features which visitors are prepared to travel long distances to see. Cheddar Gorge in Somerset and Malham Cove in Yorkshire fall into this category.

# Unique facilities in terms of size

Size can be considered in a number of ways:

# Level of event

We can define the geographical scale of an event by determining whether it is of local, regional, national or international importance.

| Local | An event which would only attract people who live in the local area<br><br>*Example*: A local swimming gala |
|---|---|
| Regional | An event which would attract people from within a region such as the south east of England or North Wales<br><br>*Example*: A county show such as the Cheshire Show |
| National | An event which would attract people from throughout the country<br><br>*Example*: The Glastonbury Music Festival in Somerset |
| International | An event which attracts visitors from several countries<br><br>*Example*: The Eisteddfod Music Festival which is held at Llangollen in North Wales every year |

# Level of attendance

Facilities or events of national significance will attract a much higher level of visitors than local or regional events. For example, the Euro 96 football tournament attracted hundreds of thousands of British and overseas visitors to football stadia throughout England (see Fig. 1.7).

# Physical size of a facility

Facilities can also be considered to be unique in terms of their size. For example, the Manchester Evening News (Nynex) Arena in Manchester can seat up to 19,500 people for pop concerts attracting top artists and sporting events such as the Manchester Storm Ice Hockey team (see Fig. 1.8).

**Fig. 1.7** *Euro 96 logo*

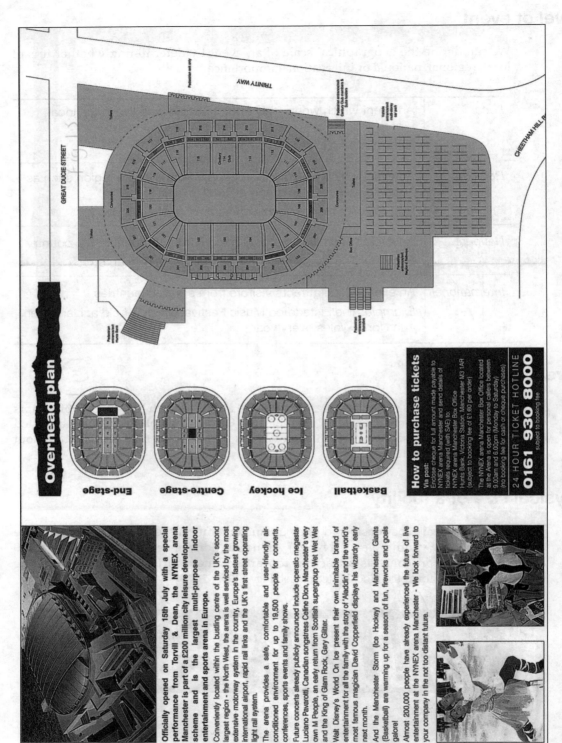

**Overhead plan**

GREAT DUCIE STREET

TRINITY WAY

CHEETHAM HILL R...

**End-stage**

**Centre-stage**

**Ice hockey**

**Basketball**

Officially opened on Saturday 15th July with a special performance from Torvill & Dean, the NYNEX arena Manchester is part of a £200 million city leisure development scheme and is the largest multi-purpose indoor entertainment and sports arena in Europe.

Conveniently located within the bustling centre of the UK's second largest region - the North West, the arena is well serviced by the most extensive motorway system in the country, Europe's fastest growing international airport, rapid rail links and the UK's first street operating light rail system.

The arena provides a safe, comfortable and user-friendly air-conditioned environment for up to 19,500 people for concerts, conferences, sports events and family shows.

Future concerts already publicly announced include operatic megastar Luciano Pavarotti, Canadian songstress Celine Dion, Manchester's very own M People, an early return from Scottish supergroup Wet Wet Wet and the King of Glam Rock, Gary Glitter.

Walt Disney's World On Ice present their own inimitable brand of entertainment for all the family with the story of 'Aladdin' and the world's most famous magician David Copperfield displays his wizardry early next month.

And the Manchester Storm (Ice Hockey) and Manchester Giants (Basketball) are warming up for a season of fun, fireworks and goals galore!

Almost 200,000 people have already experienced the future of live entertainment at the NYNEX arena Manchester - We look forward to your company in the not too distant future.

**How to purchase tickets**

Via post:
Enclose cheque for full amount made payable to NYNEX arena Manchester and send details of tickets required (with SAE) to:
NYNEX arena Manchester Box Office
Hunts Bank, Victoria Station, Manchester M3 1AR
(subject to booking fee of £1.60 per order)

The NYNEX arena Manchester Box Office located at the Arena is open for personal callers between 9.00am and 6.00pm (Monday to Saturday) (no booking fee for cash or cheque purchases)

24 HOUR TICKET HOTLINE
**0161 930 8000**
subject to booking fee

**Fig. 1.8** *Manchester Evening News (Nynex) Arena, Manchester*

Another unique facility in terms of size is Old Trafford, the home of Manchester United FC. Old Trafford is England's largest football stadium after Wembley and can accommodate up to 55,300 spectators (see Fig. 1.9).

## Historical/cultural significance

Throughout the UK there are a number of sites and relics which have a unique significance for the history of the country. They may mark the site of an historic battle, e.g. the Battle of Culloden, or the former residence of an interesting historical figure, e.g. Hampton Court and King Henry VIII.

The culture of a country or a region is the way of life. This may be represented by the homes in which people lived or the festivals and events which were unique to that area. Examples of this include the Edinburgh Festival.

## Activity

**'Give four examples of leisure and recreation facilities of national significance'**

Choose two facilities or venues of national significance for each of the following categories:

1. Unique in terms of natural landscape.

2. Unique in terms of size.

3. Unique in terms of historical/cultural significance.

Write a brief report describing the facilities, why they are significant and the products and services which are available there.

**Key skills satisfied:** *Communication* **2.3**

> Describe leisure and recreation *facilities*, *products* and *services* available in a locality and give *reasons for their location*

**Fig. 1.9** *Manchester United Football Club logo*

The provision of leisure and recreation facilities and their location is based on a combination of factors (see Fig. 1.10).

Leisure and recreation facilities are unevenly distributed and the location of any one facility is a result of a combination of these factors. It is possible to generalise about the reasons for the location of leisure and recreation facilities with reference to a theoretical model such as that described by David Waugh (*Geography – An Integrated Approach*, 1994).

By referring to the model shown in Fig. 1.11 it can be seen that certain facilities tend to be located in different parts of the urban–rural area.

# Factors which will affect the location of leisure and recreation facilities

## Accessibility

Accessibility can be measured either by physical distance or by the time which it takes to reach the facility. The more accessible a facility is, the higher the number of visitors it will attract. A city or town centre location is usually more accessible to large numbers of people.

## Availability of land

When building a leisure or recreation facility the availability and suitability of the land on which it is built must be taken into consideration. Depending upon the size of the facility there must be sufficient space, allowing for car parking and future expansion plans and the land must be flat making it suitable for building on. Land is usually more expensive in the centre of a town or city and therefore facilities which

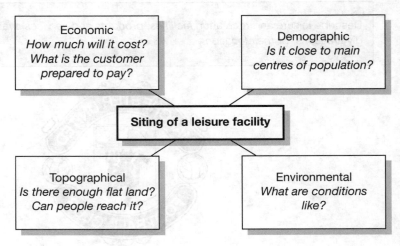

*Fig. 1.10* Factors influencing the site of a leisure facility

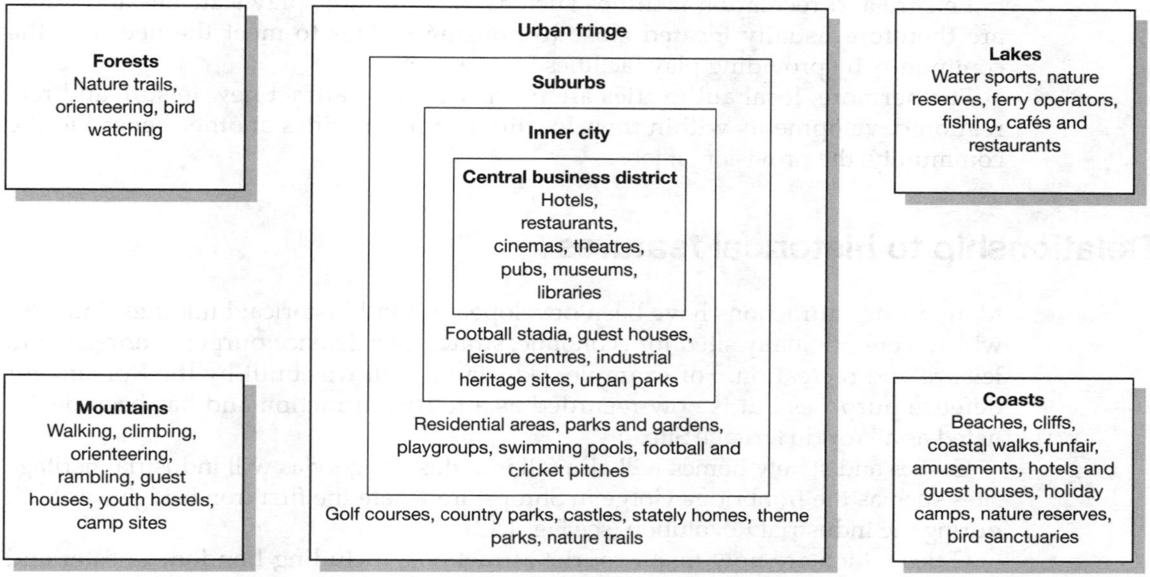

**Forests**
Nature trails, orienteering, bird watching

**Urban fringe**

**Suburbs**

**Inner city**

**Central business district**
Hotels, restaurants, cinemas, theatres, pubs, museums, libraries

Football stadia, guest houses, leisure centres, industrial heritage sites, urban parks

Residential areas, parks and gardens, playgroups, swimming pools, football and cricket pitches

Golf courses, country parks, castles, stately homes, theme parks, nature trails

**Lakes**
Water sports, nature reserves, ferry operators, fishing, cafés and restaurants

**Mountains**
Walking, climbing, orienteering, rambling, guest houses, youth hostels, camp sites

**Coasts**
Beaches, cliffs, coastal walks, funfair, amusements, hotels and guest houses, holiday camps, nature reserves, bird sanctuaries

**Fig. 1.11** *Distribution of leisure and recreation facilities*

require a large amount of space, such as football stadia, tend to be located on the outskirts of urban areas as do parks and gardens.

## Relationship to natural features

Some leisure and recreation facilities will be dependent upon natural landscape features. For example, outdoor activity centres tend to be located in the countryside areas such as national parks where there are rivers for activities such as canoeing and hills for rambling, orienteering and climbing. The natural features may also be an attraction in themselves for sightseers.

An example of a feature which occurs naturally is the Giant's Causeway in County Antrim, which is one of Northern Ireland's most popular visitor attractions.

## Proximity to population centres

The majority of facilities for leisure and recreation will be located close to the major centres of population such as the urban areas surrounding London, Manchester, Cardiff, Glasgow and Leeds where the demand for provision of facilities and accessibility is at its maximum.

## Meeting the needs of the community

Local authorities provide leisure centres close to the main centres of population to encourage the community to participate in sport at a price which is affordable to most people.

Leisure and recreation facilities such as playgrounds, play schemes and parks are therefore usually located close to housing estates to meet the needs of the community by providing play facilities for the young.

Furthermore, local authorities are usually keen to attract new leisure and recreation developments within their locality as this provides another benefit to the community; the provision of jobs.

## Relationship to historical features

Many visitor attractions have been developed around historical buildings and sites which were originally sited for economic, strategic or defence purposes unrelated to leisure and recreation. For example, Hadrian's Wall was built by the Romans for defence purposes but is now regarded as a tourist attraction and has been designated as a World Heritage Site.

Castles and stately homes will also fall into this category as will industrial heritage sites such as the Ironbridge Gorge in Shropshire where the first iron bridge was built during the Industrial Revolution (see Fig. 1.12).

Cities which are now major tourist attractions, including London, Chester and York, were originally sited for economic or strategic reasons. Their economic importance still exists today but from this has grown a massive tourist trade. For example, the Romans chose Chester as one of their main bases in England and for its strategic importance in their battles against the Welsh armies. It is the extensive Roman remains which is one of the main tourist attractions (Fig. 1.13) of Chester.

**CASE STUDY**

## Leisure and recreation facilities in Manchester and its surrounding areas

By referring to the example of the city of Manchester we can try to explain the distribution of some of the leisure and recreation products which can be found there (see Fig. 1.14).

*Zone A: Central Business District (CBD)*

| Facility | Example | Reasons for location |
|---|---|---|
| Fast food outlets | McDonalds Pizzaland | *Accessibility* – City centres have highly developed transport infrastructures which enable large numbers of people to reach them, e.g. the Manchester Metrolink provides a fast, frequent service from the suburbs into the heart of the city |
| Restaurants, pubs and theatres | Sam's Chop House Opera House Royal Exchange | |
| Concert halls | Free Trade Hall | |
| Exhibition centres | G-Mex Nynex | *Land availability* – Land is at its most expensive in the city centre |

| Facility | Example | Reasons for location |
|----------|---------|----------------------|
| Hotels<br>Museums | Piccadilly<br>Museum of Science and Industry | and therefore developments tend not to be on such a large scale as can be found in the inner city areas where many facilities also have car parks attached |

## Zone B: Inner City

| Facility | Example | Reasons for location |
|----------|---------|----------------------|
| Sports stadia<br>Retail parks<br>Parks/gardens<br>Swimming pools<br>Athletics tracks | Old Trafford<br>White City<br>Heaton Park<br><br>Belle Vue | *Land availability* – Land is slightly cheaper on the outskirts of the CBD and therefore more extensive projects are more likely to be sited here; customer car parks are often sited adjacent to the facility |

## Zone C: Suburbs

| Facility | Example | Reasons for location |
|----------|---------|----------------------|
| Water activity centres<br>Residential areas<br>Larger playing fields | Trafford Water Park | *Land availability* – Water parks such as this take up large amounts of land and are therefore located on the outskirts of urban areas<br>*Meeting community needs* – Housing estates with high numbers of children are usually located in the suburbs where there is a higher demand for play facilities |

## Zone D: Urban fringe

| Facility | Example | Reasons for location |
|----------|---------|----------------------|
| Golf courses<br><br>Country parks<br>Open air museums | Mere Golf and Country Club<br>Styal Country Park<br>Quarry Bank Mill | *Availability of land*<br>*Relationship to historical features* – Living museums are sometimes created around sites of former industrial importance |

**Fig. 1.12**  *The Iron Bridge Gorge Museum, Shropshire*

**Fig. 1.13** *The Grosvenor Museum, Chester*

*Zone E: Rural areas*

| Facility | Example | Reasons for location |
|---|---|---|
| National parks<br><br>Dry ski slopes<br><br>Forests | Peak District<br><br>Ski Rossendale | *Land availability* – Facilities which occupy large areas of land are usually located here where land is generally less expensive and more readily available<br><br>*Natural features* – Countryside areas of natural scenic beauty are usually located in Zone E<br><br>*Accessibility* – Facilities located in this zone will be less accessible to non-car owners |

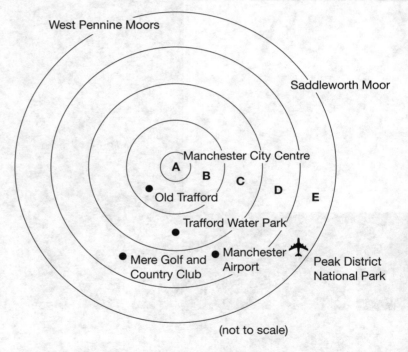

A – **Central business district (CBD)** contains major shops and restaurants and is the entertainment centre.

B – **Inner city** containing retail parks and sport stadia.

C – **Suburbs** – the main residential areas often contain larger recreational areas such as playing fields.

D – **Urban fringe** containing recreational facilities which require larger amounts of physical space such as golf courses, airports.

E – **Rural areas** with large areas of open space, e.g. the Peak District and moorland areas.

**Fig. 1.14** *Distribution of leisure facilities in Manchester and the surrounding area*

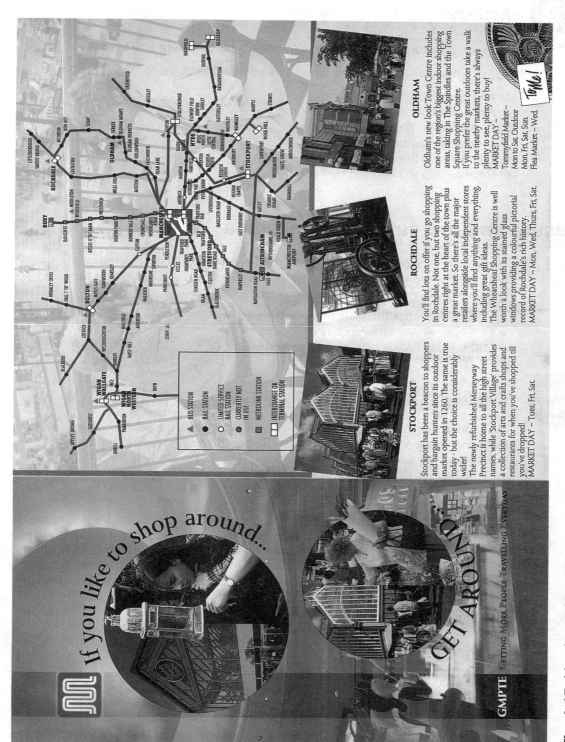

**If you like to shop around...**

**STOCKPORT**

Stockport has been a beacon to shoppers and bargain hunters since its outdoor market opened in 1260. The same is true today - but the choice is considerably wider!

The newly refurbished Merseyway Precinct is home to all the high street names, while 'Stockport Village' provides a collection of arts and crafts shops and restaurants for when you've shopped till you've dropped!

MARKET DAY – Tues, Fri, Sat.

**ROCHDALE**

You'll find lots on offer if you go shopping in Rochdale. Not one, but two shopping centres right at the heart of the town plus a great market. So there's all the major retailers alongside local independent stores where you'll find anything and everything, including great gift ideas.

The Wheatsheaf Shopping Centre is well worth a look with its stained glass windows providing a colourful pictorial record of Rochdale's rich history.

MARKET DAY – Mon, Wed, Thurs, Fri, Sat.

**OLDHAM**

Oldham's new look Town Centre includes one of the region's biggest indoor shopping areas, taking in The Spindles and the Town Square Shopping Centre.

If you prefer the great outdoors take a walk to the nearby markets, there's always plenty to see, plenty to buy!

MARKET DAY –
Tommyfield Market –
Mon to Sat Outdoor
Mon, Fri, Sat, Sun.
Flea Market – Wed.

**To Me!**

**GMPTE** GETTING MORE PEOPLE TRAVELLING EVERYDAY

**GET AROUND**

- ▲ BUS STATION
- ● RAIL STATION
- ○ LIMITED SERVICE RAIL STATION
- ● CURRENTLY NOT IN USE
- ▣ METROLINK STATION
- ▢ INTERCHANGE OR TERMINAL STATION

**Fig. 1.15** Manchester Metrolink

## Activity

**'Choose a leisure facility which is located near to where you live'**

Try to explain why it is located where it is by referring to the following factors:

1. Accessibility.
2. Availability of land.
3. Closeness to population centres.
4. Meeting community needs.
5. Relationship to natural features.
6. Relationship to historical features.

# Leisure and recreation case studies

Through a variety of case studies we will compare the characteristics of facilities from each of the three economic sectors and describe the range of products and services which they offer.

- Cottons Leisure Club (Private Sector)
- Delamere Forest Enterprise (Public Sector)
- Youth Hostel Association (Voluntary Sector)

## Cottons Leisure Club (private sector)

Many private sector organisations are diversifying their range of products and services by providing services in both the Leisure/Recreation and Travel/Tourism industries. The example which we will use for the purpose of this case study is the Cottons Leisure Club, Knutsford, Cheshire (Fig. 1.16). The Cottons Hotel, part of the Shire Inns Group.

*Reasons for location*
Shire Inns Ltd is a nationwide hotel chain which stretches from Carlisle to Southampton. The company specialises in quality hotels providing a high standard of service for business and family use. Shire Inns hotels are located on out of town sites in semi-rural areas or business parks where there is room for expansion and where there are good communication links to the main centres of business and commerce.

The number of bedrooms in each hotel ranges from 51 to 109. There is a range of facilities for the business client including:

- Conference rooms.
- Ample car parking.
- Office facilities.

**Staff structure**

The staff structure at the Cottons Hotel is shown in Fig. 1.17. All of the employees are paid workers.

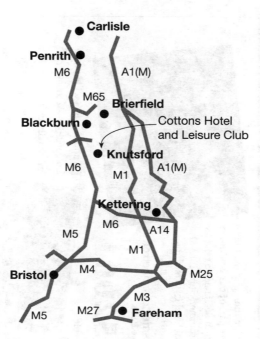

**Fig. 1.16** *Nationwide locations of Shire Inns*

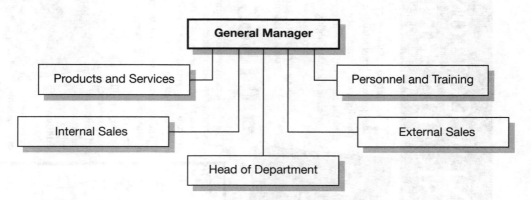

**Fig. 1.17** *Staff structure at the Cottons Hotel*

### The Cottons Leisure Complex

This privately run facility contains a range of sporting and fitness facilities for the business person and families. Each of the Shire Inns hotels, with the exception of the Millstone in Blackburn, has a similar facility.

*Products and services*
The facilities provided at the Cottons can be seen in Fig. 1.18 and include:

- 13 m swimming pool.
- Whirlpool.

**Investigate the leisure and recreation industry nationally and locally 29**

# THE NEW COTTONS LEISURE CLUB, PHYSICALLY BETTER ~ FOR YOU.

The Cottons Hotel opened in 1984, building at the time a premier hotel leisure facility. As part of our continued development, a brand new leisure club designed to take us into the next century will open this summer. Shire Inns also operate six other highly successful hotel leisure clubs throughout the country.

CALL SARAH STAFFORD, MEMBERSHIP CO-ORDINATOR FOR AN INFORMATION PACK

☎ 01565 652001

The club is designed to create an enjoyable atmosphere with professional staff on hand to supervise and provide advice to help you achieve a healthy and enjoyable lifestyle.

Flexible memberships are designed to suit your personal needs. Monthly or full year payment, full time or off peak rates. Paying for additional facilities as you use them eg squash, tennis, classes or sunbed.

In addition to a wide range of facilities we consider a full activity programme, from subsidised social events to fitness challenges and charity events, vital in creating a fun club atmosphere.

All ages are welcome. Children have their own activity club, with membership limited.

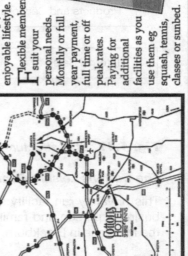

Cottons HOTEL SHIRE INNS

**Fig. 1.18** Cottons Leisure Club brochure

- Air-conditioned gym.
- All weather tennis courts.
- Beauty treatment rooms.
- TV lounge.

Qualified staff are always on hand to provide advice and assistance and will help to devise personal fitness plans for their members.

*Private sector characteristics*
The aim of the Leisure Club is to improve the overall profitability of the Cottons Hotel. Income is generated via a membership system. Following the recent refurbishment of the Leisure Club there was a 100 per cent membership uptake with 1,000 members. The income from membership subscriptions represents approximately 12 per cent of total hotel sales.

*Benefits to the community*
The Leisure Club encourages family membership and places a very strong emphasis on family image. It provides a privately run facility of a kind which did not previously exist in the locality.

Another positive benefit is the jobs which are created in the Leisure Club.

The Leisure Club therefore helps serve the needs of the community and forms an important part of the hotel and group marketing image, i.e. a high quality leisure facility attached to a hotel which appeals to the local community and national business.

## Delamere Forest Enterprise (public sector)

For our public sector case study we will look at the Forest Enterprise at the Delamere Forest Park. We will look at the management of the park at an operational level and the day to day activities.

Delamere Forest Park is located in the heart of Cheshire and is the remains of a prehistoric forest which once covered most of Cheshire and parts of Shropshire. Fig. 1.19 shows a brief history of Delamere Forest.

*Public sector characteristics*
The Delamere Forest Park is a working forest in that it survives on income from the sale of timber and receipts from tourists for recreational activities. The Forest Park is organised by the Forestry Commission which forms part of the Ministry for Agriculture, Fisheries and Foods as shown in Fig. 1.20.

Income is also derived from the advice which the forest rangers provide for land and forestry management. There is also a cycle hire facility which is provided by a voluntary body, the Groundwork Trust.

In line with many public sector organisations Forest Enterprise has recently developed along more commercial lines and all of its activities must be financially viable. As yet parking is free, however in the near future this may be changed.

**Fig. 1.19** *Brief history of Delamere Forest Park*

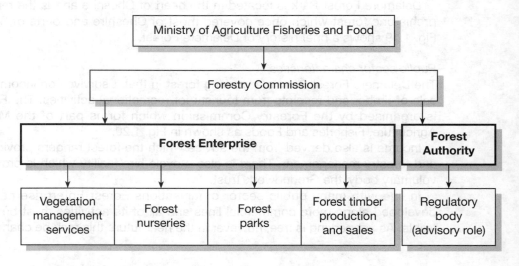

**Fig. 1.20** *Forest Enterprise within the government structure*

### Staff structure

The staffing structure at Delamere Forest Park is shown in Fig. 1.21.

Most of the posts shown in Fig. 1.21, apart from the Visitor Centre Manager and assistants, are full time and all are paid employees of Forest Enterprise.

### Forest Enterprise

*Role as a provider of leisure and recreation products and services*
Forest Enterprise provides a range of products and services at Delamere Forest Park, some of which are free and others for which a fee is payable and which must be booked in advance.

| *Recreational services (paying)* | *Educational services* |
|---|---|
| Horse riding (permit required) | Guided walks |
| Orienteering | Talks by the ranger |
|  | Use of the classroom |
| *Recreational activities (free)* | *Products for sale* |
| Bird watching | Souvenirs |
| Walking | Refreshments |
| Cycling | Maps |
| Jogging | Promotional literature |
|  | Christmas trees |
|  | Logs |

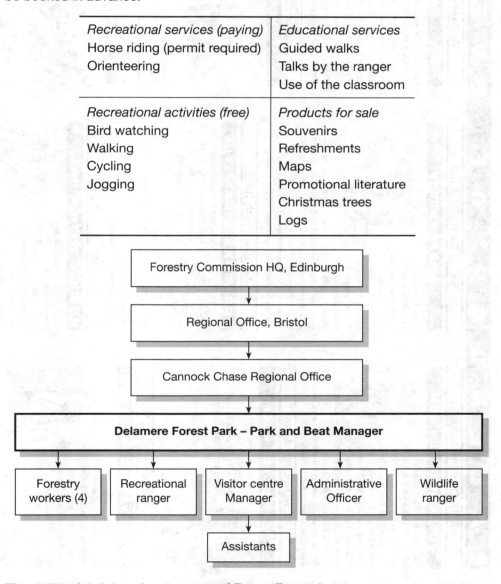

**Fig. 1.21** *Administrative structure of Forest Enterprise*

# C A L E N D A R   O F   E V E N T S

## SATURDAY 9th MARCH
### DELAMERE FUN RUN

Roll up! Roll up! For Delamere's seventeenth annual fun run. 5 or 10 miles part path, part road. Brilliant rural course! Free entry on the line! Start at 2.00 pm from Forest Enterprise Visitor Centre, Linmere, Delamere. This event, supported by Forest Enterprise, is organised by Cheshire County Council, Sport and Recreation department.
*For further details contact Cheshire County Council Sport Development Unit, 01606 871812.*

## SUNDAY 7th APRIL
### EASTER EGG HUNT

Follow the trail, solve the puzzle and win a prize.
**Meet :** 11.00 am at Forest Enterprise Visitor Centre, Linmere, Delamere.
**Charge :** £1.00 per person

## THURSDAY 16th MAY
### DISCOVERING FORESTRY

A full tour of the forestry operation in the biggest woodland in Cheshire. Follow the process from seed to mature tree, the equivalent of 55 years of tree growth in 2 hours.
**Meet :** 1.30 pm at Forest Enterprise Visitor Centre, Linmere, Delamere.
*Booking essential: 01244 603128, 2 – 4 pm*

## SATURDAY 15th JUNE
### HORSE ENDURO

If you have access to a horse this may be just the challenge you are looking for! Organised by the Cheshire Endurance Riding Group and run under strict veterinary guidance there are both competitive and non-competitive classes. Routes through Delamere and other land vary from a pleasure ride of 10 miles to the longest competitive class of 50 miles.
*For more information contact Liz Finney, Cheshire Endurance horse Riding Group, 01565 633310*

## SUNDAY 16th JUNE
### DRAGONS & DAMSELS

Discover Delamere's dragonflies with this fascinating talk by Dragonfly author *Richard Gabb*, followed by a forest walk to Black Lake for a chance to see them.

**Meet :** 10.00 am at Forest Enterprise Visitor Centre, Linmere, Delamere.
**Charge :** £1.00 per person
*Booking essential 01606 889792*

## JULY & AUGUST
### RAMBLE WITH A RANGER

Guided walk through the forest every wednesday.
**Meet :** 2.00 pm at Forest Enterprise Visitor Centre, Linmere, Delamere.
**Charge :** £1.00 per person

## WEDNESDAY 17th JULY
### BAT CHAT

Go batty in the woods whilst identifying different species of the famous flying mouse using a bat detector. Bat expert *Mike Freeman* will be on hand to demystify this creature of the night.
**Meet :** 8.00 pm at Forest Enterprise Visitor Centre, Linmere, Delamere.
**Charge :** £1.00 per person
*Booking essential 01606 889792*

## THURSDAY 15th AUGUST
### DISCOVERING FORESTRY

A full tour of the forestry operation in the biggest woodland in Cheshire. Follow the process from seed to mature tree, the equivalent of 55 years of tree growth in 2 hours.
**Meet :** 1.30 pm at Forest Enterprise Visitor Centre, Linmere, Delamere.
*Booking essential 01244 603128, 2 – 4 pm*

## SUNDAY 15th SEPTEMBER
### FRUITS OF THE FOREST

Discover Delamere's natural annual bounty on this tasty woodland walk.
**Meet :** 11.00 am at Forest Enterprise Visitor Centre, Linmere, Delamere
**Charge :** £1.00 per person
*Booking essential 01606 889792*

**Fig. 1.22** *Calender of events at Delamere Forest Park*

Delamere Forest Park also produces an annual programme of recreational events, as illustrated in Fig. 1.22.

Delamere Forest Park aims to provide a range of recreational activities to suit the needs of families, groups and individuals and to promote the forest across as wide a range of customers as possible.

*Significance in the North West region and benefits to the community*
Delamere Forest Park provides a unique opportunity for visitors to take part in outdoor recreational activities in a diverse natural habitat. It also provides the opportunity for town dwellers to observe nature at first hand.

The forest is a sanctuary for many forms of wildlife. At the visitor centre it is possible to see a range of birds such as chaffinches, wrens, blue tits, robins, woodpigeons and tawny owls (see Fig. 1.23).

*Reasons for location*
The location of Delamere Forest is rooted in history and its present day form is a result of the development of settlements and industry in the north west as land has been progressively cleared of forest.

CASE STUDY

## Youth Hostel Association (YHA) (voluntary sector)

The YHA in England and Wales was founded in 1930. Its stated aim was:

*To help all, especially young people of limited means, to a greater love and care of the countryside, particularly by providing hostels or other simple accommodation for them in their travels, and thus to promote their health, rest and education.*

This aim still holds true today and the YHA operates a total of 240 hostels in England and Wales.

### Funding

The YHA is a registered charity and receives its revenue from a variety of sources.

*Membership*
With over 250,000 members paying subscriptions the revenue from this source was equal to £1.4 million in 1995. For this members receive an accommodation and information guide on special discounts available through their periodical which is known as *Triangle*.

Members also receive details of any special courses, such as orienteering or canoeing, which are becoming increasingly popular. These courses are becoming more important as revenue earners for the YHA.

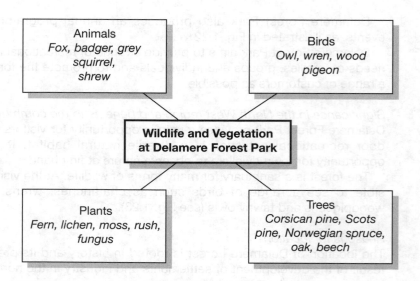

Fig. 1.23 *Wildlife and vegetation in Delamere Forest Park*

## Activity

Can you suggest why the YHA magazine is called *Triangle*?

*Accommodation fees*

This represents a substantial proportion of the YHA's annual income with a total of over £20 million in 1995. This is split into:

- £12.1 million overnight fees.
- £6.1 million from catering.
- £2.0 million in miscellaneous sales.

Visitors who are paying accommodation fees come from all over the world (see Table 1.2).

Fig. 1.24 *Youth Hostel Association logo*

**Table 1.2  Origin of international visitors to Youth Hostels in England and Wales**

| Continental areas from which the visitors came | Number of visitors |
|---|---|
| Western Europe | 336,145 |
| Eastern Europe | 16,653 |
| Far East | 26,447 |
| Africa | 6,242 |
| Australasia | 87,925 |
| Middle East | 2,263 |
| North America | 66,797 |
| South America | 14,910 |
| Other | 37,884 |
| Total number of visitors | 595,266 |

*Sponsorship*

Several large companies provide financial sponsorship to the YHA in a variety of forms. This may be direct sponsorship where the sponsoring company pays for information brochures. For example, National Express have sponsored the *Places to Stay* leaflet and the Hertz Car Rental Company have sponsored the *Accommodation Guide*.

There is also revenue in the form of paid advertising which appears in the YHA magazine.

This tends to be by companies who are associated with outdoor living and activities. A discount booklet is also produced allowing members a variety of reductions on purchases of related products around the country.

*Legacies*

An important source of funding for the YHA is legacies. A legacy can be money or properties left in a person's will to the YHA. This will usually be because the person leaving the money had an interest in the countryside. A total of £41,000 was left in legacies to the YHA in 1995.

*Donations*

In 1995 the YHA received a total of £207,000 in the form of donations. This money came from various sources such as members, companies, charitable trusts and the general public.

**Staff structure**

The structure of the YHA's staff is shown in Fig. 1.25.

The YHA is managed by paid employees but relies heavily on volunteer labour. At the local level hostels are managed by paid employees, however they receive help from volunteer workers in arranging trips and activities around the hostels.

In line with the hostels' move towards an increase in funding the hostels at Llangollen and Edale now offer outdoor pursuit courses. This means that specialist

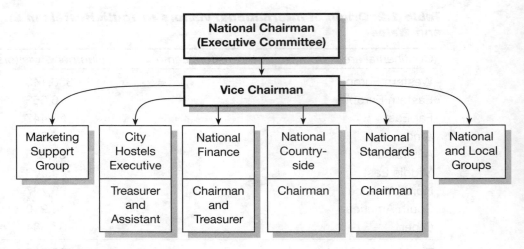

**Fig. 1.25** *National staffing structure*

(paid) instructors need to be employed to adhere to the Activity Centres (Young Persons Safety) Act, 1995.

Following market research the YHA decided that more specialist staff would be required to operate in newly identified areas such as large city centre hostels, which in some cases provide over 100 beds. Another new development is hostels which cater for specific user groups, for example school parties or educational groups.

### Products and services of the YHA

From its initial formation the aim of the YHA, to provide cheap accommodation, has remained most apparent. This aim is even more important today where a wide range of customers require services (Fig. 1.26) and accommodation:

- International travellers.
- Back packers.
- Outdoor pursuit enthusiasts.
- Families.
- School and youth groups.

Many of the hostels now provide a meal service which includes an evening meal and breakfast. The importance of this additional service is recognised in the financial statements which show that catering income contributed £6.5 million to the overall income.

The YHA walking holiday package is shown in Fig. 1.27.

### Benefits to the community

If we refer back to the original aim which was formulated in 1930 we can see that the objective of providing reasonably priced accommodation has not been lost. When we consider the work which the YHA is involved with now we can see that this aim is still being worked towards.

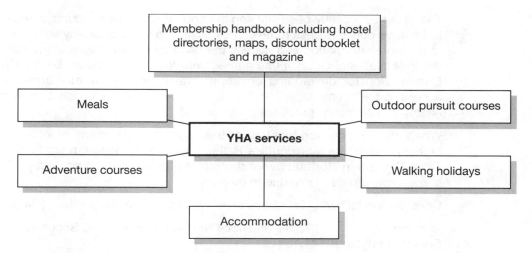

**Fig. 1.26** *Products and services of the YHA*

**Fig. 1.27** *YHA walking holidays*

The YHA has recently been working in partnership with the Countryside Commission to improve public access routes. They have also worked closely with English Nature to promote information and access the national nature reserves. In addition to this the YHA National Council has agreed with ideas put forward by the Countryside Commission for developing environmental education, nature conservation and access to the countryside. The YHA is also looking very carefully at how to improve energy and efficiency practices in its hostels.

When we consider the location of the youth hostels, many of which are in rural areas, for example Mankinholes Hall in Lancashire, Malton in North Yorkshire and Once Brewed in Northumberland, visitors staying at such hostels provide a welcome extra source of revenue to rural areas.

Consider the following list of overseas visitors to YHA regions for 1994/95:

Northern            58,754  (includes Northern England and Scotland)
Southern England  141,184
Wales              41,877
Cities            353,451

We can see the importance of the visitors in the Northern YHA region that an additional 58,000 visitors must bring to rural areas where the hostels are located. If every hosteller spends £10 per overnight stay this represents an additional income of over half a million pounds to the Northern Region alone.

### Reasons for location

Figure 1.28 shows the location of youth hostels in England and Wales. Many of these hostels are sited in rural locations where hostellers can take part in traditional outdoor activities, for example, rambling. In contrast to this some hostels are situated in city centres such as London, Manchester and Chester. City centre sites will satisfy the hostellers' desires to explore city centre attractions.

## Assignment

**'Report on local leisure and recreation facilities'**

**Evidence indicators:** A brief report describing the leisure and recreation facilities, products and services available in a locality, and giving reasons for their location. Students should consider all the reasons listed in the range and expand on those which are relevant to the local facilities.

**Key skills satisfied:** *Communication* **C2.1, C2.1b, C2.2, C2.3**
                         *Information Technology* **C2.3**

### Situation

You are an administrative assistant working for the local authority Leisure Services Department. The manager has asked your section to prepare a report describing

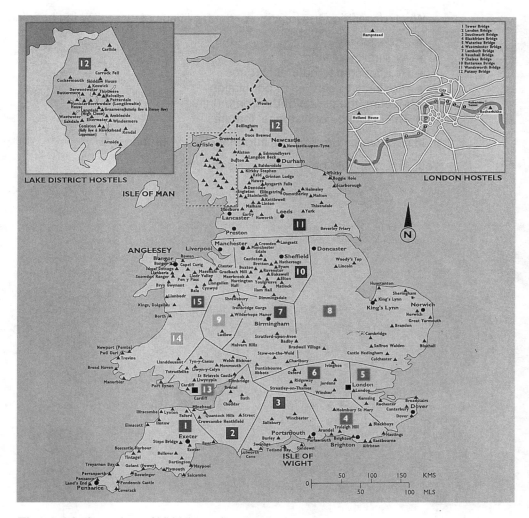

**Fig. 1.28** *Location of YHA hostels*

the provision of public and private sector leisure and recreation facilities within a five mile radius of the town centre.

### Tasks

1. Make a list of all of the leisure and recreation facilities within the area. State whether these facilities are run by the public, private or voluntary sector.
2. For each facility which you identify make a list of the products and services which it provides.
3. Construct a bar chart to show the distribution of facilities between the three sectors.
4. Draw a map of the area showing the location of the leisure and recreation facilities. Try to explain for each facility which you have identified the reasons for its location.

When describing the location of the facilities use the following headings:

- Accessibility
- Availability of land
- Relationship to natural features
- Proximity to centres of population
- Meeting the needs of the community
- The influence of historical features

5. In your teams present this information to your manager.

Your report should be word processed.

# Investigate the travel and tourism industry nationally and locally

One of the recreational activities which an individual may choose to take part in during their leisure or free time is travelling and visiting places of interest.

- **Travel** can be defined as the movement of individuals towards their destinations – How you get there.
- **Tourism** refers to the activities which the individuals take part in at their chosen destination – What you do when you are there.

## What is a tourist?

A tourist is an individual who is travelling for leisure or business purposes. They will be visiting a destination which is different from their normal place of residence. Tourist movements are short term and temporary.

Tourists can be categorised in a variety of ways:

## Length of stay at destination

- **Day tripper** – A day tripper will return home before nightfall so that the inward and outward journeys will occur within the same day. *Example*: A day visit to a theme park such as Alton Towers.
- **Weekend trip/short break** – Where less than four nights are spent away from the tourist's normal place of residence this is known as a short break, or a weekend break if the excursion occurs over Saturday/Sunday nights. *Example*: A weekend shopping break in London.
- **Long stay holiday** – A long stay holiday is where the holidaymaker is away from home for more than four consecutive nights. *Example*: A two-week holiday in Majorca.

## Activity

The adverts shown in Fig. 1.29 show a range of excursions and holidays of differing lengths of stay.

Which of these excursions/holidays can be said to be day trips, short/weekend breaks or long stay holidays?

# Reader Holidays

## AUG 23
**8 Days From**
**£369**

### BAY OF NAPLES
Flying Manchester

There can be few more idyllic setting for a week by the sea  than the Sorrento Peninsula. If you simply look forward to days lazing in the sun and nights of wining, dining and dancing; then this is the perfect place, and Vesuvius, Pompeii, Naples and Capris are just a sample of the unforgettable sights and scenery close at hand.

### LEGOLAND - windsor

This special trip includes coaching throughout. One nights accommodation in a comfortable, modern hotel with all private facilities and full English breakfast. Entrance fee to Legoland and Thames River Cruise with barbeque.

## AUG 10
**2 DAYS From**
**£79**
Children £39

## AUG 15
**4 DAYS from**
**£144 Adults**
**£99 Child**

### BOURNEMOUTH BONANZA

Included in this holiday is 3 nights half board at the New Durley Dean Hotel. All rooms en suite, free use of indoor pool, steam room and gym. Visits to Warwick and Gloucester.

### BRITTANY

For a holiday with something for all tastes, there could be nothing better than our tour of Brittany.
Firstly, we have magnificent scenery, one of the most beautiful coastlines in Europe, very reminiscent of Cornwall but without the crowds and Brittany is synonymous with good weather - we are way south of the Channel Islands.

## AUG 28
**5 Days From**
**£224**

## SEPT 13
**3 DAYS from**
**£119**

### ANTIQUES WEEKEND

2 nights half board at the Oak Hotel, Brighton. Visit to Summers Place, Billingshurst with special "Antiques" talks.

### HIGHLANDS & COUNTRY GARDENS

Join us for this fabulous weekend to Strathpeffer, a most attractive Highland Spa resort set in the beautiful wooded Strath Canon Valley and experience the easy- going atmosphere that Queen Victoria loved so much. The imposing peak of Ben Wyvis is the backdrop to this charming village.

## AUG 16
**4 DAYS from**
**£125**

## JULY 29
## AUG 18
**3 Days From**
**Adults £95**
**Child £65**

### EURO DISNEY - PARIS

* Return journey through Eurotunnel on Le Shuttle
* 2 nights' accommodation in a shared twin, three bedded or four bedded room at a good two star hotel in the Greater Paris area.
* Continental breakfasts
* A full day at DISNEYLAND Paris including a one day admission pass
* A visit to central Paris

### ROMANTIC RHINE VALLEY

4 nights accommodation in Kamp-Bornhofen staying in a Gasthof or Hotel such as the Kurfust or Singender Wirt on a half board basis (breakfasts and 3 course evening meals). The holiday price is based upon 2 people sharing a twin or double bedded room with washbasin. Twin or double room with private facilities and single rooms with and without private facilities are available in limited supply at the supplement.
* Optional excursions.

## AUG 31
**5 Days From**
**£109**

---

# READER HOLIDAYS
## British Trips

| DEPARTING | No. OF DAYS | DESTINATION | PRICES FROM |
|---|---|---|---|
| 10 Aug | ONE | Legoland | £79.00 |
| 10 Aug | TWO | Riverdance | £99.00 |
| 17 Aug | ONE | Shrewsbury Flower Show | £25.50 |
| 24 Aug | ONE | Southport Flower Show | £23.50 |
| 31 Aug | TWO | Les Miserables | £69.00 |
| 24 Aug & 28 Sept | TWO | Buckingham Palace | £79.00 |
| 7 Sept | TWO | Burghley Horse Trials | £79.00 |
| 13 Sept | THREE | Antique Weekend | £119.00 |
| 14 Sept | TWO | Miss Saigon | £69.00 |
| 25 Oct | ONE | Healthcliff in Birmingham | £59.95 |

*specially selected reader holidays*

Breakaway is committed to choosing quality holidays at affordable prices. Furthermore we insist on the highest possible standards from our tour operators who are all bonded with ABTA, ATOL or AITO.

For enquiries and Credit Card bookings:
**01625 531121**
Monday-Friday 10am-3pm

24 hour brochure request line
**0891 777326**
Calls charged at 39p per min cheap, 48p per min at all other times

---

**Fig. 1.29** *Holidays of differing lengths of stay*

## Purpose of visit

Tourists will have individual reasons for their choice of destination. This will depend upon a number of factors including personal choice, circumstances and leisure time available.

| Purpose | Reason | Example |
|---------|--------|---------|
| Leisure | Education | School exchange trip to France |
|         | Relaxation | A beach holiday in Greece |
|         | VFR | Visiting friends and relatives in Australia |
|         | Activity | Pony trekking in the Welsh mountains |
|         | Event | European football supporters travelling to an event e.g. Euro 96 |
|         | Religion | To visit a holy shrine such as Lourdes, France |
|         | Cultural | A trip to the opera |
|         | Sports event | Commonwealth Games, Manchester 2002 |

People travelling for business purposes are also tourists.

| Purpose | Reason | Example |
|---------|--------|---------|
| Business | Conferences | To find out about business developments e.g. in IT in the USA |
|          | Exhibitions | To visit or exhibit at trade fairs and shows e.g. British Travel |
|          | Meetings | To meet clients and arrange business deals e.g. Trade Fair, NEC |

In order to reach the chosen destination a tourist will need to make use of travel services.

> Describe the *main components* of the UK travel and tourism industry

> Give examples of *products and services* available through the travel and tourism industry nationally

In this section we shall be looking at the structure of the travel and tourism industry within the UK and the types of tourist movement. We shall also examine the products and services which the different sectors of the industry offer.

The travel and tourism industry can be broken down into a number of component areas (see Fig. 1.30).

# Travel services

*Travel services are the services which enable an individual to travel.*

Travel services are provided by:

- Retail travel agencies.
- Business travel agencies.
- Tour operators.
- Transport principals.

## Retail travel agencies

Retail travel agencies are the shop window of the travel market. They sell holidays and travel to the general public and provide a range of other services.

Lunn Poly, Going Places and Thomas Cook are amongst the most well known travel agencies whose branches can be found in the high streets of most towns and cities throughout the UK.

They are all multiples, which means they have at least ten branches, and are often referred to as the 'Big 3' because of the way in which they dominate the holiday market. There also exists thousands of smaller independent travel agencies.

Retail travel agencies provide the following products and services:

- Making holiday bookings.
- Providing travel insurance.
- Checking availability of holidays.
- Arranging car hire.
- Checking travel details.
- Exchanging foreign currency.
- Providing advice on destinations.
- Sale of travellers cheques.

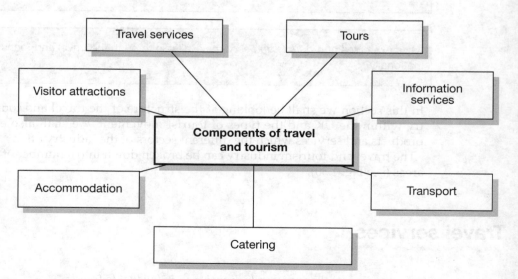

**Fig. 1.30** *Component areas of the travel and tourism industry*

## Activity

Visit your local town and list the names of the travel agencies.

Divide your list into multiples and independents (your tutor may have to advise you about this) and draw a pie chart to show the split between the two categories.

Visit two of the travel agencies and make a note of some of the tour operators who display their brochures there. Do certain names appear more than others?

**Important:** Remember to check with the travel agency staff before removing any brochures!

**Key skills satisfied:** *Application of Number* **N2.1, N2.3**

# Tours

*A tour is any kind of trip or journey which may involve one or a number of destinations. A tour may be domestic, incoming or outgoing.*

Examples of tourist movements which are inbound and outbound to the UK and those which are domestic are shown below:

| | |
|---|---|
| *Domestic flow* | Birmingham to Blackpool |
| | Birmingham to Newquay |
| *Incoming tours* | USA to Manchester |
| | Amsterdam to London |
| *Outgoing tours* | London to Brussels |
| | London to Paris |

## Activity

Look at the following tourist journeys and decide which of the three categories of tourist flow they belong to:

| Route | Purpose |
|---|---|
| Birmingham to Lloret del Mar | Holiday |
| Burnley to Newquay | Holiday |
| Seattle to Manchester | VFR |
| Dublin to Belfast | Business |
| Newcastle to Stavanger | Activity holiday |
| Hull to Stratford upon Avon | Cultural |

All of the above routes are with respect to the UK

# Domestic tours

Domestic tourism refers to holidays and visits which are made within a tourist's home country. The domestic holidays industry in the UK has changed dramatically over the past forty years as the importance of traditional 'bucket and spade' type family holidays at British seaside resorts has declined.

As holidays abroad have become cheaper and technology has made transport faster, the more accessible domestic resorts have struggled to compete with the obvious climatic attractions of the Mediterranean resorts of Spain, France, Italy, Greece and more recently the North African destinations of Morocco, Tunisia and Egypt.

There has however been a compensatory rise in the number of day trips and weekend breaks taken in the UK as car ownership has become more widespread throughout Britain.

# Outgoing tours

The rising trend in outgoing tours continues as British holidaymakers continue to take their main summer holiday abroad. Tour operators such as Thomson put together inclusive packages which include accommodation and transport by charter flight. Spain is the top charter flight destination followed by the Canary Islands and Greece and the Greek Islands. Package holidays are usually sold through the high street travel agents although it is possible to buy a package holiday directly from the tour operator. Some tour operators will only sell directly to the public, for example Portland and Eurocamp. The advantage to the customer of buying direct is that it will be cheaper as the travel agent's commission is cut out but the customer will lose the other benefits of booking via a travel agency, such as advice and information.

# Incoming tours

The number of overseas visitors to the UK on incoming tours has also increased significantly since the 1960s although not at the same rate as the number of British people travelling abroad.

In 1965 there were approximately 2.5 million visitors to the UK. This had risen to 25.5 million by 1997.

In order to cater for overseas visitors the domestic holiday market has to provide a range of products and services including:

- Accommodation.
- Catering.
- Guiding and information services.
- Visitor attractions.
- Entertainment.
- Transport.

# Tour operators

Tour operators organise a range of holidays and inclusive packages which include transport and accommodation.

The UK's largest overseas tour operators are Thomson Tour Operations, First Choice JMC and Airtours. Thomson and Airtours own two of the major retail travel agencies, Lunn Poly and Going Places respectively. Thomas Cook is a tour operator as well as being a travel agent.

Domestic tour operators play a much smaller role in the holiday market as most people will make their own travel and accommodation arrangements within the UK. Most domestic tours are organised by transport principals. For example, coach operators such as Wallace Arnold and Shearings organise a range of domestic and overseas packages.

# Transport

*Transport forms the link between the tourist's point of origin and destination enabling tourism to take place.*

The UK has a very well developed transport infrastructure making it easy for passengers to travel around the country – but also easy to leave!

On outgoing tours to overseas destinations a tourist is most likely to travel by air as it is the fastest and most efficient method of transport and forms the travel component of most package holidays.

The UK's busiest airports are shown in Table 1.3.

### Table 1.3  The UK's busiest airports

| Airport | Passengers, 1998 (millions) |
| --- | --- |
| London Heathrow | 60,336 |
| Manchester | 17,206 |
| Glasgow | 6,481 |
| Birmingham | 6,608 |
| London Stansted | 6,831 |
| Edinburgh | 4,542 |
| Newcastle | 2,919 |
| Aberdeen | 2,649 |
| Belfast International | 2,626 |

*Adapted from*: BAA plc Civil Aviation Authority

The supremacy of air travel however is being challenged for short haul destinations as the building of the Channel Tunnel has opened up Europe to rail travel.

The cross channel ferry companies are also being challenged by Le Shuttle service which enables a motorist to take a car to Europe via the Channel Tunnel.

For domestic tours the private car is undoubtedly the most common form of transport.

## Transport principals

Transport principals are the companies which provide the main forms of transport which enable tourists to reach their chosen destinations. The following list shows the main forms of transport, who provides it and the products and services which the transport principals offer.

| Method of travel | Principal | Products/services |
| --- | --- | --- |
| Air travel | Airlines, e.g.: British Airways, Air France, Qantas | Flights, catering, in-flight entertainment |
| Road travel | Coach operators, e.g.: National Express, Stagecoach, Wallace Arnold | Coach tours, day trip excursions, theatre visits |
| Sea travel | Ferry companies, e.g.: Stena Sealink, Brittany Ferries, North Sea Ferries | Sea crossings for cars and passengers, hovercraft crossings, on-board entertainment, cabin accommodation |
| Rail travel | Virgin Eurostar, Le Shuttle | Fast Intercity routes, London to Paris direct, rail tours, catering facilities |

## Activity

Find two more examples of transport principals who provide coach, air and sea travel.

Can you think of any other products and services which these transport principals provide?

# Visitor attractions

*Visitor attractions are the reason why tourism takes place.*

In order for tourism to take place there must be an attraction which draws people to a destination.

Visitor attractions can take many forms. One person's attraction could be another person's distraction.

A resort such as Blackpool is immensely popular with millions of visitors. For example, in 1997 a total of 1.2 million people visited Blackpool Tower. Other tourists however prefer the rural charms of a countryside area such as the Lake District National Park.

Visitor attractions includes a wide range of facilities ranging from theme parks to heritage sites, each providing its own unique range of products and services.

Take, for example, the Salt Museum, Northwich; the products and services of this visitor attraction are:

| Main product | Services |
| --- | --- |
| The artefacts (objects) on display | Guided tours |
| | Talks on the history of salt |
| The interpretation panels which explain them | Sale of souvenirs and refreshments |
| | Information booklets and leaflets |

## Activity

Working in groups carry out a survey of the visitor attractions in the UK which your class has visited. Collate the results and list them under the headings of:

1. Heritage          e.g. museums, stately homes, castles
2. Entertainment     e.g. theme parks, pubs, discos, restaurants
3. Natural attractions  e.g. national parks, hills, geological features
4. Seaside resorts

Draw a bar chart to summarise the results. State what proportion of the class visited each type of visitor attraction.

**Key skills satisfied:** *Application of Number* **N2.3**

# Information services

Providing information to tourists is part of a visitor attraction's marketing strategy.

- If no one is aware of the attraction it will not receive visitors.
- If the promotional literature is not distributed to information points the public will be unaware of its existence.

Tourist Information Centres (TIC) can be found in most towns and cities in the UK. Figure 1.31 lists the services provided by the TIC in Keswick. TICs provide a wealth of information and advice to visitors on the surrounding area, what to see and where to stay.

Tourist boards also provide information on attractions in their own region. England, Scotland, Wales and Northern Ireland each has its own national and regional tourist boards.

**Fig. 1.31** *Information services available at Keswick Tourist Information Centre*

The kind of information which is contained in the tourists boards' regional brochures includes:

- Where to stay – with advice about accommodation and details of classification schemes.
- Details of visitor attractions and opening times.
- Transport details.
- Location maps.
- Phone numbers for further details.

The British Tourist Authority provides information to overseas visitors through its network of international offices.

The Tourism Department of local authorities also provides an information service for visitor attractions in their area. They ensure that literature is available in public places within the community, e.g. at libraries, other visitor attractions, leisure and community centres.

## Activity

Visit your nearest TIC and make a note of the range of services which it provides in addition to the provision of literature on visitor attractions.

# Guiding services

Tour guides will lead a visit or a tour and will require an in-depth knowledge of the area or attraction which they work in. This is a specialised, seasonal job which is often performed by retired people or volunteers who have close links with the area.

A unique guiding system operating in Canterbury, the Canterbury City Centre Initiative (CCCI), helps provide information for visitors to the city. These guides (shepherds) are available to meet incoming coaches and help provide information for the tourists either in the form of local city centre maps or information in the tourist's own language. The Canterbury scheme has been so successful that guides are employed on a full-time basis.

The tourist boards offer a regional guiding service known as the 'Blue Badge' Guide system.

# Accommodation

*The provision of shelter is one of the basic elements of a tour package.*

One of the primary considerations for tourists when visiting a destination is the type of accommodation which is available.

The choice of accommodation will depend upon a number of factors including the individual's circumstances, as shown in Fig. 1.32.

All tourists require the basic provision of shelter but the differing needs and wants of tourists will determine the type of accommodation chosen.

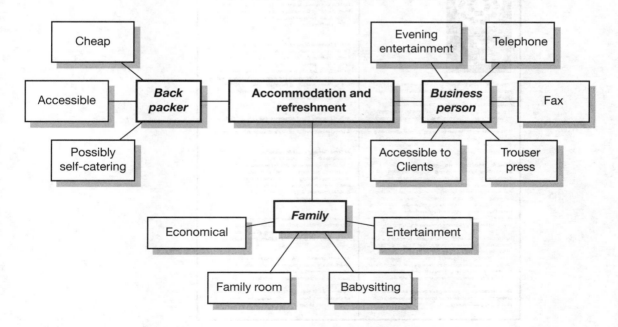

**Fig. 1.32** *Factors influencing choice of accomodation*

# Types of accommodation available

There is a wide range of different types of accommodation available in the UK offering a variety of products and services. Tourists can choose from:

| Serviced accommodation – meals and housekeeping are included | Self catering accommodation – no meals are included, housekeeping may be included |
| --- | --- |
| Hotels | Camping and caravanning |
| Motels | Apartments |
| Guest houses | Timeshare properties |
| Bed and breakfast | Holiday cottages |
| Farmhouses | Chalets |

Guest Accommodation

English Tourism Council    Information Sheet 06
QUALITY ASSURANCE SCHEMES

# Ratings you can trust

**English Tourism Council**

◆ ◆ ◆
GUEST ACCOMMODATION

When you're looking for a place to stay, you need a rating system you can trust. The **English Tourism Council's** ratings are your clear guide to what to expect, in an easy-to-understand form. Properties are visited annually by our trained, impartial assessors, so you can have confidence that your accommodation has been thoroughly checked and rated for quality before you make a booking.

Using a simple one to five Diamond rating, the new system puts a much greater emphasis on quality and is based on research which showed exactly what consumers are looking for when choosing accommodation.

"Guest Accommodation" covers a wide variety of serviced accommodation for which England is renowned, including guesthouses, bed and breakfasts, inns and farmhouses. Establishments are rated from one to five Diamonds. The same minimum requirement for facilities and services applies to all Guest Accommodation from one to five Diamonds. Progressively higher levels of quality and customer care must be provided for each of the one to five Diamond ratings. The rating reflects the unique character of Guest Accommodation, and covers areas such as cleanliness, service and hospitality, bedrooms, bathrooms and food quality.

Look out, too, for the English Tourism Council's new Gold and Silver Awards, which are awarded to those establishments which not only achieve the overall quality required for their Diamond rating, but also reach the highest levels of quality in those specific areas which guests identify as being really important for them. They will reflect the quality of comfort and cleanliness you'll find in the bedrooms and bathroom and the quality of service you'll enjoy throughout your stay.

**The new ratings are your sign of quality assurance, giving you the confidence to book the accommodation that meets your expectations.**

## What to expect at each rating level

The Diamond ratings for Guest Accommodation reflect visitor expectations of this sector. The quality of what is provided is more important to visitors than a wide range of facilities and services. Therefore, the same minimum requirement for facilities and services applies to all Guest Accommodation from One to Five Diamonds, while progressively higher level of quality and customer care must be provided for each of the One to Five Diamond ratings.

**At One Diamond Guest Accommodation you will find:**
Clean accommodation, providing acceptable comfort with functional décor and offering, as a minimum, a full cooked or continental breakfast. Other meals, where provided, will be freshly cooked. You will have a comfortable bed, with clean bed linen and towels and fresh soap. Adequate heating and hot water available at reasonable times for baths or showers at no extra charge. An acceptable overall level of quality and helpful service.

**At Two Diamond Guest Accommodation, you will find:**
(in addition to what is provided at One Diamond)
A sound overall level of quality and customer care in all areas.

**At Three Diamond Guest Accommodation, you will find:**
(in addition to what is provided at Two Diamond)
A good overall level of quality. For example, good quality, comfortable bedrooms; well maintained, practical décor; a good choice of quality items available for breakfast; other meals, where provided, will be freshly cooked from good quality ingredients. A good degree of comfort provided for you, with good levels of customer care.

**At Four Diamond Guest Accommodation, you will find:**
(in addition to what is provided at Three Diamond)
A very good overall level of quality in all areas and customer care showing very good levels of attention to your needs.

**At Five Diamond Guest Accommodation, you will find:**
(in addition to what is provided at Four Diamond)
An excellent overall level of quality. For example, ample space with a degree of luxury, an excellent quality bed, high quality furniture, excellent interior design. Breakfast offering a wide choice of high quality fresh ingredients; other meals, where provided, featuring fresh, seasonal local ingredients. Excellent levels of customer care, anticipating your needs .

***Fig. 1.33*** *English Tourism Council – Diamond Classification System*

# Hotel and guest house accommodation

Following the Development of Tourism Act 1969 there was a move towards the rationalisation of accommodation classification systems. In 1999 the English Tourism Council, the AA and the RAC amalgamated a joint star rating system for hotels and a diamond rating system for guest accomodation.

## Hotels

English Tourism Council     Information Sheet 04
QUALITY ASSURANCE SCHEMES

# Ratings you can trust

**English Tourism Council**

★ ★ ★

**HOTEL**

When you're looking for a place to stay, you need a rating system you can trust. The **English Tourism Council's** ratings are your clear guide to what to expect, in an easy-to-understand form. Properties are visited annually by our trained, impartial assessors, so you can have confidence that your accommodation has been thoroughly checked and rated for quality before you make a booking.

Based on the internationally recognised rating of one to five Stars, the new system puts greater emphasis on quality and is based on research which showed exactly what consumers are looking for when choosing a hotel.

Ratings are awarded from one to five Stars – the more Stars, the higher the quality and the greater the range of facilities and level of services provided.

Look out, too, for the English Tourism Council's new Gold and Silver Awards, which are awarded to properties achieving the highest levels of quality within their Star rating. While the overall rating is based on a combination of facilities and quality, the Gold and Silver Awards are based solely on quality.

***The new ratings are your sign of quality assurance, giving you the confidence to book the accommodation that meets your expectations.***

### What to expect at each rating level

In a One Star hotel you will find an acceptable level of quality, services and range of facilities. Moving up the One to Five Star rating scale, you will find progressively higher quality standards providing ever better guest care as well as a wider range of facilities and a higher level of services.

**At a ONE STAR hotel you will find:**
Practical accommodation with a limited range of facilities and services, but a high standard of cleanliness throughout. Friendly and courteous staff to give you the help and information you need to enjoy your stay. Restaurant/eating area open to you and your guests for breakfast and dinner. Alcoholic drinks will be served in a bar or lounge. 75% of bedrooms will have en-suite or private facilities.

**At a TWO STAR hotel you will find:**
*(in addition to what is provided at ONE STAR)*
Good overnight accommodation with more comfortable bedrooms, better equipped – all with en-suite or private facilities and colour TV. A relatively straightforward range of services, including food and drink and a personal style of service. A restaurant/dining room for breakfast and dinner. A lift normally available.

**At a THREE STAR hotel you will find:**
*(in addition to what is provided at ONE and TWO STAR)*
Possibly larger establishments, but all offering significantly greater quality and range of facilities and services, and usually more spacious public areas and bedrooms. A more formal style of service with a receptionist on duty and staff responding well to your needs and requests. Room service of continental breakfast. Laundry service available. A wide selection of drinks, light lunch and snacks served in a bar or lounge.

**At a FOUR STAR hotel you will find:**
*(in addition to what is provided at ONE, TWO and THREE STAR)*
Accommodation offering superior comfort and quality; all bedrooms with en-suite bath, fitted overhead shower and WC. The hotel will have spacious and very well appointed public areas and will put a strong emphasis on food and drink. Staff will have very good technical and social skills, anticipating and responding to your needs and requests. Room service of all meals and 24 hour drinks, refreshments and snacks. Dry cleaning service available.

**At a FIVE STAR hotel you will find:**
*(in addition to what is provided at ONE, TWO, THREE and FOUR STAR)*
A spacious, luxurious establishment offering you the highest international quality of accommodation, facilities, services and cuisine. It will have striking accommodation throughout, with a range of extra facilities. You will feel very well cared for by professional, attentive staff providing flawless guest services. An hotel setting the highest international standards for the industry, with an air of luxury, exceptional comfort and a very sophisticated ambience.

**Fig. 1.34** *The expected facilities at graded hotel accomodation*

# Ratings you can trust

English Tourism Council

★ ★ ★
HOLIDAY PARK

English Tourism Council

★ ★ ★
TOURING PARK

English Tourism Council

★ ★ ★
CAMPING PARK

When you're looking for a place to stay, you need a rating system you can trust. For the year 2000, a new Star rating scheme has replaced the (Q) Tick scheme for Caravan and Camping Parks. It is a completely new scheme, but with quality still at its heart and reflecting consumer expectations even more strongly. The Star rating reflects the overall quality of the park and the highest rating of Five Star is reserved for those parks of exceptional quality which also provide specific key facilities and services.

This is a new scheme with a new symbol and new ratings reflecting the ever higher standards which Holiday, Caravan and Camping Parks have to offer in the new millennium. It is the result of extensive research into what visitors are looking for, ensuring that you can easily find a park that meets your expectations.

The new Star ratings offer you more than the (previous) corresponding Tick ratings and should not be compared with them.

**Star Quality**

★ ★ ★ ★ ★    Exceptional Quality

★ ★ ★ ★    Excellent Quality

★ ★ ★    Very Good Quality

★ ★    Good Quality

★    Acceptable Quality

Parks are visited annually by trained, impartial assessors. A rating of from one to five stars is awarded, based on cleanliness, environment and the quality of facilities and service provided.

*Look for the English Tourism Council ratings, and book with confidence!*

***Fig. 1.35*** *Caravan and Holiday Park Rating System*

The rating system is managed by the three organisations and was introduced to help travellers to know what kind of facilities to expect in hotels and guest houses. The system is more customer friendly and more easily understood.

The kind of products and services which a guest would expect at a hotel which had been awarded five stars would include colour TV, radio, telephone, ensuite facilities, hair dryer, shoe cleaning equipment as well as meals and a laundry service.

A grading system also now exists covering other areas of accommodation such as the key system for self-catering accommodation and the star rating for caravan parks. Figure 1.35 shows the rating system for caravan and holiday parks.

## Activity

Working in teams of 3 or 4 students carry out a survey of your local area investigating both the types of catering establishments and types of accommodation which are available.

Classify the accommodation under the tourist board crown rating systems and produce a bar/pie chart to illustrate your results.

When collecting information about catering outlets classify your results in the following way:

1. Traditional café.
2. Fast food outlet.
3. Licensed restaurant.
4. Brewery group chain.
5. Ethnic restaurant, e.g. Indian, Chinese.
6. A la carte (exclusive) restaurant.

Show your results as a bar/pie chart.

Produce a word-processed report of your findings including an analysis of the bar charts.

**Key skills satisfied:** *Communication* **C2.2, C2.3**
*Application of Number* **N2.1, N2.2, N2.3**
*Information Technology* **IT2.1, IT2.2, IT2.3**

# Catering

The provision of food and drink has always been an important part of a holiday or business trip. Consequently the types of catering outlets available are very wide and varied.

Small independently owned restaurants and cafés tend to specialise in regional dishes, e.g. tea shops in the West Country which serve cream teas and aim to project a quaint, rustic image.

In contrast to this, many seaside resorts promote fish and chips as the national dish, for example seafront cafés in Blackpool, as does the Harry Ramsden chain of restaurants.

The current trend in catering is for themed family pubs which are being developed by the large brewery groups. Such pubs sell food for all the family and provide play facilities for children.

A successful example of this is the Brewers Fayre chain which is owned by the Whitbread Group.

Some catering venues are tourist attractions in themselves because of their reputation and the image they promote. The Hard Rock Café and Planet Hollywood in London are good examples of this type of restaurant.

## Activity

**'Describe the main components of the travel and tourism industry, supported by examples of its products and services'**

Describe each of the components of the travel and tourism industry.

Identify two examples of facilities or providers from each component area and list the products or services which they offer.

> *Compare* the characteristics of public, private and voluntary sectors in the travel and tourism industry supporting the comparison with examples

In Element 1.1 we discussed the differences in operation and funding between the private, public and voluntary sectors. In this section we are going to study three contrasting facilities, one from each of economic sectors of the travel and tourism industry.

We will describe the differing methods of funding and operation and the various services which they provide. We will also consider the impact which they have on their local environment.

- Private sector     Shire Inns plc and the Cottons Hotel, Knutsford
- Voluntary sector    National Trust – Quarry Bank Mill, Styal
- Public sector      Vale Royal Tourism and Anderton Boat Lift

# The private sector in travel and tourism

The private sector tends to dominate the travel and tourism industry in the UK. It is an expanding industry in which private sector operators hope to make substantial profits.

If we consider the component areas which make up the travel and tourism industry we can see that they are dominated by large corporations:

- **Travel services**
  - British Airways
  - Wallace Arnold
  - Lunn Poly
  - Going Places

  The exception here is British Rail which is currently changing from public to private ownership.
- **Tour operators**
  - Thomson
  - First Choice
- **Visitor attractions** (many are owned by leisure corporations)
  - Waterworld (Rank Leisure)
  - Alton Towers (Tussauds Group)
  - Rank Leisure are currently bidding to take over the Hard Rock Café chain of restaurants

- **Accommodation**
  - Forte Travel Lodge (see Fig. 1.36)
  - Stakis
  - Ladbrokes
- **Catering**
  - McDonalds
  - Harry Ramsdens
  - Brewery chains, e.g. Whitbreads

There are at the same time however thousands of small independently owned operators in all of these areas.

**Fig. 1.36** *Forte Travelodge*

## Cottons Hotel, Knutsford (private sector)

We described earlier how a private company, Shire Inns, has diversified across the component areas of sport, leisure, catering and accommodation.

As mentioned earlier in the case study of the Cottons Hotel Leisure Centre the complex is part of a nationally based company known as **Shire Inns**.

**KNUTSFORD**

**A A**

**4**

**S T A R**

**Cottons HOTEL SHIRE INNS**

*I*n the heart of Cheshire, the Cottons Hotel is surrounded by a wealth of exciting places to visit. The Hotel is located on the A50, just five minutes from junction 19 or 20 of the M6 motorway making it easily accessible from Birmingham, Leeds and North Wales.

Situated in the pretty village of Knutsford, the Cottons is a perfect place to stay for a weekend or even longer. Its old colonial style is a clever recreation of French New Orleans and is reflected in the sumptuous furnishings and decor, providing the ultimate feeling of seclusion and comfort.

Fine cuisine comes high on the list of priorities and the splendidly furnished Magnolia Restaurant sets the mood for a memorable eating experience. Speciality Creole and Cajun dishes feature along with traditional favourites, whilst the adjoining Magnolia Conservatory Lounge offers an all-day menu and is ideal for coffee and a light snack.

The Bourbon Street Bar provides a relaxing atmosphere for both pre-dinner drinks and late evening nightcaps. Some of Britain's most unspoilt countryside is within easy driving distance of the Cottons Hotel, including the spectacular Peak District.

**AT YOUR LEISURE**

The Cottons Hotel's outstanding leisure complex has been designed to create an enjoyable atmosphere with professional staff on hand to supervise and provide advice. In addition to the wide range of facilities are a 13m pool, mixed steam rooms, air conditioned gym, all-weather tennis courts, beauty treatment rooms and both wet and dry lounges to relax in.

**MANCHESTER ROAD**

**KNUTSFORD**

**CHESHIRE**

**WA16 0SU**

TEL : 01565 650333

FAX : 01565 755351

**Fig. 1.37** Cottons Hotel, Knutsford

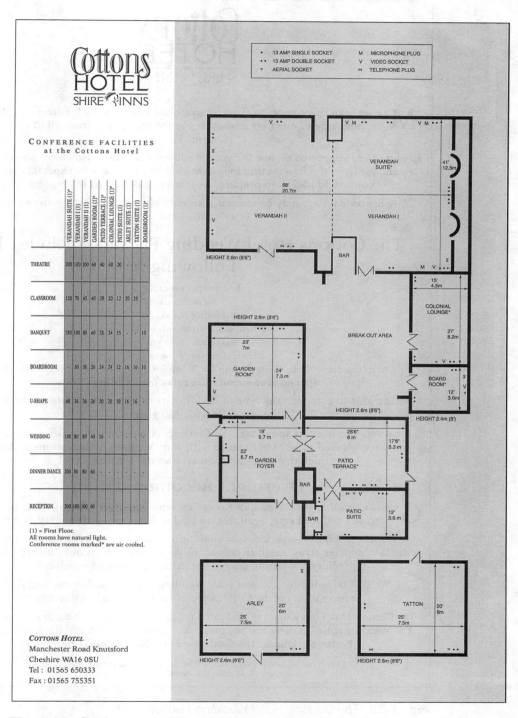

**Fig. 1.38** *Conference facilities at the Cottons Hotel, Knutsford*

M ay we take this opportunity to congratulate you on your forthcoming Wedding and extend our best wishes to you for the future, from all of us at the Cottons Hotel.

Enclosed are suggested menus for your Wedding Reception. However, please feel free to choose from the Banqueting menus available, or if there is a special dish which you would like us to prepare, we would be delighted to arrange this.

Any drinks package may be chosen, alternatively, please select from the enclosed wine list.

## The Cottons Hotel Wedding Package Includes The Following :

Red carpet on arrival
Menu cards
Wedding Breakfast
Floral decorations on all tables
Cakestand and knife
Changing room
Complimentary "Four Poster" suite for Bride & Groom with a bottle of champagne
**Special accommodation rates for wedding guests**

We are able to cater for any type of wedding from a small intimate celebration to a reception for 180 guests.

Please do not hesitate to contact the Conference & Banqueting Office, who will be only too pleased to be of assistance with your Wedding preparations and will be delighted to show you around the Cottons Hotel.

## Overnight Accommodation

G uests attending your Wedding Reception who would like to stay overnight, can do so at a reduced rate, available on Friday, Saturday and Sunday nights only.

The rate includes superb accommodation with en suite facilities, full English breakfast, courtesy tray, satellite colour television, free use of our Leisure Club which offers swimming pool, gymnasium, sauna and whirlpool.

We will be delighted to send your Wedding Invitations for you and include information on the Cottons Hotel for your guests' information.

The Cottons Hotel has a team of dedicated professionals who are able to guide you along the 'wedding path'.  If there are any particular questions which you have, please do not hesitate to contact the Conference and Banqueting Department.

All prices and menus are subject to availability and may change without prior notification.
All prices include VAT @ 17.5%.

***Fig. 1.39*** *The Cottons Hotel Wedding Package*

Shire Inns is a subsidiary of Daniel Thwaites Brewing Group which was founded in Blackburn in the early nineteenth century. Although predominantly a brewing company the group now owns hotels throughout the country, as shown in Fig. 1.16.

The hotel has recently undergone a refurbishment and the accommodation now includes 99 bedrooms including a range of single, double and family rooms. There is also a conservatory coffee lounge, public bar area and restaurant.

The majority of customers who visit between Monday and Friday are individual business travellers and conference delegates. Weekend customers are mainly from the Weekend Break market or are attending functions.

The hotel now has a range of ten conference suites (see Fig. 1.38) which can accommodate from 10 to 200 guests. In line with the trend towards providing a wide range of conference facilities it is now possible to equip rooms with:

- Video players and monitors.
- Audio equipment.
- Overhead projectors and screens.
- Slide projectors.
- Lecturn.
- Telephone/fax facilities.

Also available are flip charts, pens and essential writing stationery.

The business trade is predominantly from Monday to Friday. In order to improve the weekend business the hotel has concentrated on developing facilities for wedding receptions. Figure 1.39 gives an example of the type of wedding package which the Cottons Hotel can offer.

## National Trust – Quarry Bank Mill (voluntary sector)

In our voluntary sector case study we will look at Quarry Bank Mill, a site of great significance for industrial heritage.

*Fig. 1.40* Quarry Bank Mill and the National Trust logos

### National Trust

The National Trust was founded in 1895 for the preservation of places of historic interest or natural beauty. The properties are held in trust which means that they cannot be sold. They are held in trust for future generations.

The National Trust is a charity which depends upon the voluntary support of the public and its members. Much of the property which it owns has been left to the nation by landowners. It is a good example of a voluntary sector organisation which is involved in the travel and tourism industry. There are few examples of such organisations at the national scale as the majority of voluntary groups are run on a local basis in response to meeting the needs of the community.

The National Trust is the UK's largest private land owner after the Queen. Its range of properties includes:

- Industrial heritage sites.
- Stately homes.
- Castles.
- Villages.
- Forests.
- Lakes.
- Nature reserves.
- Antiquities.
- Coastal footpaths.
- Parks and gardens.

The National Trust also provides self-catering holidays throughout the UK with cottage accommodation.

*National Trust facts and figures*
The National Trust:

- Attracts more than 10 million visitors every year.
- Owns more than 365 houses and gardens.
- Has over 2 million members.
- Owns over half a million acres of land.

Quarry Bank Mill is situated in Styal Country Park in the countryside of north Cheshire, close to Manchester Airport. The mill was founded in 1784 by Samuel Gregg. It is an excellent example of industrial heritage, being one of the first water-powered spinning mills and symbolises the beginning of the Industrial Revolution in the UK. It possesses the only remaining water-powered cotton shed in the world.

Figure 1.41 shows the location of Quarry Bank Mill.

The Power Project aims to make the Quarry Bank Mill the only site in the world where visitors can see water and steam power working on site, powering machines The Project includes:

- A working 1840's Boulton and Watt type Beam Engine.
- Wooden water wheel in 1784 mill.
- New audio visual theatre.
- Exciting interactive displays and exhibitions.

**Fig. 1.41** *Products and services at Quarry Bank Mill*

*Scale of operation*

The site is managed by a registered charity, the Quarry Bank Mill Trust, who lease the site from the National Trust. In 1978 Quarry Bank Mill opened as a museum. The mill is a unique facility of international significance as it is the only operational cotton mill in the UK which can be water powered and attracts visitors from all over the world.

### Products and services

The museum comprises a number of features:

| | |
|---|---|
| *Museum and site* | Mill (see Fig. 1.42)<br>Living museum – costumes<br>Working machines<br>Spinning and weaving demonstrations<br>Apprentice house<br>Country park<br>Workers village<br>Exhibitions |
| *Visitor services* | Car park<br>Mill shop<br>Restaurant – 'The Mill Kitchen'<br>Café – 'The Mill Pantry'<br>Toilets<br>Picnic benches<br>Baby changing facilities<br>Signage |
| *Education services* | Guided tours<br>Education resource centre with<br>    taught sessions<br>'Hands on' exhibits<br>Publications |
| *Conference and banqueting* | Two conference rooms<br>Restaurant<br>Exhibitions<br>Private functions<br>Weddings and parties<br>Business conferences<br>Dinner dances |

### Staff

Quarry Bank Mill is operated by a combination of paid employees (of which there are approximately 100) and local volunteers.

The personnel chart shown in Fig. 1.43 shows the range of jobs connected with the management and operation of Quarry Bank Mill.

The majority of the workforce are unpaid volunteers, as indicated on the chart.

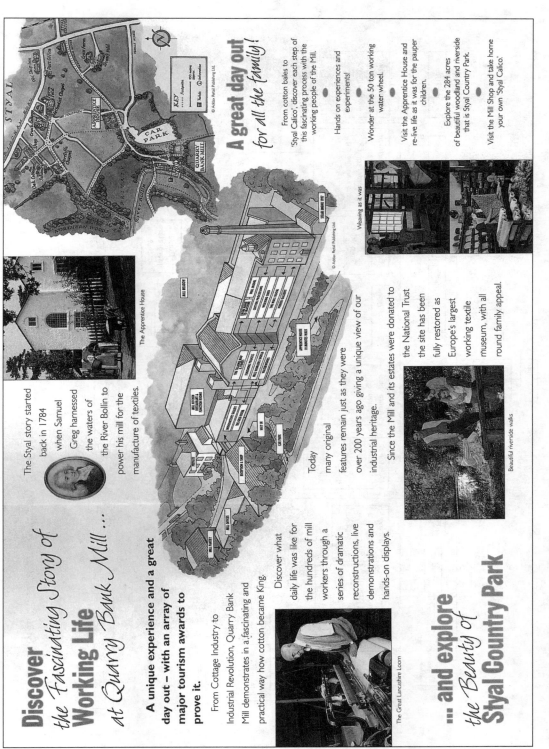

# Discover *the Fascinating Story of* Working Life *at Quarry Bank Mill...*

**A unique experience and a great day out – with an array of major tourism awards to prove it.**

From Cottage Industry to Industrial Revolution, Quarry Bank Mill demonstrates in a fascinating and practical way how cotton became King.

Discover what daily life was like for the hundreds of mill workers through a series of dramatic reconstructions, live demonstrations and hands-on displays.

*The Great Lancashire Loom*

## ...*and explore the Beauty of* Styal Country Park

The Styal story started back in 1784 when Samuel Greg harnessed the waters of the River Bollin to power his mill for the manufacture of textiles.

*The Apprentice House*

Today many original features remain just as they were over 200 years ago giving a unique view of our industrial heritage.

Since the Mill and its estates were donated to the National Trust the site has been fully restored as Europe's largest working textile museum, with all round family appeal.

*Beautiful riverside walks*

## A great day out *for all the family!*

From cotton bales to 'Styal Calico', discover each step of this fascinating process with the working people of the Mill.

Hands on experiences and experiments!

Wonder at the 50 ton working water wheel.

Visit the Apprentice House and re-live life as it was for the pauper children.

Explore the 284 acres of beautiful woodland and riverside that is Styal Country Park.

Visit the Mill Shop and take home your own 'Styal Calico'.

*Weaving as it was*

**Fig. 1.42** *The Quarry Bank Mill site*

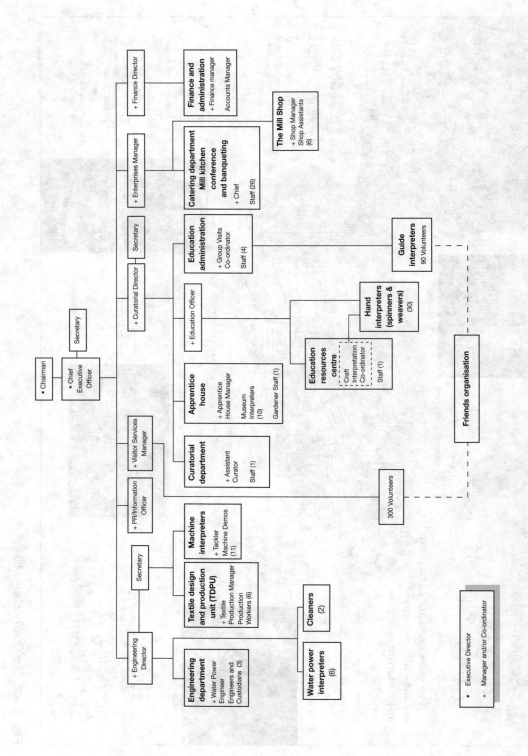

**Fig. 1.43** *Staffing structure at Quarry Bank Mill*

## Method of funding

Quarry Bank Mill derives its income from a variety of sources and is funded in a number of ways.

Quarry Bank Mill recently received funding of £537,000 from the National Lottery Heritage Fund towards the £826,000 total cost of the Power Project. The aim is to make up the shortfall by using all its available sources of income as fully as possible.

## Impact on the locality

To help the visitors find Quarry Bank Mill and Styal Country Park the attraction is signposted around the local community and from the M56 motorway. Visitor numbers are in the region of 200,000 per annum and approximately 60,000 of the visitors are school children or group educational visits.

The site is open all year round but the majority of non-school visitors come in the summer months, especially between April and September, reaching a peak in August during the school summer holiday.

The majority of visitors are National Trust members (61 per cent).

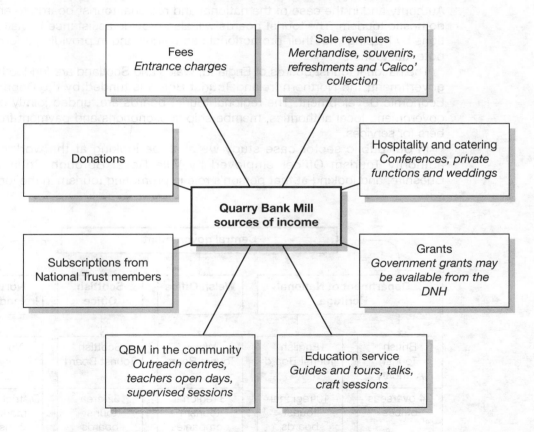

**Fig. 1.44** *Sources of funding for Quarry Bank Mill, Styal*

The authenticity of the mill has attracted television and film companies to visit the site and use it as an authentic setting for film productions. For example, the BBC TV programme 'Landmarks' featured Quarry Bank Mill in its series on Victorian Britain.

## CASE STUDY

## Tourism Department, Vale Royal Borough Council, Mid Cheshire area (public sector)

The public sector is funded and organised by central and local government. At central government level this is through the Department of National Heritage and the Welsh, Scottish and Northern Ireland Offices, as illustrated in Fig. 1.45, who have the responsibility of organising the national and regional tourist boards which were set up under the Development of Tourism Act in 1969 (the Northern Ireland Tourist Board was established in 1948).

The role of the tourist boards in conjunction with local government is to encourage overseas tourists to visit the UK in the case of the British Tourist Authority and in the case of the national and regional tourist boards to encourage domestic tourism. The tourist boards will also provide assistance to visitor attractions by helping with their promotional campaigns and in providing information to potential tourists.

The national tourist boards of England, Wales and Scotland are funded by central government; the Northern Ireland Tourist Board is funded by the Department of Economic Development. The regional tourist boards are funded jointly by central government, local authorities, membership subscriptions and payment from members for services.

In our public sector case study we shall be looking at the work of a local authority Tourism Officer employed by Vale Royal Borough Council in Mid Cheshire, and looking at that person's role in promoting tourism in the local area.

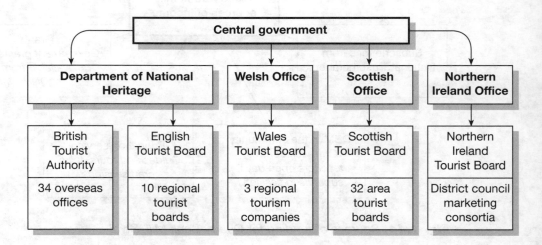

*Fig. 1.45*

### Role of local government in travel and tourism

Tourism departments exist within local authorities often as part of the Leisure Services Department. In the case of Vale Royal Borough Council (VRBC), tourism is organised by the Tourism Unit which is part of the Community Services Directorate.

Local authorities are keen to develop the tourism industry in their area as it is an expanding industry which helps to create jobs for local people. Tourism also attracts visitors to the area who will spend money on local services, thus boosting the local economy.

### Role of the Tourism Unit at VRBC

- To promote Vale Royal as a tourist destination in order to:
  - create jobs in Vale Royal
  - increase spending by tourists in Vale Royal
  - enhance tourism services and facilities for the benefit and enjoyment of the local community
- To encourage and promote the development of the tourism industry in Vale Royal. This will be achieved by providing advice on:
  - finance
  - marketing and publicity
  - funding for new projects
  - event management
  - planning and development
- To act as a co-ordinating body bringing together bodies with a vested interest in tourism organising and distributing promotional material, e.g. Fig. 1.46 shows the *Where to Eat in Vale Royal Guide* which was produced and distributed by the Tourism Unit.
- To provide an information service to the public. The Tourism Unit produces leaflets which describe the tourist attractions in the area such as the publication shown in Fig. 1.46, *Discover Vale Royal*. Information is distributed to and made available in public places such as libraries, other visitor attractions and the Information Centre in Northwich. Vale Royal does not have its own Tourist Information Centre (TIC) at present but hopes to in the near future.

The Tourism Officer for Vale Royal sees the chief attractions of the area as being:

| Attraction | Example |
| --- | --- |
| Heritage | e.g. The local salt industry |
| Countryside | Vale Royal is a predominantly rural area set in the Mid Cheshire countryside |
| Retail outlets | Northwich is an attractive market town which has many black and white Tudor style buildings |
| Natural history | e.g. Delamere Forest |
| Waterways | formerly important for industry but they now have a high recreational value, e.g. The Weaver Navigation and the Trent and Mersey Canal |

**Fig. 1.46** *Where to Eat in Vale Royal*

An example of the Tourism Unit's work is its commitment to restore into working condition the Anderton Boat Lift.

### Anderton Boat Lift

The restoration of the Anderton Boat Lift is an excellent example of the public, private and voluntary sectors working together in a collaborative project.

Figure 1.48 describes the historical significance of the Anderton Boat Lift in terms of feats of engineering and its former economic importance to the Mid Cheshire region. The photographs show the lift in its former industrial context.

Figure 1.49 shows both the location and the present industrial setting of the Anderton Boat Lift.

#### Ownership
The Anderton Boat Lift is a unique example of industrial heritage of national significance. Because of its importance it has been designated as a scheduled monument by the government. It is the only lift of its kind in the UK.

**Fig. 1.47** *Discover Vale Royal*

The lift fell into disuse in 1982. British Waterways are its custodians and are responsible for its maintenance and upkeep.

In 1994 the Anderton Boat Lift Trust was established, made up of a number of partners including representatives from the public, private and voluntary sectors, as illustrated in Fig. 1.50.

*The work of the Anderton Boat Lift Trust*
The Trust has been involved with the siting of a temporary visitor centre which provides information on the history of the ABL and the reasons for its siting in connecting the Weaver Navigation with the Trent and Mersey Canal. The future development plans for both the lift and the surrounding area as a tourist attraction which will also provide guided walks and tours for people who are interested in the area's heritage.

Another body which is involved in the restoration work is the Friends of Anderton Boat Lift. This voluntary group has established a temporary visitor centre providing information on the history of the Anderton Boat Lift and other tourist attractions. This group works alongside the Trust and shares the same vision statement. Its

# THE FIRST ANDERTON BOAT LIFT

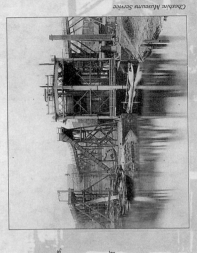

Cheshire Museums Service

In the early part of the 1870s, the Weaver Navigation Trustees decided to build a physical link between the canal and river at Anderton to eliminate the cost, effort, and wastage involved in hand transportation. Edward Leader Williams, the Trustees' engineer (who later became Sir Edward and famous for designing the Manchester Ship Canal), suggested the idea of a "boat carrying lift". In consultation with Edwin Clarke, a prominent civil engineer, he produced a design that was a unique and magnificent example of the Victorian's mastery of cast iron and hydraulics.

Completed in 1875, graceful in appearance, simple in use, and above all efficient, the Lift was hailed as a marvel of the era, and became a prototype for larger versions on the waterways of France, Belgium and Canada.

The operating mechanism consisted of two vertical sets of interconnected hydraulic cylinders and pistons set into the bed of the river and each piston supported a boat carrying tank 22.86 metres long and 4.72 metres wide. At rest, one tank was level with the canal and the other level with the river and to move the tanks, a small amount of water was removed from the bottom tank making it lighter than the top tank.

Because the two hydraulic cylinders were connected, the heavier top tank moved down and forced hydraulic liquid through the connecting pipe into the other cylinder pushing that piston and the lighter tank upwards. Watertight gates both on the tanks and at the entrance to the canal contained the water while the tanks were in movement. A steam driven hydraulic pump supplied the small amount of additional energy required to effect a reasonably rapid movement and to enable the tanks to be precisely levelled at the end of their journey.

All went well for the first ten years, then pitting and grooving of the cylinders and pistons occurred and increased to the point where it caused grave anxiety. Investigations showed that the canal water used as the hydraulic liquid was contaminated by chemicals, was corrosive, and therefore causing the damage.

It was immediately changed to condensed water from the steam engine powering the hydraulic pump. Corrosion was dramatically reduced but the damage had been done, repair bills continued to rise and it became increasingly difficult to keep the Lift in operation.

In addition, the boiler for the steam engine needed renewing, so the Weaver Trustees chose a radical solution to their problems, and in 1906 they gave the order for a new Lift to be constructed to a design by J A Saner, their current engineer.

*a wonder of the waterways*

# INTRODUCTION

The industrial history of the area around the Anderton Boat Lift stretches back at least as far as 1670 when rock salt was found at a depth of 33½ yards from the surface of the ground near Marbury.

By the 18th century, cargo boats carrying 60-70 tons could reach Winsford, the limit of navigation of the River Weaver. This, together with the completion of the Trent and Mersey Canal in 1777, provided easy means of transporting both salt and the large quantities of fuel needed to produce it, and the Alkali industry as we know it was born.

Anderton had a very important place in these activities, as there were three large salt works near the site of the present Boat Lift. More importantly, Anderton was the place the Weaver Navigation Trustees chose to transfer goods between the new canal and the river as here the navigations were very close, although the canal was over 15 metres above the river. Soon after the canal opened in 1777, a river basin was excavated to provide docking for boats, and pathways, inclined planes, and chutes were constructed to ease the task of moving every ton of cargo by hand. Primitive railways were laid to assist in moving cargoes, cranes were built and later steam engines were installed to power some of the inclined planes.

# THE SECOND ANDERTON BOAT LIFT

he Lift was to be re-built on the existing site, but there needed to be minimum interference to traffic while the work was underway. The solution adopted by Saner was as classic in its simplicity as the design of the original Lift and again confirmed the faith that the Weaver Trustees had in their own engineer.

The new Lift was built over the top of the Victorian structure, utilising the Victorian front and rear columns, some walkways and lattice work, and retaining intact the aqueduct leading to the canal. The main structure comprised tubular columns,

made up of lengths of cast iron short enough to be easily transported to the site, then bolted together to form the framework of the new Lift. The top of the framework formed a platform on which was located a system of shafts, pulleys and gears which was the new operating mechanism.

Each of the boat carrying tanks was now suspended on wire ropes which ran from the tank to the top of the Lift, over pulleys, and down to a set of cast iron weights equal to the weight of the water filled tank. Turning the pulleys one way or

the other moved the ropes and raised or lowered the tank. Because the tanks were counterbalanced, only a small amount of power was required to overcome friction in the pulley bearings and move the tanks, and this power was supplied by a small electric motor.

Completed in 1908 the Lift was an instant success. It was reliable, cheap and easy to operate. Unlike the Victorian Lift it was not the least bit graceful, but it was functional and it worked. Amazing as it may seem, during the two years of construction, boat passages through the old Lift were only interrupted for three periods, each only of two weeks.

Although the new Lift was a massive engineering undertaking, all the machining, turning, boring, fabrication of the girders to form the main top structure, and the drilling of the tubular columns was done locally in the Weaver Navigation Trustees' Maintenance Yard close by at Northwich (now British Waterways), unusual for an operation on that scale.

Even more surprising is that all the construction and building work, installation of the shafts, gearing and pulleys, and the electrical installation was also done by Weaver Navigation staff working under the supervision of Saner. It says much for his ability that he was able to motivate and control a workforce with no previous experience of such a complex civil engineering project, and complete it on time with minimum disruption during the construction period.

# THE LIFT IN USE

oth the original 1875 Lift and the present version were used extensively by commercial traffic and the principal cargoes carried were coal, china clay, salt, manufactured goods, including china ware, and agricultural produce. Sadly, trade on inland waterways in Britain declined dramatically in the 1950s, and the use of the Lift by commercial traffic effectively ended by the mid 1960s. The increase in the use of inland waterways for pleasure boating after the end of commercial traffic gave the Lift a new, but short, lease of life, as it was the navigational link joining the River Weaver to the rest of the inland waterways system and allowed visitors access to one of the most beautiful parts of England, the Weaver Valley.

History has, however, a trick of repeating itself, and in 1982 the Lift was closed because of structural faults. It has remained closed since then.

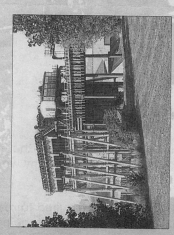

**Fig. 1.48** *The Anderton Boat Lift*

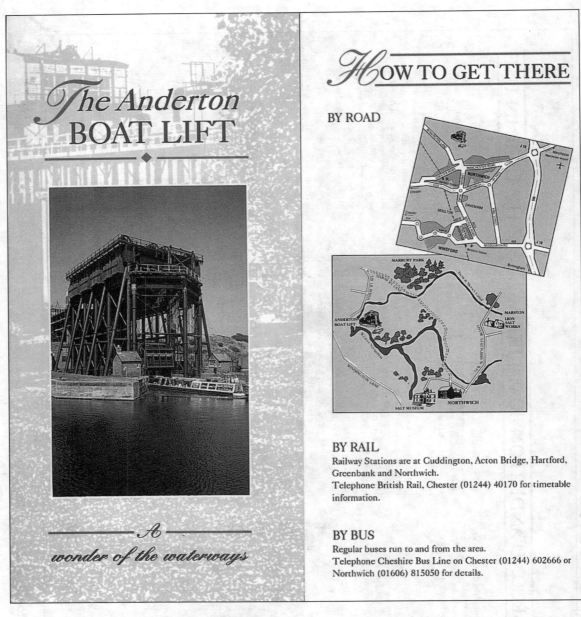

# The Anderton BOAT LIFT

### A
### wonder of the waterways

# HOW TO GET THERE

## BY ROAD

## BY RAIL
Railway Stations are at Cuddington, Acton Bridge, Hartford, Greenbank and Northwich.
Telephone British Rail, Chester (01244) 40170 for timetable information.

## BY BUS
Regular buses run to and from the area.
Telephone Cheshire Bus Line on Chester (01244) 602666 or Northwich (01606) 815050 for details.

**Fig. 1.49** *Location of the Anderton Boat Lift*

members are unpaid volunteers from the local community who rely on donations and fund-raising activities to finance any work which they undertake.

*Funding*
An estimated £10.9 million is required to restore the Anderton Boat Lift, establish a significant visitor centre and carry out the associated landscaping work. It is anticipated that the money will come from a variety of sources as shown in Fig. 1.51.

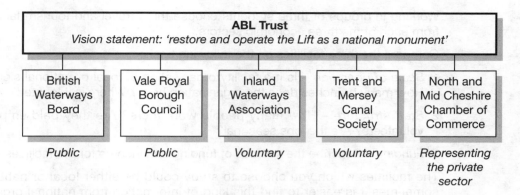

**Fig. 1.50** *Membership of the Anderton Boat Lift Trust*

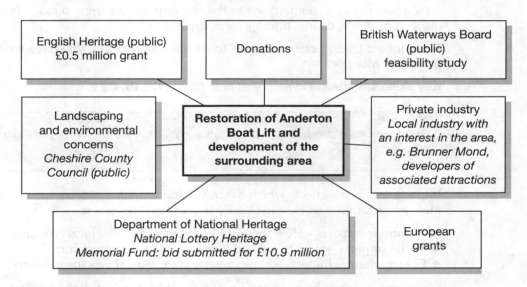

**Fig. 1.51** *Funding of the Anderton Boat Lift restoration project*

*Reasons for the restoration of Anderton Boat Lift*
Anderton Boat Lift is a facility of **national significance** as it is unique in terms of its history and culture.

The redevelopment of the Lift and its surrounding area will be of significant **benefit to the local community**.

In order to obtain funding from the National Lottery the Trust must demonstrate that the restoration project will benefit the local community.

## Activity

'**Compare the characteristics of the public, private and voluntary sectors of the industry – supported by examples of three facilities, one from each sector'**

Working in groups of three students choose three travel and tourism facilities, one from each of the three economic sectors.

Compare the three facilities on the following basis:

1. *Scale of operation* – Is it a facility/organisation of local or national significance? How many branches does the organisation have? Where is it located?

2. *Staff structure* – How many people work there? Are they paid employees or volunteers? Are the jobs seasonal?

3. *Funding* – Describe the sources of funding and income for the facilities.

The facilities which you choose to study could be either local or national – but sometimes it is easier to find this kind of information from national organisations who have published sources such as information packs or company reports.

As a group present your findings to the rest of the class using a range of visual displays, e.g. OHPs, charts, photographs, brochures.

**Remember:** Swap notes with your team members so that you have sufficient evidence for your portfolio.

**Key skills satisfied:** *Communications* **C2.1a, C2.1b, C2.2**

Give examples of the positive and negative *impacts in the UK* of the travel and tourism industry

Impacts means the effects which the travel and tourism industry has on its environment or surroundings. We can classify impacts in three ways:

- **Economic impacts** – How travel and tourism affects the local economy.
- **Social impacts** – How travel and tourism affects the community.
- **Environmental impacts** – How travel and tourism affects the local environment.

Some impacts may be positive, i.e. they will have a beneficial effect on the local areas, or they may be negative and have a detrimental effect on the area.

We can summarise typical impacts as follows:

| Type of impact | Positive | Negative |
| --- | --- | --- |
| Economic | Job creation<br>Attracting income to the local area which other businesses will benefit from | Loss of local industry as traditional jobs are replaced<br>Seasonal nature of employment |
| Social | Services may be provided for the community which did not previously exist, e.g. leisure centres, parks | The tranquillity of rural areas may be disrupted by hordes of tourists; the nature of the community may be altered |

| Type of impact | Positive | Negative |
|---|---|---|
| Environmental | The appearance of the area may be improved or landscaped to attract tourists<br><br>Areas which have become derelict may be redeveloped | The increasing volume of tourist traffic may result in air pollution and traffic congestion, and the countryside footpaths may be eroded |

The following extract from the North West Tourist Board publication 'Strategy for Success' illustrates the economic benefits which tourism can bring to the region:

*Tourism is already a potent force in economic terms with visitor spending in the Region amounting to £1,412m and directly supporting some 275,000 jobs in tourism-related sectors of the economy such as hotels, catering, transport and entertainment in 1990. The benefits of tourism are not just restricted to the economic sphere, however, and in some parts of the Region the social and environmental benefits may be of greater significance than the economic.*

*Tourism has the potential to:*

- *Create and support employment and generate local income.*
- *Establish a flourishing economic sector, diversifying, complementing and strengthening the regional economy.*
- *Enhance the image of the Region as a place in which to work, live and invest.*
- *Provide an enriching and enjoyable experience for the visitor.*
- *Help support the arts, heritage, sport and local services.*
- *Stimulate improvements to the environment and infrastructure.*
- *Generate pride, awareness and appreciation of the Region amongst local residents.*

If we look at the case of the Anderton Boat Lift restoration project we can see that it will have significant benefits for the Vale Royal area. There will inevitably be some negative aspects of the project. The following table summarises the potential positive and negative impacts.

## Economic impacts

| Positive | Negative |
|---|---|
| One of the main benefits to the Vale Royal area will be the creation of jobs in the visitor attractions and facilities which will surround the boat lift<br><br>Local businesses should benefit from the increase in trade which the tourists will bring | Taxpayers money will be used to develop tourist attractions – local residents may feel that the money would be better spent elsewhere, e.g. on education<br><br>Substantial amounts of money will have to be spent on improving the infrastructure, e.g. widening roads and strengthening bridges |

## Social impacts

| Positive | Negative |
|---|---|
| The development will create a tourism focus for the community which will also include marinas, cafes chandlery shops and a visitor centre | The infrastructure improvements may cause short-term disruption to local residents |
| The development will help to strengthen the community identity and its association with heritage | The increased tourist trade may bring with it social problems such as rising crime rates and noise |

## Environmental impacts

| Positive | Negative |
|---|---|
| The local community will be involved in upgrading an industrial site which has fallen into dereliction | Possibility of traffic congestion in the narrow country lanes leading to the site |
| The overall appearance of the area will be enhanced through landscaping | Air and litter pollution are amongst some likely impacts |

The restoration of the Anderton Boat Lift and redevelopment of the surrounding area for recreational purposes is an extremely important project for the Mid Cheshire area. It is envisaged that the project will act as a focal point strengthening the area's image as a provider of heritage attractions. A heritage package will include other facilities which are unique to the Mid Cheshire area, such as:

- **Lion Salt Works** – The only open pan salt works remaining in the UK
- **Salt Museum** – The history of the salt industry
- **Hunt's Lock** – The lock has been redeveloped to demonstrate the water control scheme on the River Weaver

Planning for the Heritage Package has already started with the development of a recognised walk known as the Victorian Trail. This is a pleasant country walk of approximately six miles which encompasses many of the area's important heritage attractions (see Fig. 1.52).

## Activity

**'Give six examples illustrating both the positive and negative impact which the travel and tourism industry has in the UK'**

**Fig. 1.52** *The Victorian Trail*

Choose six visitor attractions or tourist destinations in the UK.

Write a **brief** description of each destination and list the positive and negative effects which the tourism industry might have on them.

Try to identify a range of economic, social and environmental impacts.

## Assignment

**Title:** A theme park on your doorstep?

**Evidence indicators:** A report of an in-depth investigation of the travel and tourism industry in a locality which descibes the facilities, products and services available at the locality, identifies which sectors provide these facilities and explains the economic impact made by the industry on the locality.

**Key skills satisfied:** *Communication* **C2.1a, C2.1b, C2.2**
*Application of Number* **N2.1**

**Situation:** A leisure corporation wishes to build a new theme park providing a range of exciting 'white knuckle' rides on the outskirts of your town.
  The class should be divided into two groups:

● Group 1 – Working for the leisure services department of the local council who will support the project.
● Group 2 – Volunteers in a local environmental pressure group who will oppose the development.

### Tasks

*Part A*
First of all you will need to carry out some background research into the travel and tourism industry in your area:

1. Write a descriptive account of the tourist attractions in your area and the products and services which they provide. Use a range of leaflets to illustrate your answer.
2. List the facilities for travel within your area – this could be for travel within your town and also the facilities for a tourist to leave the area to visit other parts of the UK or to travel abroad.
3. Identify which economic sectors the travel and tourism facilities which you have identified belong to. Show your results as a bar chart and describe the results in words.
4. Explain the kind of jobs which the travel and tourism facilities are providing for your local area.

*Part B*
Discuss in class the arguments for and against the theme park development.
  The discussion should be centred around the impact which the development will have on the local area and should include economic, social and environmental impacts.
  Make notes on the issues which are discussed and these can be used as evidence for your portfolio.

# Prepare for employment in the leisure and tourism industries

Leisure and tourism is one of the world's fastest growing industries and therefore is a major job provider. It is estimated that by the year 2000 it will be the world's largest industry.

It is important that when you are seeking work in the leisure and tourism industry that you are aware of the importance of career planning and the best way of presenting yourself to prospective employers in order to achieve your career goal.

One of the problems associated with finding a job in the leisure and tourism industry is the range and diversity of opportunities which exist.

Typical job roles range from administrative officer for a tourist board to travel courier to an outdoor pursuit instructor or a receptionist at a leisure centre.

Finding out what is available to you and how you might go about achieving your career goal is therefore a complicated process. One of the first things which you should do is to look at a variety of sources of information about job opportunities which might help you to identify the types of job you would like to do.

> Identify, using main sources of information, jobs within the leisure and tourism industries which are likely to suit him/her and explain why

## Typical jobs in leisure and tourism

There is a wide range of job opportunities in the leisure and tourism industry. Some of the jobs are working directly in leisure and tourism whereas others are as a result of the industry. These are known as indirect jobs.

The following list shows some of the jobs which you might be able to apply for when you have completed your GNVQ qualification and the managerial positions you can aim for once you have acquired further qualifications or more experience.

The prospects for progression and promotion in the leisure and tourism industry are excellent as it is a fast moving industry and one in which it is possible to progress quickly along the promotional ladder to a managerial position.

There is a variety of sources of information which you might consult to identify job vacancies in the leisure and tourism industry. Sources include:

- Trade press and specialist magazines.
- Newspapers.
- Employment agencies.
- Job centres.
- Careers service.
- Press articles on new developments.

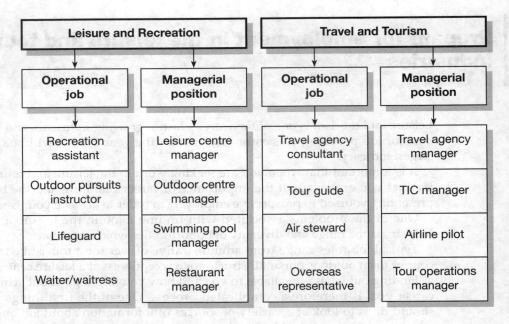

**Fig. 1.53** *Career pathways in leisure and tourism*

# Trade press and specialist magazines

One of the main sources of information is the trade press. The trade press includes magazines, journals and newspapers which are written specifically for the leisure and tourism industry. They include features and articles of interest such as news, forthcoming developments and job advertisements.

Typical trade journals include:

| Travel industry | Travel Trade Gazette<br>Travel Weekly |
| --- | --- |
| Leisure industry | Leisure Management<br>Leisure Opportunities |
| Hospitality industry | Caterer and Hotel Keeper<br>Hospitality |

## Activity

**'Main sources of information for employment in leisure and tourism'**

You should be able to find copies of trade journals either in your college/school library or in the local lending library.

By using the classified section of such journals identify 3 jobs in the travel industry and 3 jobs in the leisure/hospitality industry which would be of interest to you in the future.

Make a note of the details of the jobs as follows:

- Job title.
- Name of organisation.
- Description of the job.
- Skills and qualifications required.
- Salary/wages offered.
- Sources of information – The name of the journal where you found the vacancy.

**Key skills satisfied:** *Communication* **C2.1a, C2.2**

# Newspapers

Jobs in leisure and tourism are also advertised in local and national newspapers.

Managerial positions are usually advertised in national newspapers such as the Guardian, the Daily Telegraph or the Daily Mail whereas more junior positions are more likely to be advertised in local or regional newspapers such as the Manchester Evening News, Liverpool Echo or the Bolton Evening News.

Figure 1.54 shows a selection of job advertisements in leisure and tourism.

### Activity

**'Main sources of information for employment in leisure and tourism'**

Start collecting examples of job advertisements for the leisure and tourism industry which you can find in national and local newspapers. Keep a record of which newspaper the vacancy was advertised in.

Which kind of jobs are advertised most frequently?

**Key skills satisfied:** *Communication* **C2.1a, C2.2**

# Employment agencies

Employment agencies advertise jobs on behalf of employers. The employment agency will advertise the job and may conduct an initial interview for suitability for the post. If the candidate appears to be suitable the agency will then refer the interviewee to the company or organisation which is advertising the post. Commission is paid to the employment agency by the company which has advertised the vacancy.

**Fig. 1.54** *Employment opportunities in leisure and tourism*

## Activity

**'Main sources of information for employment in leisure and tourism'**

Employment agencies advertise a range of jobs in their shop window. Visit the employment agency in your town and make a note of any jobs which are displayed for the leisure and tourism industry.

**Key skills satisfied:** *Communication* **C2.1a, C2.2**

# Job Centres

Job Centres advertise vacancies for a wide range of employment from engineers to van drivers. The vacancies are usually based in the area which is local to the Job Centre.

The Department of Employment is responsible for managing Job Centres where specially trained staff are employed to help prospective job applicants by providing advice to identify suitable opportunities.

# Careers Service

The Careers Service employs careers advisers who provide advice, guidance and information to pupils in schools and colleges through talks and careers interviews.

To help provide this service careers advisers will visit schools and colleges and arrange interviews with pupils and students or it is also possible to call into your local Careers Service office and arrange an interview. At the careers office there will also be an adult careers adviser who is specially trained in identifying the needs of adults who are either returning to work or wish to make a career change.

The services which careers advisers can offer include:

- Occupational information about jobs.
- Advice and details of courses in further and higher education.
- Discuss youth training courses.
- Carry out psychometric/diagnostic tests to assess career suitability.
- Advice on how to apply for a modern apprenticeship.

The careers/employment adviser will also advise pupils and students on how they should present themselves for interviews. This advice will cover areas such as:

- Personal appearance.
- Letters of application.
- Writing CVs.
- Telephone techniques.
- Mock interviews.

Most schools and colleges usually appoint one member of staff as the Careers Teacher/Co-ordinator who has special responsibility for dealing with matters concerning careers advice and guidance.

Much careers information is now stored on computers and CD-ROMs. The Careers Teacher will be trained in how to use software programs such as ECCTIS which is a database of higher education courses and MicroDoors which contains occupational information on jobs. From the databases the Careers Teacher should be able to produce a printout of training courses or careers which might be suitable for you.

## Reports of developments

Leisure and tourism is a fast moving industry and companies are always looking for other opportunities to expand and diversify their business. Some examples of this include:

- Hotels which add leisure centres to their range of facilities.
- Theme parks such as Alton Towers which build hotels at their sites.

Such developments require specially trained staff and are leading to an increasing number of vacancies in the industry.

It is important for people who are seeking employment in the leisure and tourism industry to be aware of developments as this will indicate the way in which the industry is moving and is an indicator of where the future job opportunities are likely to be.

Figure 1.55 shows the First Leisure expansion plan.

It is also important to be aware of new developments in the leisure and tourism industry in your area. For example, if a new leisure centre is being built or a new travel agency is being opened there will be jobs to be filled. An example of this is the new Excel Centre in Bolton. This is a leisure centre which was built as a partnership between Bolton Borough Council Leisure Services Department and Bolton College. This development is described in Figure 1.56.

# First Leisure expansion plan

**First Leisure's Brannigans music bars are set for expansion**

After achieving record interim results, First Leisure is set to embark on its biggest ever expansion programme across all of its sectors.

In the six months to 30 April, pre-tax profits were up 5 per cent to £18.1m, thanks to a return in consumer confidence and the novelty of scratchcards wearing off, as well as further investment. Chair, Michael Grade, says: "The Group comprises a well-balanced portfolio, within which the more mature businesses continue to generate substantial cashflow and the newer ones demonstrate significant opportunities for profitable developments."

Four nightclubs are scheduled to open next year, and work has started, or is due to start, on seven Riva bingo clubs. The health and fitness expansion is underway (LO, 24 June) and sites are being sought for the successful Brannigans music bar and more Snowdomes. Details: 0171 437 9727

**Fig. 1.55** First Leisure expansion plan

> **BOLTON College's aim to encourage all members of the community to fit learning into their lives whatever their age, academic background or status will be given a big boost this autumn with the opening of the EXCEL Learning Centre.**
>
> Part of the £2M EXCEL – Centre of Excellence for Leisure and Learning Complex, being built in partnership with Bolton Council's Leisure Services Department with support from the Further Education Funding Council, the Excel Learning Centre will promote flexible, non-classroom based learning methods. It will make learning more accessible to a wider range of students helping them to pick up knowledge and skills at their own pace and at time to suit them.
>
> The Excel Learning Centre is part of Bolton Excel – Centre of Excellence for Leisure and Learning, a unique partnership between Bolton College and Bolton Metro Leisure Services to give the people of Bolton and College students a first class sports, leisure, exhibition and events facility plus valuable training and work experience opportunities for a wide range of College students.
>
> The Centre will feature a Multi-purpose Sports Hall, a Great Hall with full Theatre Facilities, an Exhibition Hall, Two Squash Courts, Climbing Wall, Travel Agency and Hair and Beauty salon, Full Bar and Catering Services and a wide range of leisure courses including Yoga, Golf Techniques, Stress Management, Community Sports Leaders Award and Aromatherapy, Massage and Holistic Therapy.

**Fig. 1.56** *Bolton Excel, Centre of Excellence for Leisure and Learning*

Some organisations also produce careers information to help guide your career choice. For example, the English Tourist Board produces a number of guides which provide advice on the qualifications and skills required to work in the travel and tourism industry. For example, Figure 1.57 shows the English Tourist Board's *Your Future in Tourism*.

# Identifying jobs which will suit you

Now that you have looked at some job vacancies in the leisure and tourism industry you will be starting to form opinions as to the type of career you would like to pursue. But is the job you have chosen suitable for you?

One of the first things that you will need to do is to take stock of your personal situation by analysing your current position. You will need to consider your:

- Personal skills.
- Current circumstances.
- Existing qualifications and those you are working towards.
- Experience.
- Interests.

**Fig. 1.57** English Tourist Board career guidance

## Personal skills

The skills which an employer will be looking for in you will depend upon the job for which you are applying. There are certain common or key skills however which all jobs demand:

- **Communications skills** – All candidates will need to demonstrate good interpersonal skills and the ability to communicate effectively with customers and other members of staff. If you are applying for a job abroad you may well be required to speak a foreign language.
- **Numeracy skills** – You may well need to show your ability to handle figures and money; e.g, this would be necessary if you were applying for the position of a leisure centre receptionist.
- **IT skills** – These are increasingly important in a business world where many administrative functions are carried out by computers.

Above all, however, you must have enthusiasm, a high level of self-motivation and show initiative and a flexible approach towards work.

## Activity

Make a list of what you consider to be your personal skills. Analyse your strengths and weaknesses.

Discuss your analysis with your tutor and try to identify how you might improve in any areas where you think you are weak.

## Personal circumstances

It is pointless applying for a job which is situated 100 miles from where you live – unless you are prepared to move house. You must therefore analyse your personal circumstances and make sure that they match the requirements of the job you are considering applying for. You will therefore need to consider the practicality of travel arrangements and, if you have children, think about how you might make arrangements for child care.

## Qualifications

The job advert will usually list the required qualifications for the position. Your *present* qualifications may already match the requirements of the job. You may however be awaiting the results of the examinations which you have just sat, in which case you would be able to apply for the job in *anticipation* of receiving your grades.

## Experience

If you are a school leaver you are unlikely to have sufficient experience for many of the jobs which you would eventually wish to apply for. However you could draw on the experience which you have gained through your part time job if you have one or through voluntary work or work experience.

For example, if you have a Saturday job working in a supermarket then you would have acquired some experience in dealing with customers.

## Interests

Your interests say a lot about you. If you have no interests you may appear unmotivated to your prospective employer.

If you have interests which involve you organising events or leading groups, e.g. if you have been a Young Leader in your local Guide movement, this will show the employer that you are actively involved in your hobbies and with the local community.

Your interests should also help you to identify the correct job for you. If all of your interests are in sport and you are applying for a desk bound job in a travel agency, the interviewer may question your suitability for the job.

## Activity

Select one of the job adverts shown in Figure. 1.58.

Consider how your personal situation matches the needs of the vacancy which you have chosen by completing the following chart:

| Personal situation | Matched | Not matched | How can improve |
|---|---|---|---|
| 1. Personal skills | | | |
| 2. Interests | | | |
| 3. Qualifications | | | |
| 4. Experience | | | |
| 5. Personal circumstances | | | |

Identify and describe *qualifications, skills and experience* required for these jobs

You will have noticed from looking at job adverts that employers are not only looking for good qualifications but also a range of skills which they feel are necessary to carry out the job successfully.

When you apply for a job in the leisure and tourism industry you will need to look at your existing circumstances, skills and qualifications and consider whether you would be a suitable candidate. If you are still at school or college it is unlikely that you will currently have the correct skills to match the requirements of the jobs which are advertised, therefore you will need to consider how you might acquire these.

It is useful to analyse your current situation by asking yourself a few questions which can form the basis of a Personal Career Plan.

## RECREATION ASSISTANT £9,450 pa

How would you like to work in a dynamic, forward thinking leisure environment?

We are looking for recreation assistants with energetic personality and flexible attitude who can perform effectively as part of a team and work on their own initiative.

Successful applicants will have a wide range of experience in a similar leisure environment and must possess the RLSS pool lifeguard qualification. Coaching qualifications would also be an advantage.

A 40 hour per week shift system is worked which includes evening and weekends.
For an application form and further details contact: **Grendale Borough Council**, St Patricks Way, Grendale, North Yorks.

The council operates a no-smoking policy.
We are an equal opportunities employer.

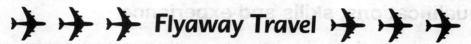

**Flyaway Travel** require sales consultants for their busy friendly offices in Gloucester.

Applicants must have a minimum of 2 years' experience and an excellent telephone manner and the ability to work under pressure. Galileo essential.
First class salary to the right applicant!
Please apply in writing to: R. Branston, Flyaway Travel, Runway Road, Gloucester GLI 3ZZ

**Fig. 1.58** *Typical job advertisements*

# Personal Career Plan

| Goals | Information |
|---|---|
| Where am I now? | Student |
| | School leaver |
| | Unemployed |
| Where do I want to be? | Job advertisements |
| | Careers guidance |
| How will I get there? | Qualifications |
| | Training |
| | On the job experience |

## Activity

**'Identify and describe qualifications, skills and experience required for these jobs, and how to acquire them'**

Using the headings listed above try to complete your own word-processed Personal Career Plan. How has the use of a word processor improved the presentation of your Personal Career Plan?

If you are uncertain about your career goal it is well worth making an appointment either with your school/college careers adviser or with the careers service.

**Key skills satisfied:** *Communication* **C2.1a, C2.1b, C2.2**
*Information Technology* **IT2.1, IT2.2, IT2.3**

# Qualifications, skills and experience

An employer will be looking for a combination of qualifications, skills and experience in a prospective job candidate.

The range of qualifications and the routes which students and pupils can take is quite complex. Figure 1.59 shows the national qualification framework and indicates the equivalence between academic and vocational qualifications at the various levels.

## The national framework for qualifications

There is a variety of qualification routes which a student will encounter and might take to reach their career goal. It is not essential to follow one pathway as a combination of the different types of qualifications might suit the needs of the student.

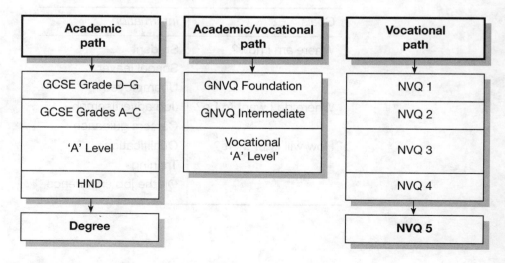

*Fig. 1.59* National qualification framework

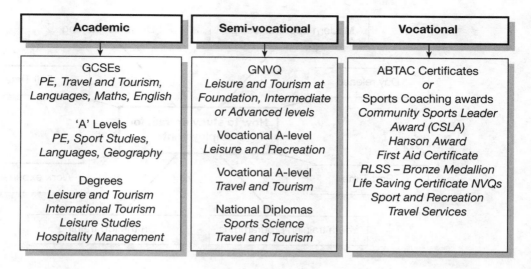

**Fig. 1.60** *Academic and vocational pathways*

The first pathway which most students will encounter is the schools based GCSE Academic pathway which traditionally leads on to 'A' Levels for those who remain at school. The distinction between pathways is becoming more blurred now as increasingly schools are also offering GNVQs at Foundation and Intermediate Levels. A pupil might therefore study a combination of 3 or 4 GCSE subjects whilst at the same time studying for a GNVQ Intermediate qualification. Alternatively a pupil who has studied 7 or 8 subjects to GCSE standard at school might decide to opt for a Vocational A-level qualification at a College of Further Education rather than remaining at school to study 'A' Level subjects.

An NVQ is a practical work-based qualification which is usually taught in the workplace. An NVQ tests an individual's capabilities to perform a specific job or task whereas a GNVQ qualification contains a combination of practical skills and theoretical study which is more broadly based than an NVQ.

Figure 1.60 suggests some typical qualifications which are relevant to careers in leisure and tourism.

For most jobs employers will be looking for basic skills in Maths and English which could be achieved either through GCSEs or through the study of core skills which are taught as part of GNVQs. Some qualifications are essential for certain jobs. For example, a pool lifeguard would require an RLSS pool life saving qualification.

It is possible to study for qualifications by a variety of methods of study as well as the traditional full-time route.

## Activity

**'Identify and describe qualifications, skills and experience required for these jobs and describe how to acquire them'**

Think about the sort of career in leisure and tourism which you would like to pursue.

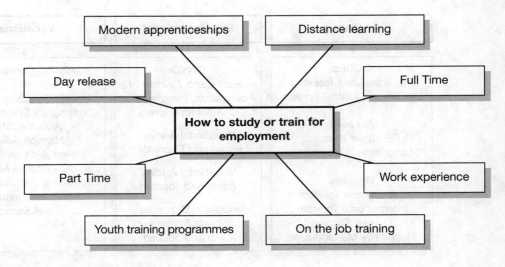

**Fig. 1.61** *Methods of study*

Visit your local college of further education and with the help of a prospectus identify four different courses which will help you to achieve your career aims.

What other personal skills might help you to achieve your career goal?

Enter this information into your Personal Career Plan.

Word process your Personal Career Plan and discuss it with your tutor.

**Key skills satisfied:** *Communication* **C2.1b**
*Information Technology* **IT2.3**

Describe how to acquire qualifications, skills and experience required for these jobs

There are a number of academic and training routes which can be taken to reach your chosen career goal. Your choice of route will be influenced by your personal circumstances (see Fig. 1.61).

# Full-time courses

Many young people now progress straight from school into further full-time study either by remaining at school, attending a local sixth form college or college of further education.

All of these establishments offer 'A' Levels and GNVQs although there is usually a stronger emphasis on GNVQs and vocational courses such as NVQs in colleges of further education. For example, if you wanted to study NVQ Travel Services as a full-time course you would need to attend your local college of further education. Many colleges of further education now offer an opportunity to study in a realistic working environment by providing 'in house' travel agencies. These travel agencies provide the necessary practical experience students are likely to encounter, if they obtain work in a travel agency.

After completing your 'A' Level programme or Vocational A-level you may then wish to continue your studies at university where there is a wide range of HNDs and degrees in Leisure and Tourism.

For example, Sheffield Hallam University offers the following courses:

- HNDs
  - Hotel, Catering and Institutional Management
  - Home Economics
- Degrees, BA/BSc (Honours)
  - Hotel and Catering Management
  - Hotel and Tourism Management
  - Recreation and Tourism Management
  - Recreation Management
  - Countryside Recreation Management

# Part-time courses

It is also possible to study towards a qualification in Leisure and Tourism on a part-time basis. Depending upon the requirements of the course this could be on an evening basis, e.g. many travel agency qualifications such as the ABTAC Primary Certificate are delivered as evening programmes.

This method of study might suit your personal needs if, for example, you are a parent with young children.

Many employers are keen for their workforce to learn new skills and will therefore encourage them to study further by offering a day release arrangement. On this basis you would spend one of your normal working days at college. Many NVQ courses are studied in this way.

## Distance learning

If you are unable to attend college because of your personal circumstances you may choose to study by distance/open learning methods. This could be achieved by a correspondence course where the learning materials are sent to you by post at the beginning of the study period and you would return your completed assignments by post. You would then be contacted by a distance learning co-ordinator either by phone, letter or e-mail to discuss your progress and to see if you have any problems or queries.

You may also be required to attend the college for a very short period of time for a study/summer school in order to gain support from tutors and other students on the course.

Many universities now offer this method of study as does the Open University. It is a method of study which is most appropriate to higher level courses such as HNDs and degrees where students are able to work without supervision.

## On the job training

Whilst you are in the workplace doing a job you will constantly be learning new skills through experience. Your supervisor or trainer will ensure that you are performing tasks in the correct way and will provide advice and guidance.

### Work experience

As part of your GNVQ Leisure and Tourism course you will probably undergo a period of work experience in a local leisure and tourism organisation. This is a very valuable experience for although much of your time will be spent observing or *shadowing* other members of staff it will give you a taste of the industry and help you to identify whether this is the correct job for you.

Many leisure and tourism organisations have very well structured work experience programmes, e.g. British Airways and Servisair, which give students a real feel of working in the industry.

### Training programmes

Many employers offer specific training programmes to equip their staff with the practical skills necessary to perform their work effectively. This may be carried out on site by an in-house trainer or supervisor or at a specialised training centre or college.

An example of a training programme which is widely used in the leisure and tourism industry is the Youth Training scheme. This is a two year programme sponsored by the government. The trainee is employed by the leisure and tourism organisation who are committed to train the young person (age 16–18) in the skills necessary to perform the job. This may be through in-house training or at a specialised training centre.

## Career pathways

To illustrate the variety of pathways which might be taken we will show a number of typical career routes highlighting the qualifications, skills and experience which might be required to achieve the stated career goals. All of these positions will also require the candidate to have gained experience and to have acquired work based skills as they have progressed up the career ladder.

## Situation 1: 16-year-old student progressing to further education

| Career goal | Method |
|---|---|
| Tour Operations Contract negotiator working for a major tour operator such as Thomson or Airtours | Full-time position plus on the job training |
| Degree in International Tourism | Full-time study for 3 years at university |
| Vocational A-level Travel and Tourism | Full-time study for 2 years at college of further education plus work experience in a related field |
| School leaver with 4 or more GCSEs at grades A–C | Full-time study at school |

## Situation 2: School leaver wishing to find employment with on the job training

| Career goal | Method |
|---|---|
| Leisure Centre Manager | Professional qualifications: Institute of Leisure and Amenity Management (ILAM) Certificate of Leisure Management, NVQ level IV (day release) |
| Duty Manager | NVQ Facility Operations level III (part-time study) |
| Leisure Centre Assistant | NVQ Facility Operations level II (on the job training plus day release at college of further education) |
| School leaver with 4 or more GCSEs at grades A–C | Full-time study at school |

## Situation 3: Career change – an adult returner to education who needs to reskill

| Career goal | Method |
|---|---|
| Travel Agency Manager | British Airways fares and ticketing Certificates levels I and II |
| Senior Consultant in a travel agency | Job related qualifications: e.g. ABTAC Primary, Advanced and Air Certificates |

| Career goal | Method |
|---|---|
| Junior Consultant in a travel agency | On the job training plus training days |
| Adult with qualifications and experience in an unrelated field | NVQ Travel Services level II – part-time study at a college of further education with an in-house travel agency |

It is important to plan your qualification route in order to achieve your chosen career goal. A careers adviser will provide you with advice and guidance as to suitable careers and the ways in which you might achieve the necessary qualifications and experience to meet the needs of the job and help you to build up a personal action plan.

## Activity

Figure 1.54 shows a number of advertisements for typical jobs in leisure and tourism.

Read through the adverts and make a list of the following:

- Vocational qualifications required.
- Academic qualifications required.
- Skills necessary.
- Experience necessary.

Describe different *ways of presenting* personal information to prospective employers

When you are applying for a job you will be in competition with many other candidates. It is essential therefore that you spend time planning your application, identifying the needs of the job so that you can present yourself in the best possible light.

In this section we will study the case of a typical applicant who is applying for the position of Trainee Travel Consultant, as illustrated in the job advertisement shown in Fig. 1.59.

We will follow through the job application procedures from the identification of the initial job advertisement to the interview stage.

## Applying for a job

The following job vacancy is advertised in the Job Centre and the local newspaper:

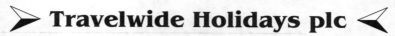

# Travelwide Holidays plc

Require an enthusiastic *Trainee Travel Consultant.*

Applicants require a sound general education with GCSE passes in maths and English.
Candidates must have a polite manner and good communication skills.
On the job training will be provided.
Apply in writing to:
Miss B. Cook, Travelwide Holidays plc, 110 High Street, Casterbridge, Dorset CA2 4PQ

☎ Tel.: 01407 330669

**Fig. 1.62** *Typical job advertisement*

## The application process

Mark Owen has just read the advert for a Trainee travel consultant in his local news-paper, the Casterbridge Gazette. He has been looking for a vacancy in a travel agency since leaving Casterbridge College of Further Education where he studied GNVQ Leisure and Tourism.

Mark decides to write a letter to Travelwide Holidays asking for more informa-tion about the job and also to provide them with his personal details.

## Activity

**'Describe different ways of presenting personal information to prospective employers'**

Write a letter of application for one of the jobs which you identified previously.

Remember that your letter of application will be the first impression you make on the employer. Poor spelling and sloppy handwriting are unlikely to impress an employer.

- Are all the words spelt correctly?
- Is your letter neatly written?
- Word process the letter if possible.

Why do you think it is important to word process your letter of application?

**Key skills satisfied:** *Communication* **C2.3**
*Information Technology* **IT2.2, IT2.3**

Mark has received a reply to his letter of application. Travelwide have asked him to complete an application form. The application form provides an employer with most of the information which they need to know about a candidate, e.g. date of birth, qualification details. There is usually a section in which you need to state why you are applying for the job – this is often the most difficult part to complete.

*67 Harkness Road*
*Casterbridge*
*Dorset CA6 6LL*

Miss B. Cook,
Travelwide Holidays plc,
110 High Street,
Casterbridge,
Dorset CA2 4PQ

23 July 1997

Dear Miss Cook,

| | |
|---|---|
| **Job title** | **Trainee Travel consultant** |
| **Source of job advert** | I would like to apply for the position of Trainee Travel Consultant which was advertised in the Casterbridge Gazette on 19th July 1997. |
| **Personal details** | I am 17 years old and have the following qualifications: |

GCSE English      Grade C
GCSE Maths       Grade B
GCSE French      Grade D
GCSE Geography   Grade D
GNVQ Intermediate Leisure and Tourism (merit)

[*Also include details of qualifications you are working towards*]

**Work experience** 
Since leaving Casterbridge College of Further Education I have been working on a part-time basis in Burger King. Whilst at college I had a period of two weeks work experience at Going Places in Casterbridge.

**Referees** 
If you need referees please contact:

| | |
|---|---|
| Mr G. Barlow, | Mr R. Williams, |
| Head Teacher, | Personnel Manager, |
| Smithills High School, | Burger King, |
| Croft Road, | 110–116 The Mall, |
| Casterbridge CA4 1BB | Casterbridge CA1 8NZ |

**Sound enthusiastic** 
I am very keen to pursue a career in the travel industry. I am friendly and outgoing and I enjoy travelling and meeting new people.

**Interview time** 
I am available for interview at any time which is convenient to you.

Yours sincerely

**Mark Owen**

***Fig. 1.63*** *Letter of application*

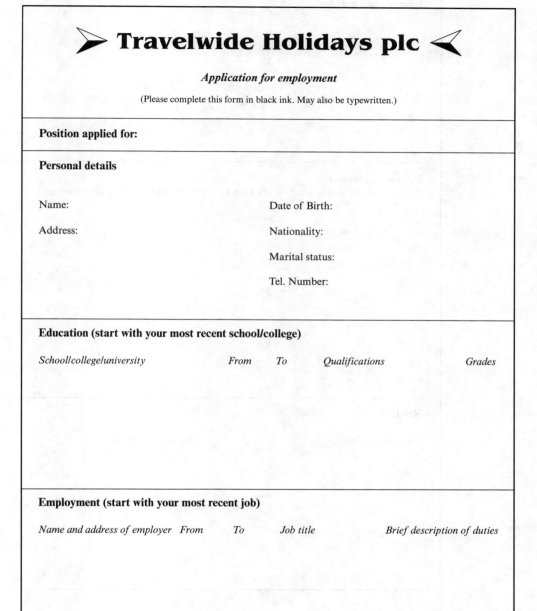

**Fig. 1.64** Employment application form

**Interests and hobbies**

**Personal statement**
*Explain why you wish to apply for this post. Continue on a separate sheet if necessary.*

**Referees**

Name and address:

Name and address:

Tel:

Tel:

Signed.......................................................................... Date................................

**Fig. 1.64** *(Continued)*

## Activity

**'Describe different ways of presenting personal information to prospective employers'**

Complete the details on the application form as if you are applying for one of the vacancies which you have selected.

- Always read the application form carefully before filling in any of the sections.
- It is advisable to complete it in pencil first which can be erased, or to take a photocopy to avoid having to cross bits out.
- Read the instructions at the top of the application form – are you required to complete the form in black ink, capital letters, should it be hand written or type written?
- Keep your answers short and concise – show that you can identify the appropriate information
- If you are unsure about the correct spelling of any words always check them using a dictionary – or use the spell check facility if you are using a word processor.
- In the educational details section do not list your primary school – the employer is only interested in your secondary education plus any further or higher education courses which you have undertaken.
- In the section on interests avoid including pastimes such as 'socialising' – it might give the employer the impression that you like to stay out all night.
- Keep a copy of the completed application form as you may wish to read it again before the interview.
- Write a short covering letter to accompany the completed application form.
- Proof read the completed application form and letter and check for mistakes.

Discuss the completed form with your tutor.

**Key skills satisfied:** *Communication* **C2.3**
*Information Technology* **IT2.3**

---

Produce a *suitable CV* for submission to prospective employers

---

Mark Owen has now been selected for interview for the position of Trainee Travel Consultant. He will need to take his curriculum vitae (CV) and National Record of Achievement (NRA) to the interview.

# Curriculum vitae

CV is short for 'curriculum vitae' which is a compilation of personal details and achievements. For example, if you had played in a school sports team you would probably want to include this in your CV.

Mark Owen's CV, which he will take with him to his job interview, is shown in Fig. 1.65.

## Curriculum Vitae

### Personal details

| | |
|---|---|
| Name: | **Mark Owen** |
| Address: | 67 Harkness Road, Casterbridge, Dorset CA6 6LL |
| Telephone: | 1407 889880 |
| Date of Birth: | 03/04/79 |
| Marital status: | Single |

### Education and qualifications

**1995–97**  *Casterbridge College of Further Education*
Intermediate GNVQ Leisure and tourism Grade: Merit

**1990–95**  *Smithills High School*
GCSEs in English (C), Maths (B), French (D), Geography (D)

### Employment

**1995**  Part-time kitchen assistant at Burger King, Casterbridge.
*The work involved kitchen duties and dealing with the general public.*

**March 95**  Two weeks' work experience at Going Places in Casterbridge.
*The work involved general administrative duties including filing, making
telephone calls and shadowing the senior travel consultant.*

### Other achievements

Duke of Edinburgh award
First aid certificate
Driving licence

### Interests

Playing football for a Sunday league team. I am also interested in mountain biking
and music. At school I was captain of the first XI cricket team.

### Referees

| | |
|---|---|
| Mr G. Barlow, | Mr R. Williams, |
| Head Teacher, | Personnel Manager, |
| Smithills High School, | Burger King, |
| Croft Road, | 110–116 The Mall, |
| Casterbridge CA4 1BB | Casterbridge CA1 8NZ |

**Fig. 1.65**  *A curriculum vitae ('CV')*

## Activity

**'Describe different ways of presenting personal information to prospective employers'**

Using Mark's CV as a guide, prepare your personal CV for the job vacancy which you have identified.

- Ideally your CV should be word processed, making it easy to read.
- Present your CV on A4 paper – try not to make it longer than two pages.
- Check that all the details are correct.
- Ensure that all spelling, punctuation and grammar are correct.

**Key skills satisfied:** *Information Technology* **IT2.3**

# National Record of Achievement *(NRA)*

Every pupil should have a National Record of Achievement which they will update at various stages throughout their academic career.

Your Record of Achievement should include the following:

- Personal details.
- Details of qualifications achieved.
- Progress statements by teachers/tutors.
- Records of other achievements, e.g. swimming certificates, music awards, participation in school events or events in the community.
- Employment history – include details of all part-time and full-time jobs plus work experience.
- A personal statement of your goals and targets.

It is always useful to take an NRA to an interview as this provides the employer with much background information about yourself, such as academic achievement, character references, interests and hobbies. It helps to give the employer an immediate impression about you and your personal qualities.

## Activity

**'Describe different ways of presenting personal information to prospective employers'**

Bring your National Record of Achievement to the classroom and discuss with your tutor how you might update it in order to prepare yourself for seeking employment or for use in applying for higher level educational courses.

Word process any additional information which you choose to insert into your NRA.

Explain how you feel the use of information technology has helped you to present your personal information more effectively.

# What is the National Record of Achievement?

*"I interview staff and it is very hit or miss. The NRA gives me a much broader view of people, and what they are capable of."*
(David Williams, General Manager of University Student Union Services)

### Recording achievement

The Government launched the National Record of Achievement (NRA) in 1991. It is a system that people all over the country can use to summarise their achievements in education, training and throughout life.

Whether you are at school, college or work, a record of your achievements helps you to make the most of your strengths. The NRA has been designed to:

- give a clear picture of your past successes;
- give you a foundation to build future plans on; and
- help you track your progress towards your targets.

### What does the NRA include?

The NRA is made up of a number of standard sheets stored in a folder. It is up to you to decide exactly what information you put on these sheets. But usually you will discuss this with an adviser (perhaps a college tutor, or a work supervisor). The NRA sheets cover:

- personal details – including your education and training history;
- personal statement – your views on how you are doing;
- qualifications and credits – details of your exam results (you can also store certificates in the NRA);
- achievements and experiences – including your progress in core skills, personal qualities, sports you like and social interests;
- employment history – details of full-time and part-time jobs you have held; and
- individual action plan – a summary of your future goals. This section can help you plan for the future.

School leavers can also use the NRA for their school achievements and attendance record.

### How can the NRA help me?

You can use the NRA to take control of the way you learn and develop. It can help you to:

- show what you have achieved and your abilities;
- make the most of your strengths;
- make future plans;
- take charge of your development; and
- work towards NVQs.

If you want to change your job or go to college, the NRA can help by summarising the information you need to think about when you make decisions about the move. It will help you prepare for interviews, and give employers, trainers and colleges a clear idea of what you have to offer.

If you want to go further in education, training or work, the NRA can help you base your future career or training decisions on firm ground. You can use it to set goals for your future and to keep track of your progress.

The NRA is recognised by employers, trainers and colleges all over the country and it can give you support through all stages of learning and decision-making.

**Resources**
For further
Information contact:
**The National Council
for Vocational
Qualifications**
222 Euston Road
London NW1 2BZ

***Fig. 1.66*** *National Record of Achievement*

# The interview

Before Mark's interview date he discusses how to present himself with the Careers Adviser at the Careers Service in Casterbridge. The Careers Adviser gave Mark the following advice.

- Find out the location of Travelwide Holidays and plan your travel arrangements.
- Be punctual.
- Dress smartly and appropriately.
- Speak slowly and clearly – don't mumble.
- Find out about Travelwide Holidays in case you are asked questions about the company at the interview.
- Think carefully before answering questions – take your time.
- Prepare in advance answers to these typical questions:
  - 'Why do you want this job?'
  - 'How will your role benefit the company?'
- Try to identify some questions to ask the interviewer – it is your chance to find out whether the position will suit you.
- Body language:
  - don't fidget or look bored
  - maintain eye contact with the interviewer – it shows that you are interested
  - don't look out of the window
  - have a pleasant manner – smile and show an interest

## Revision questions

1. Name the component areas of leisure and recreation.
2. Describe one facility from each of the component areas of leisure and recreation.
3. Name the component areas of travel and tourism.
4. Describe one facility from each of the component areas of travel and tourism.
5. Describe one facility from each of the three economic sectors.
6. Describe what is meant by negative impact of the travel and tourism industry.
7. Describe when you would use a CV.
8. What else can you use to present personal information for a job interview.

# Unit 2

# MARKETING IN LEISURE AND TOURISM

**Investigate the marketing and promotion in leisure and recreation and travel and tourism organisations**

**Plan a leisure and recreation or travel and tourism promotional campaign**

**Run and evaluate a leisure and tourism promotional campaign**

In this unit we shall be looking at some of the basic principles of marketing and how these can be related to the promotional activities of leisure and tourism organisations. We shall be considering marketing activities such as market research, target markets and market segments. The marketing mix and promotional activities are then considered in relation to examples of leisure and tourism organisations.

In Chapters 2 and 3 you are required to put these principles into practice by designing and running your own promotional campaign and evaluating its success.

# Investigate marketing and promotion in leisure and recreation and travel and tourism organisations

Leisure and tourism is a fast moving, competitive industry. For companies to be successful they need to 'market' their products effectively in order to achieve sales and profits. This means finding out what product the public wants (marketing) and then letting the public know that the product is available and how they can obtain it (promotion).

> Explain how marketing applies to leisure and recreation and travel and tourism organisations

## Marketing and promotion in the leisure and tourism industry

By carrying out marketing activities companies are able to identify customer requirements and to provide the public with the products which they want. The results of marketing can then be used to prepare promotional campaigns which make customers aware of the range of products available, thus encouraging the consumer to buy or use that particular product.

## Marketing

- Identifying customer needs.
- Identifying of the potential market for a product/service.

Marketing involves identifying the needs and wants of the buying public (market) through techniques such as market surveys, customer feedback forms and questionnaires. This will indicate the potential number of people who may want to buy the product; for example, a market survey may reveal that there is a demand for cycling holidays in Ireland.

### Activity

Design a questionnaire which you can use to investigate the leisure interests of your students in your college/school.

**Key skills satisfied:** *Information Technology* **IT2.1, IT2.2**

# Product design

- Meeting customer needs.
- Influencing product development.

A product is designed and produced to meet the identified needs of the target market. This is vital as customers will not buy a product which they do not want.

## Activity

Using the information which you have gathered for the questionnaire work out how many people might be interested in playing in a college netball match.

Design a second questionnaire aimed specifically at people (**target market**) who showed an interest in playing netball and try to determine whether there is sufficient interest to put together a team to represent the college in a tournament (**product design**).

**Key skills satisfied:** *Application of Number* **N2.1, N2.2, N2.3**

# Promotion

- Informing customers
- Promoting products
- Influencing consumer choice

These are the methods by which the public is made aware or informed of the products, e.g. by advertising or by specific sales promotions, which indicate where the product can be purchased and how much it will cost.

A leisure or tourism organisation will hope to influence consumer choice by using its promotional materials to make the product look attractive and will try to convince the public that they need the product.

## Activity

You will now need to promote the forthcoming netball tournament. Design a poster which is aimed at encouraging spectators to attend (**influencing consumers**). You may find it useful to word process the poster and make some use of graphics.

**Key skills satisfied:** *Information Technology* **IT2.2**

# Sale of product

- Generating income
- Generating profit

The customer has been informed of the product; the product meets the customers needs; the customer buys the product. Was the sales target achieved?

The ultimate aim of many private sector organisations is to make money.

All organisations will need to make enough money to cover the cost of their overheads such as wages, equipment, material costs. Hopefully there will be sufficient funds left over to make a profit.

$$Profit = Income - Overhead\ costs$$

In a specific promotional campaign a leisure or tourism company will have set an anticipated level of sales and profit which it will hope to achieve from the campaign.

## Activity

It has been suggested that refreshments are made available at the netball tournament. Think about how much it will cost you to provide the refreshments and how much you will have to charge in order to make a profit.

**Key skills satisfied:** *Application of Number* **N2.1, N2.2**

## Customer feedback

- Achieving customer satisfaction

It is important to evaluate the success of a product and its promotion. The organisation will need to analyse whether the product was available at the right time and in the right place at the right price.

Is the customer satisfied?

## Activity

You have received some favourable comments about the netball tournament and you are wondering whether a larger competition with more players, teams and spectators would be possible.

Working in groups try to think of the questions you would ask in order to collect the information on which you could make a decision.

You might need to have two lists of questions; one for spectators and one for competitors.

## Response

If the product sells well the company should make a profit and continue to produce that product.

If product sales are poor the company will look back to the product design stage and consider its marketing strategy and may either produce a modified version of the product or discontinue its sale.

## Social profit

Social profit is the benefit to the community which the leisure or tourism product or service brings. This is not measured in terms of money. Many public sector leisure and tourism facilities such as local authority leisure centres are more concerned with providing a service to the community by providing facilities which may not otherwise exist. The cost of providing them may result in very little financial profit being made, however local authorities must try to ensure that the cost of providing the service does not exceed the income from sales otherwise a financial loss will be made.

The promotional materials which a local authority leisure centre uses to inform the public of its services will not be as glossy or expensive as those which a private leisure centre uses.

# The marketing process

We can consider the marketing process in relation to a travel product such as Le Shuttle, the rail service whose route is the Channel Tunnel.

- **Marketing** – The marketing department of Le Shuttle will analyse the needs and wants of holidaymakers and businesses who use the English Channel as their route to continental Europe. Market information indicates that customers would like a faster service than is provided by the traditional car ferry crossing.
- **Product design** – Le Shuttle: a vehicle- and passenger-carrying rail service linking the UK with France with a journey time of only 40 minutes.
- **Promotion** – Le Shuttle is advertised in brochures and newspapers so that the public is made aware of the services available. Promotional offers such as special rates may be made.
- **Sales of product** – The success of Le Shuttle's promotional campaign will be determined by the number of passengers using Le Shuttle and whether they are satisfied with the service they have received, and whether the company has made a financial profit through running the service.
- **Customer feedback** – The level of sales and customer opinion will be fed back to the marketing team who may modify the product or its promotion as appropriate.

## Activity

Choose two products, one from the leisure industry and one from the travel industry, which are available nationally and which are widely promoted in the press or on TV.

Gather a range of advertising materials for the products, or make a note of the TV advertisements.

With help from your tutor try to analyse the market for the products and the way they have been promoted, as follows:

1. Marketing – Identify the target market.

2. Product design – How do you think the product might have been designed to meet the needs of the market?

3. Promotion – Describe the promotional methods that have been used.

4. Sales of product – Where is the product sold? Is the product competitively priced?

5. Customer feedback – What is your opinion of the product? How would you modify the product?

---

Describe the *marketing mix* and explain how *promotional activities* fit into it

---

The marketing mix refers to the ingredients of marketing and can be compared to a recipe for baking a cake. As with the cake each of the ingredients in the marketing mix is vital to producing a successful product. Unlike a cake recipe, however, the ingredients in the promotional mixture can be varied. For example a facility may decide to reduce the price of its products as a special promotion to attract new customers. The marketing mix has four interrelated parts which are known as product, place, price, promotion.

- **Product** – This is the leisure or tourism product/service which an organisation sells or hires out, e.g. swimming lessons, guided tours, flights.
- **Place** – Where the product can be bought or where the facility offering the service is located, e.g. the place where swimming lessons (product) can be bought is a swimming pool.
- **Price** – How much the product or service will cost, e.g. entry fees may vary depending upon the time of day or time of year (peak and off peak tariffs), group discounts may apply as might special offers.
- **Promotion** – The methods by which the public is made aware of the product or service on offer, e.g. leaflets and advertising.

For a leisure or tourism organisation to be successful it must get its marketing mix right. This means getting the right product to the right people, at the right price, in the right place at the right time whilst ensuring that the customer is informed about the product or service on offer.

# Waterworld

The following example illustrates how the marketing mix can be applied to Waterworld. Waterworld is a water theme park which is owned by Rank Leisure. It is located in Hanley, near Stoke on Trent.

The centre offers a range of activities including water chutes, flumes, slides, wave machines and an outdoor pool. There is also a café and licensed bar adjacent to the pool.

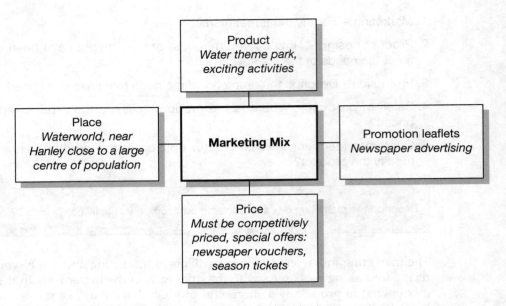

**Fig. 2.1** The 4 Ps of marketing at Waterworld, Hanley

## Activity

Name the place where the following products can be purchased:

| Product | Place | Price range |
|---|---|---|
| Package holiday | | |
| Riding lessons | | |
| Latest blockbuster film | | |
| Watch a play | | |
| Late night entertainment | | |
| Replica football shirt | | |
| Ride on a rollercoaster | | |
| Visit the Crown Jewels | | |

To complete the table try to find the prices charged for the products in the places which you have identified.

List the sources of information which you used to complete the table.

# Promotional activities

There is a wide range of promotional activities which are used by organisations to inform the public of the range of leisure and tourism products and services which they offer. The choice of promotional activity will depend upon a number of factors including:

- The type of the product.
- The nature of the target market.
- The financial resources of the organisation.

## Advertising

An advertisement will inform the public of the products or services which a facility can offer.

Advertising will use one of the following media channels, which may be either at a local or national level:

- Television.
- Radio.
- Newspapers and magazines.
- Billboards and posters.

Television advertising is one of the most expensive methods of promotion. Some of the large tour operators such as Thomson and First Choice run extensive television advertising campaigns which cost hundreds of thousands of pounds.

Not all advertising is so expensive though. For example, a coach company may advertise its services in a local newspaper for a modest fee.

The scale of advertising is relative to the size of company and its financial resources. The First Choice TV advertising campaign will reach millions of viewers whereas the coach company's press advertisement will be targeting the local market.

## Sales promotion

Special offers or the promotion of a certain feature of a facility are specific sales promotions. They are designed to produce a fast response from the customer. For example, a money off voucher may only be valid for a certain period of time, therefore encouraging the customers to buy the products within a specified time period.

Figure 2.2 shows a money off promotion which has been used by Jodrell Bank in Cheshire.

Another type of specific promotion is free gifts. For example companies selling timeshare apartments often offer a free gift to encourage people to attend their presentations. Restaurants may provide the incentive of half price children's meals where two adult meals are being purchased.

Tour operators offer special rates for late availability bookings during the summer months. If you look in a travel agents window you will see that it is full of special offers with tour operators competing against each other in order to sell unbooked holidays at the last minute (see Fig. 2.3). Private leisure clubs such as the Cottons

**Fig. 2.2** *Money saving promotion at Jodrell Bank, Cheshire*

Leisure Club in Knutsford, Cheshire, offer special rates for family membership to encourage the whole family to use the leisure facility.

## Public relations

Many leisure and tourism organisations will want to build up an image of the company which makes it attractive to its existing customers and potential customers. It may then become involved in projects which are not directly advertising but in which the company name is used to support a project and thus raising the public's awareness of the organisation.

The fast food chain McDonalds is very aware of its image and supports a number of good causes. For example, McDonalds will not buy beef for its burgers from suppliers whose cattle have grazed on land which has been cleared of tropical rain forest. McDonalds also supports a number of children's charities and has set up a number of Ronald McDonald Houses for parents of sick children. By doing this the profile of the company is enhanced, thus encouraging people to eat at McDonalds.

## Personal selling

This occurs when a customer meets the sales person face to face. This sale may not necessarily be the sale of a tangible product, for example a pair of sports shoes, but may be the sale of a service, for example a sports coaching course to be held at a local park to develop football skills. Successful personal selling depends on the skills of the seller by providing good customer service as discussed in Unit 3.

## Direct marketing

When you receive a mail shot, through your letter box, from a local cinema which you have recently visited, this is an example of direct marketing. Your name and address have been obtained by the cinema because, on your recent visit, you took

**Fig. 2.3** *Last minute bargains available at Going Places*

the trouble to fill in and return a customer survey form. The cinema could then identify you as a potential customer. Consequently they sent you details of forthcoming attractions in order to encourage new business.

## Activity

Produce a poster or collage displaying advertising material sent directly to your house. Try to identify from all the leaflets and brochures which you feel is directly targeted to your family.

## Sponsorship

Nowadays many leisure and tourism organisations try to increase revenue from as many sources as possible. Let us assume that a local hotel is holding a wedding fayre to promote the hotel as a suitable venue for weddings. In order to support this venture many local companies may be asked to contribute to this event. Contributions may be made in many forms. One method might be an advertisement for a local taxi firm which is included in the main wedding fayre advert (see Fig. 2.4). The taxi advertisement is paid for by the taxi company, thus reducing the advertising costs of the full page advert to the hotel.

**Fig. 2.4** *Example of a sponsored advertisement*

A second example might be a local dressmaker supplying wedding gowns to display at the fayre.

## Activity

Look through your local newspaper and try to find advertisements of a similar nature to the one described above. Cut out these adverts and keep them as evidence in your portfolio. Highlight the sponsors of the adverts.

## Production of brochures

Many leisure and tourism organisations need to produce brochures to display their range of products and services. The idea of the brochure is that the customers can take it home and select their choice of products or services at their own convenience.

Examples of these are holiday brochures, shopping catalogues and hotel and accommodation guides.

## Price

Getting the price right can be very difficult. The leisure or tourism facility must consider a number of factors when pricing its products and services.

## Profit

Is the price high enough to allow the company to make a profit after the overheads have been paid?

*Profit = Price charged for product – Cost of making product (materials, wages, fuel bills)*

If the facility is in the private sector making a profit will be the company's chief objective. In the public and voluntary sectors the chief objective will be to provide a service without losing money and where possible to make a financial surplus.

## Competitors

What prices are competing facilities charging for similar products?

The customer will compare prices and will choose the lower price if the products appear to have the same features with the same quality. The customer will therefore demand the best value for money.

# Place

Where can the leisure or tourism product/service be purchased?

It may be possible to buy the leisure and tourism product directly from the organiser or it may be necessary to purchase the product via a distribution channel.

## Travel and tourism distribution channels

| Tour operators | Airtours | Thomson | Thomas Cook |
|---|---|---|---|
| Travel agents (distribution channels) | Going Places | Lunn Poly | Thomas Cook |
| Selling to | Customer | Customer | Customer |

For example, many tour operators operate through distribution channels which are travel agents and for this purpose the 'Big 3' tour operators own their own retail outlets, as illustrated above.

Not all tour operators sell via distribution channels. Some tour operators sell directly to the public, e.g Eurocamp, which advertises its products in newspapers and magazines. Many smaller tour operators will also sell directly to the public as this shortens the distribution channel thereby cutting costs for suppliers which will be passed on as a lower cost to the customer.

## Leisure services distribution channels

Most leisure services are purchased directly from the supplier, e.g. hire of squash court or pony trekking.

However the leisure products and merchandise required to participate in leisure and recreation activities are usually sold via distribution channels, i.e. the retail trade:

| Manufacturer | e.g. Adidas |
|---|---|
| Wholesaler or Retail outlet | e.g. Allsports |
| Selling to | Customer |

## Activity

Choose two organisations, one leisure and recreation and one travel and tourism.

What do you think would be the target market of these organisations?

How have these companies used marketing and promotion to reach their target markets?

**Fig. 2.5** *Eurocamp 1997 brochure*

> Describe the main *types of information* gathered by *marketing research*

Leisure and tourism organisations need to know what products and services the market requires so that it can supply appropriate goods. The market is the public who buy the products.

| Supplier | Airtours | Football club |
|---|---|---|
| Market | Potential holidaymakers | Potential football supporters |

Leisure and tourism suppliers need information from the market to help them decide which products to sell and at what price. This information will also help suppliers develop new products which the customer wants.

# Primary research

Primary data is information which is gathered directly from the public. It is usually gathered through questionnaires, surveys and customer feedback forms. Figure 2.6 shows the Visitor Survey used by the Salt Museum in Northwich to gather primary data.

Market research will provide information on the characteristics of customers, as illustrated in Fig. 2.7.

## Activity

Conduct a survey amongst your class/group (primary research)

Design a data collection form and carry out a survey to find out the following information:

1. Who you go on holiday with?
   - family
   - peer group (college or school)
   - peer group (outside college or school)
   - girl/boyfriend
   - by yourself

2. Destinations:
   - within the UK
   - abroad (Europe)
   - abroad (rest of world)

Each group must consider the different destinations that members of the individual groups visit and try to explain why.

<u>Salt Museum Visitor Survey</u>

We would be grateful if you could spend a few minutes answering the following questions.
The information you provide will help us improve the service to our customers.

**<u>Getting here</u>**

1  Date .....................................

2  How many are there in your party?　Adults　........................
　　　　　　　　　　　　　　　　　　　Children　........................

3  Where is your permanent place of residence?
.............................................................................................................

4  Where have you travelled from today?
Please state both town and county  ...................................................

5  How much time have you spent at the Salt Museum today?

　　　　　　Up to $^1/_2$ hour　　　　☐
　　　　　　$^1/_2$ – 1 hour　　　　　☐
　　　　　　1 – $1^1/_2$ hours　　　　☐
　　　　　　$1^1/_2$ – 2 hours　　　　☐
　　　　　　Over 2 hours　　　　　☐

6  How did you hear about the Salt Museum?

　　　　　　Salt Museum leaflet　　☐
　　　　　　Other tourism leaflet　☐
　　　　　　Press story　　　　　　☐
　　　　　　Advertisement　　　　　☐
　　　　　　Word of mouth　　　　　☐
　　　　　　Road sign　　　　　　　☐
　　　　　　Local knowledge　　　　☐
　　　　　　Other  ................................................................................

7  Was your decision to visit the museum today pre-planned? ☐ Please
　　　　　　　　　　　　　　　　　　　　　　　　　　　　　　tick
　　　　　　　　　　　　　　or spontaneous? ☐

P.T.O

**Fig. 2.6**  *Salt Museum Visitor Survey*

8   Do you feel your visit has been value for money?  YES/NO

9   Would you like to see more or less of the following in the museum?
    (Please tick.)

|                  | More | As now | Less |
|------------------|------|--------|------|
| Original Objects | ☐    | ☐      | ☐    |
| Models           | ☐    | ☐      | ☐    |
| Videos           | ☐    | ☐      | ☐    |
| Information       | ☐    | ☐      | ☐    |
| Photographs      | ☐    | ☐      | ☐    |
| Reconstructions  | ☐    | ☐      | ☐    |

Other . . . . . . . . . . . . . . . . . . . . . . . . . . . . . . . . . . . . . . . . . . . . . . . . . . . . . . . . . .

10  Is there anything you particularly enjoyed about your visit?

. . . . . . . . . . . . . . . . . . . . . . . . . . . . . . . . . . . . . . . . . . . . . . . . . . . . . . . . . . . . .
. . . . . . . . . . . . . . . . . . . . . . . . . . . . . . . . . . . . . . . . . . . . . . . . . . . . . . . . . . . . .
. . . . . . . . . . . . . . . . . . . . . . . . . . . . . . . . . . . . . . . . . . . . . . . . . . . . . . . . . . . . .

11  Have you any criticisms or suggestions for improvements?

. . . . . . . . . . . . . . . . . . . . . . . . . . . . . . . . . . . . . . . . . . . . . . . . . . . . . . . . . . . . .
. . . . . . . . . . . . . . . . . . . . . . . . . . . . . . . . . . . . . . . . . . . . . . . . . . . . . . . . . . . . .
. . . . . . . . . . . . . . . . . . . . . . . . . . . . . . . . . . . . . . . . . . . . . . . . . . . . . . . . . . . . .

**Thank you very much for your time. We hope to welcome you back to the Salt Museum in future.**

*If you would like information about school visits and other group visits please leave your name at the desk.*

**Fig. 2.6**  (Continued)

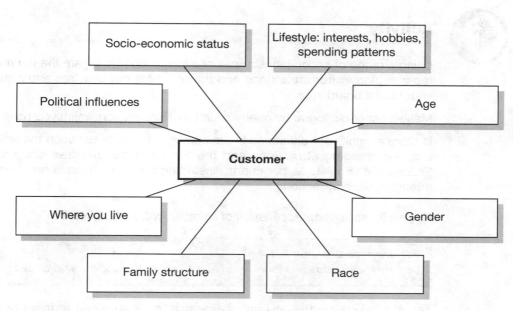

**Fig. 2.7** *Customer characteristics*

# Secondary research

Secondary data is information which can be obtained from published sources. Examples of secondary data include statistical reports such as Social Trends and the General Household Survey. The use of this type of information is known as desk research, which means that you can find information without having to ask questions.

The main types of information which leisure and tourism organisations require from market research include:

| Market information | Specific details |
|---|---|
| Personal details | Profile of customers, e.g. age, gender, interests |
| Opinions and views | Feedback from products already used |
| Buying habits | The type of product the customer usually buys |
| | When, where and how it is bought and how much the product costs |
| Competitor details | Analysis of what products other organisations offer and why customers buy certain products in preference to others |
| | Identifying gaps in the market |

# Activity

Using a range of secondary sources of information investigate the ten most popular fee charging visitor attractions and the ten most popular free entry attractions in your tourist board area.

Make a list or bibliography of any sources of information which you have used.

Is there a significant difference in the number of visitors between the ten most popular fee charging attractions and the ten most popular free entry attractions? Present the two lists as bar charts illustrating the differences in numbers of visitors attending each attraction.

**Key skills satisfied:** *Application of Number* **N2.1, N2.2, N2.3**

---

**Performance Criterion 2.1.4**
Describe how leisure and tourism *target markets* are divided into *market segments*

---

Target markets are the customers at which the leisure and tourism providers aim their products. If we look at the total potential market it is composed of a wide range of people, all of whom have different characteristics and interests.

Not all people will want to or be able to afford to buy every leisure and tourism product which is on offer. It is useful therefore to divide the total potential market into a number of categories or segments, each of which has similar characteristics. There are a number of ways in which this can be done, for example:

| Segment type | Characteristics |
| --- | --- |
| Age groups | 10–20 |
| | 21–30 |
| | 31–40 |
| | 41–50 |
| Gender | Male/female |
| Family structure | Single |
| | Young family: 2 parents |
| | Single parent family |
| | Mature family |
| | Empty nest (children left home) |
| | Senior citizens |
| Socio-economic status | The type of job you have |
| | How much money is available for leisure, i.e. level of disposable income |
| | **Note:** Disposable income = Money left over after paying essential household items, (mortgage, rent, food, bills, etc.) |

# Socio-economic status

A person's socio-economic status is determined by the type of job they have. The higher up the socio-economic scale an individual is placed the higher their salary and the greater amount of disposable income is available for leisure or non-essential items.

| Socio-economic category | Typical job role |
|---|---|
| **A**   Upper middle | Professional and managerial jobs (e.g. lawyer, doctor) |
| **B**   Middle | Managerial and administrative jobs (e.g. leisure centre manager) |
| **C1**   Lower middle | Junior managerial and supervisory positions (e.g. senior consultant in a travel agency) |
| **C2**   Skilled working | Skilled manual workers (e.g. coach driver) |
| **D**   Working | Semi-skilled and unskilled jobs (e.g. chambermaid in a hotel) |
| **E**   Unemployed | Senior citizens, students and the unemployed |

Socio-economic status will affect an individual's lifestyle and this may be reflected in

- Type of activities an individual takes part in.
- Aspirations.

# Geographical location

How accessible is the target market?
Where an individual lives will also affect customer buying habits. This can be classified by the type of environment in which the consumer lives:

- **Rural areas** – In rural areas there are fewer leisure products available due to the lower population densities. There is also less public transport available making it more difficult for non-car owners to reach facilities.
- **Urban areas** – The market in a urban area is far more diverse, containing a variety of target groups. Public transport systems are more developed offering greater accessibility to leisure facilities and tourist attractions.

For example consider the range of target markets which a facility such as the Nynex Arena in Manchester can attract through the various events which are staged there:

- **Manchester Storm Ice Hockey Team** – Young males, families.
- **Pop concert by former group** (Take That 1995 tour) – Teenage girls from a wide catchment area including the UK, Ireland and Germany.

## Activity

Choose a concert hall or arena in a city or town which is near to where you live. Investigate the range of products which it offers.

Repeat the exercise, but base it on a village hall or community centre close to where you live.

Suggest reasons for the differences between the products offered by the two venues.

Suggest the geographical catchment area for these products and the characteristics of the people who might participate at the different venues.

> Explain how the *marketing mix relates to target markets* for products and services in selected leisure and recreation and travel and tourism organisations

In this section we shall look at the marketing strategy of Jodrell Bank which is located in rural Cheshire. In the following case study we shall examine how the marketing mix can be related to their promotional activities.

## CASE STUDY

## Jodrell Bank

### Background information

Jodrell Bank is a science centre to which visitor facilities have been added. The radio telescope was completed in 1957 by the scientist Sir Bernard Lovell to help with the research work which he was carrying out at Manchester University.

The most well known feature of Jodrell Bank is the Lovell telescope which forms a distinctive feature of the Cheshire plain. At 76 metres in diameter it is the third largest radio telescope in the world.

The purpose of its construction was astronomical research, however, due to public demand and a growing interest in space research an experimental two weeks of open days in the summer of 1964 resulted in a total of 35,000 people attending. This success was repeated in 1965 leading to a decision by the university to build a visitor centre which was opened on 3rd May 1966 and was extended in 1971 to include:

- 1971 – Planetarium.
- 1972 – 30 acres of adjoining land for arboretum.
- 1987 – Telescope renamed the Lovell Telescope.
- Visitor centre recently renamed Science Centre.

To keep pace with the competition from other visitor attractions, and in line with the growing popularity of experiential attractions, the marketing department at Jodrell Bank decided to formulate a professional marketing policy.

The rationale behind the Jodrell Bank marketing policy is:

*Marketing is the management function of identifying, anticipating and satisfying customer requirements profitably*

The marketing team has produced a series of fact sheets which summarise their marketing strategy. The information is summarised under the following headings:

- Origins and objectives
- Organisation, operations and services
- Visitor statistics
- Site and facilities
- Marketing

### How the marketing mix applies to the promotional activities of Jodrell Bank

*Methods of promotion*
Figure 2.8 shows the 4 Ps of marketing and Fig. 2.9, from the 1996 promotional campaign, clearly illustrates these.

The aim of the marketing team is to keep Jodrell Bank in the public eye so that people know about it.

*Objective 1*
This objective lists the products which Jodrell Bank wish to inform the public about:

*To interest, inform and educate people in astronomy and the environment through:*

1. *Provision of displays and exhibits on astronomy, the exploration and utilisation of space, energy and the environment*
2. *Planetarium shows of both a traditional and interactive nature*
3. *Interactive science exhibits which demonstrate scientific and technological concepts and stimulate curiosity*
4. *A botanical collection of trees and interpretative trails and displays*

To help achieve this objective Jodrell Bank produces a variety of promotional leaflets, for example Fig. 2.10 shows the Jodrell Bank Arboretum. This is an example of how they are trying to achieve Objective 1.

**Fig. 2.8** *The 4 Ps of marketing at Jodrell Bank*

**Fig. 2.9** *Jodrell Bank brochure illustrating the 4 Ps of marketing*

Jodrell Bank analyses details of visitors to the site and breaks them down into target market groups based on:

● Geographical location.
● Visitor types, as determined by party groups.

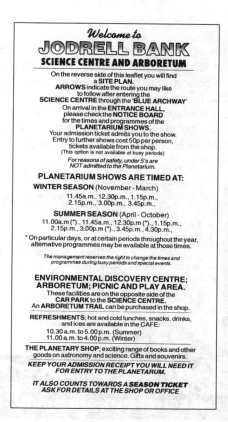

**Fig. 2.10** *Jodrell Bank Arboretum*

## Geographical location

Market segments can also be classified by geographical location based on catchment areas and will depend upon the distance travelled to visit Jodrell Bank.

Within the 26 to 50 mile radius are some of the country's largest centres of population including Manchester, Liverpool, Sheffield, Leeds and the Potteries.

## Visitor types

Jodrell Bank breaks down the types of visitors into the following categories:

- Educational, e.g. Schools.
- Non-educational, e.g. Women's Institute, Rotary Clubs.

### Group composition
The groups are then broken down into two further categories:

- Adults, including senior citizens.
- Children.

### Length of stay

The type of attractions which Jodrell Bank offers determines the average length of visitor stay. Over 75 per cent of customers stay for more than two hours. This allows Jodrell Bank the opportunity to put on displays which may take up to an hour to see but still allow time for visitors to use the cafe and visit the souvenir shop.

If we look at some examples of promotional activity designed or initiated we can start to identify the groups at which these activities are targeted.

Figure 2.11 shows examples of specific, targeted promotions.

**Fig. 2.11** *Targeted promotions at Jodrell Bank*

Look at the two promotional adverts for Jodrell Bank which are shown in Fig. 2.11.

Who do you think they are aimed at? Justify your answers.

The editorial features which appeared in the Manchester Evening News (Fig. 2.12) is on a topic of general interest which would appeal to all groups and may encourage or stimulate interest in potential visitors.

If you refer to Fig. 2.9 you will see the standard admission prices. However at certain times of the year Jodrell Bank may try to boost visitor numbers by offering specific offers or price reductions such as a 50 per cent discount for the Planetarium.

# Just space for a tweet dream

A squatter has put the sun out of bounds. Jodrell Bank's mini-telescope, which can pull in solar radio signals, is out of action while a nesting mistle thrush tends her brood.

The 28ft structure near Goostrey, Cheshire – one of the most popular exhibits in the science centre – now carries a notice on its controls explaining the problem.

Centre manager Sylvia Chaplin said: 'The thrush has built a nest in the telescope and to move it would evict the chicks.

'I suppose this is one of the problems with putting some of the exhibits outside, but all the visitors are very sympathetic and understanding.'

The thrush set up its home on the 30-year-old telescope at Easter and at once began to build her nest.

### HATCHED

Staff at the centre planned to move it to a nearby tree so they could continue using the hands-on exhibit in the shadow of Jodrell Bank's giant radio dish.

But when technician David Lucas climbed up to peer inside he found four eggs waiting to be hatched.

Sylvia said: 'We have never had a bird nesting like this before. It's all very exciting.

'At first we thought we would be able to move it but when David reported it had four eggs inside we decided not to disturb her.

'We have immobilised the telescope so it can't be tipped up or down but visitors can still turn it in a horizontal direction and the bird doesn't seem to mind.'

Now the thrush has four lively chicks and is a constant attraction for groups of visitors and school children as she comes and goes with a constant stream of worms and other titbits.

Sylvia added: 'We have no idea how long the chicks will be there until they fly the nest – and we can have our telescope back.'

**Fig. 2.12** *Editorial feature, Jodrell Bank*

# Assignment

'Good practice in marketing'

**Key skills satisfied:** *Communication* **C2.2, C2.3**
*Application of Number* **N2.1, N2.2, N2.3**

***Situation*** You are working for a consortium known as the Development of National Tourism and have been asked to prepare a visual display for a conference. The conference is being held for the benefit of its members and the theme is 'good practice in marketing'.

## Tasks

1. Your display will be required to compare and contrast two organisations. Jodrell Bank has already been selected as an organisation from the travel and tourism sector which demonstrates good practice in marketing. You must now choose a contrasting organisation from the leisure and recreation sector within your regional Tourist Board area.

2. The four components of the marketing mix are:

   ● Product
   ● Place
   ● Price
   ● Promotion

   Your display should highlight in detail how the 4 Ps are reflected in the literature and promotional material of your chosen organisation.

3. To make your display more interesting and more informative you should highlight the number of visitors received annually by each attraction and how the visitors numbers vary throughout the seasons of the year. You must decide the best way to present this data making sure that it is clearly presented and informative.

4. Using information from the available literature calculate the annual income from entrance fees and work out the average monthly takings. Use graphical methods such as pie charts and bar graphs to display this data.

# Plan a leisure and recreation or travel and tourism promotional campaign

In this element you must plan a promotional campaign for either a leisure and recreation or a travel and tourism event. In doing this you will be putting into practice the marketing theories which were illustrated in the case studies in the previous element.

It is important that the campaign you are going to plan is feasible and practical and that you have the resources to run the campaign.

Once you have run your campaign you must evaluate its success or failure.

By following the special evidence-gathering activities in this unit you will produce evidence for your portfolio. Make notes and keep a record of the meetings you hold with your team, and the decisions that you make.

## How to design your promotional campaign

Organise yourselves into groups of 4 or 5 students then discuss any event you might like to develop and become involved with. This could be a brainstorming session where suggestions are discussed in depth once a list has been made.

## Brainstorming ideas

Each of the possible events identified through the brainstorming activity should be considered in detail in relation to your identified target market, which in this case will probably be young people 16 to 19 years of age.

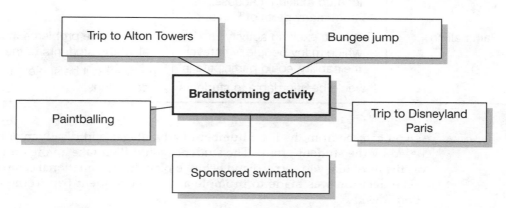

**Fig. 2.13** *Ideas generated through discussion*

Draw up a list of proposed events and discuss the advantages and disadvantages of each – as illustrated below.

| Proposed event | Advantages | Disadvantages |
|---|---|---|
| Bungee jump | Exciting to watch<br>Easy to promote<br>High profile activity | Expensive to hire necessary equipment<br>Supervision is required<br>Success of event will be subject to weather conditions<br>Insurance/danger factor |
| Trip to Disneyland Paris | Exciting combination of foreign travel and exciting rides should appeal to target market | It will be expensive to participate in this visit<br>The trip will be time consuming<br>May also require tutor help due to complexity of organising overseas visits |
| Sponsored swimathon | The event would promote a healthy image and one which would enhance the reputation of the group | It may be expensive to hire the swimming pool<br>Only swimmers can participate in the actual event<br>There may be problems collecting the sponsor money |
| Alton Towers | This event would have wide appeal to the target market<br>There is a range of exciting rides.<br>Alton Towers is centrally located making it accessible from many parts of England | The theme park is remote from some parts of the UK, e.g. Scotland<br>The entry fees are quite high<br>The event would be subject to weather conditions |
| Paintballing | This is an exciting activity which many people, whatever their ability, could participate in<br>It would be affordable to students | There may be problems transporting all of the students to the venue<br>The event will be subject to weather conditions |

As you can see from the list a number of advantages and disadvantages were discussed by the student group. The students could then take a vote on which event was the most likely to succeed and begin to plan their promotional campaign.

The decision was made to promote a possible student trip to the theme park Alton Towers.

**Activity**

Choose a number of similar activities and discuss the advantages and disadvantages of each in the same format as those above.

Describe the stages of a leisure and recreation or a travel and tourism promotional campaign

# Promotional campaign for student visit to Alton Towers

In the same way in which leisure and tourism organisations plan promotional campaigns for their products and services, students can plan a campaign to promote a student organised visit or event.

In planning the campaign you will need to consider five stages:

## Research – Idea of an event

- Market survey
  - Is there a demand?
- Research
  - Confirms demand for idea
- **What** is being promoted?
  - Identify the product
- **Who** to?
  - Identify the target market: Do the students want to go?

## Planning

- **What?**
  - Identify the objectives of the campaign. What will the promotion be?
- **When?**
  - When should the event be promoted?
- **Where?**
  - Where will the promotional material appear?
- **How?**
  - How will the campaign be carried out?
  - How much will it cost?

## Preparation of materials

- Preparing the promotional materials.
- Roles and responsibilities must be clear.
- A time plan must be produced.

## Implementation – The plan in action

- Roles allocated to team members.
- The event is promoted and advertised.
- Posters are produced.
- Students are recruited to display posters.
- Posters placed in appropriate areas.
- Travel arrangements are made.
- Students are made aware.
- Students commit themselves to the event.
- Deposits are paid.

## Evaluation – How did it go?

- **Product**
  - Did the students want the product?
  - Was the promotional campaign a success?
- **Place**
  - Were posters placed in appropriate places?
- **Promotion**
  - Were the posters noticed?
  - As a result of seeing the posters – did students ask to buy tickets?
- **Price**
  - What was the customers' reactions to the prices which were charged?
  - Were all the tickets sold?

> Describe with examples the objectives of a leisure and recreation or travel and tourism promotional campaign

# Objectives of a promotional campaign

An objective is a method of achieving your aims. Objectives must have measurable outcomes and must be:

- Clear.
- Concise.
- Realistic.
- Measurable.

The main objective of any promotional campaign is to make the public aware of the products and services which are available, which should ultimately result in an increased level of sales. By referring to the objectives of the campaign this will guide the organisation towards a series of actions which will form the basis of the marketing and promotional plan.

The type of objectives which will influence a promotional campaign are:

- Financial – To make a profit.
- Educational – To inform.
- Social – For enjoyment.
- Environmental – To make the public aware of environmental concerns.
- Image – To enhance the image of the organisation and its products.
- Time constraints – Achieving the promotional campaign within a given time period.

## Inform customers

One of the main objectives of a promotional campaign will be to inform customers of the products and services which are available. This may be to inform the public of:

- New products.
- Changes in existing products.
- New facilities.
- Special offers.

## To raise awareness

Another objective may be to raise awareness of products of an organisation or the organisation itself. This may be achieved through public relations or sponsorship which will help to raise the profile of the company rather than the products it manufactures and sells.

For example Stella Artois, the lager brewers, sponsor a major tennis tournament. The Stella Artois tournament is held annually at the Queen's Club, London, and forms the traditional run up to the Wimbledon Championship.

## To make people buy

The chief objective of most promotional campaigns will be to make the customer want to buy the product or service. This may be achieved by making the product look desirable, a product you cannot afford to be without. The objective of the campaign could therefore be to create a desire for the product.

For example, the summer holiday brochures of most tour operators depict an image of sun, sand, entertainment and enjoyment. This image will appeal to many people and may create the desire to travel to sunny destinations.

## To improve/enhance the image of the product or organisation

Advertising and promotional materials which are of a high quality with a good visual impact will reinforce the image of the product as one of high quality.

The objectives of the Alton Towers promotional campaign which is being run by our Intermediate students include:

- **Financial** – To ensure that the cost of the campaign and the trip is met by the student contributions. The trip and the associated promotional materials costs must not exceed the income.
- **Educational** – Organising the trip and the promotional campaign will enable the students to claim competence in their GNVQ unit.
- **Social** – One of the attractions of the trip will be that it is a social occasion which the students should enjoy.
- **Image** – The image created by the promotional campaign will be important in persuading students to participate.
- **Informative** – Students must be informed of the trip, when it will take place and how much it will cost.
- **Time constraints** – All of the activities associated with the promotional campaign must be achieved by given deadlines.

## Activity

Choose two adverts, one for a leisure and recreation product and one for a travel and tourism product.

State what you think the objectives of the advertisements might be.

## Evidence-gathering activity

Through your brainstorming activity you will have identified some potential events which your group can plan. Hold a meeting at which you decide the objectives of the chosen event; one member of your group could take minutes of the meeting. Word process the minutes.

**Key skills satisfied:** *Communication* **C2.1a, C2.2b**
*Information Technology* **IT2.2**

> Explain the factors which could affect the success of a promotional campaign

Before carrying out the promotional campaign for the Alton Towers trip you must consider the following factors:

## Market research

- Identify your customers.
- Describe your target market.
- Consider how many potential customers you think there will be for your event.
- Consider how many customers you need to run the event.

## Evidence-gathering activity: Target market and, promotional techniques

In your groups discuss the market at which you are aiming your event. Make a note of this 'target market' in your portfolio.

You could then test your event idea on the target market by designing a questionnaire.

Consider the promotional techniques which will be most appropriate for your campaign. Refer back to the promotional campaign process which was described on page 141.

Make a note in your portfolio of the promotional techniques you have chosen to use and justify your reasons.

# Media

- Choose which methods are you going to use to promote the trip.

Use the following table to help justify the methods you plan to use. Whether a method is appropriate depends on the nature of the product which is being promoted. We are considering this in relation to students planning a trip for themselves.

| Media | Advantages | Disadvantages |
| --- | --- | --- |
| Television | Wide coverage | Very expensive |
| | Very visual and dynamic | Inappropriate for a college trip |
| Radio | Audiences can be targeted through choice of appropriate radio station | |
| Press advertising | Local newspapers can be used for local events | The cost is relative to the scale of the event |
| Word of mouth | Cheap | Not reliable |
| | Influence of peers may encourage participation | Information will be biased |
| Flyer | Cheap to produce | Time involved in distribution |
| | Could be produced in house and distributed by friends | May be unprofessional and lack impact |
| Poster | Can be cheaply produced by students and displayed free of charge | The artistic skills to produce an eye catching poster may not be available in house |
| | Good visual impact | |
| Promotional video | Could be cheaply produced in house or it may be possible to borrow a commercially made video from the visitor attraction | In house – may be unprofessional |
| | | Visitor attraction video – would not contain information specific to the visit |

## Evidence-gathering activity: choice of media

Consider each of the media shown in the previous table and decide on the most appropriate medium which can be used for promoting your event.

Make a note about your choice of media in your portfolio. Justify the decision you have made.

## Timing of campaign

An action plan needs to be produced stating tasks which need to be achieved by certain dates, e.g. the collection of deposits, balance of monies and bookings to be made.

Dates must be allocated by which the promotional material must be displayed and the people concerned with the campaign are informed of what is happening when.

Produce a plan indicating dates by which the various parts of the campaign have to be completed.

## Available budget

In organising a promotional campaign the costs of materials and services to be used must be budgeted for, as must any other resources which are required to carry out the campaign.

For our students to determine whether or not these resources are within their means a series of questions must be asked:

● How much money is in the budget?
● What materials are required and how much will they cost?
● What resources or methods are you planning to use?
  **Remember:** You must make sure that the costs of the promotional campaign do not exceed the profits which you might make from running the trip.
● Have the figures been checked by another member of your team?

## People's perceptions

The students' choice is Alton Towers, a destination which conjures up the image of a fun packed day for young people.

Does the advertising material which you have produced reflect the image which Alton Towers projects?

Do the students expect the trip to take place and be well organised?

Does your promotional material give the impression of efficiency and organisation which would give people the confidence to take part?

# Legal constraints

In designing promotional material companies must be aware of the legislation which exists to protect the consumer, e.g. the Trades Descriptions Act. Under this act the product which is advertised must be clearly and accurately described and the advertisement must not be misleading in any way.

Other consumer acts which need to be considered are:

- Sale of Goods Act.
- Supply of Goods Act.
- Consumer Protection Act.
- Trade Descriptions Act.

## Activity

Working in four groups choose one of the acts of parliament named above. Visit the college/school library and prepare notes on the act you have chosen. You will then be required to present this information to the other groups.

**Key skills satisfied:** *Communication* **C2.1b**

# Professional constraints

Professional bodies which uphold advertising standards include the Advertising Standards Agency and the Citizens Advice Bureau. If customers are dissatisfied with the product they have purchased they can register their complaint with the Citizens Advice Bureau or the local trading standards officer.

Holidaymakers who have had a disastrous holiday can report their complaints in the following way:

- To the travel agent where they purchased the holiday.
- The travel agency will suggest writing to the tour operator.
  **Note:** If no satisfaction is received from the tour operator the travel agent may suggest that the customer writes to ABTA (the Association of British Travel Agents) enclosing copies of all correspondence that has been sent to the tour operator.
- ABTA would not normally be involved with the complaint until at least three unsatisfactory replies had been received by the consumer.

# Staff skills

The necessary staff skills for marketing and promotion may not be present within every company. Sometimes smaller leisure and tourism organisations may recruit the specialist services of professional publicity and marketing consultants to help them with specific projects.

**Fig. 2.14** ABTA logo

## Evidence-gathering activity

Look at the promotional material you have produced for your student event.

Analyse the promotional material by considering the following factors:

1. Does the poster inform?

- the date and time of the event
- the venue for the event
- how much it will cost to participate in the event
- how to buy a ticket for the event

2. Does it accurately describe the event?

- Are all the details correct?
- Is the poster misleading?

3. Does the poster have visual impact?

- Are the colours bright and bold?
- Does the wording stand out?

4. Siting of the posters:

- Are the posters placed on appropriate notice boards? For instance, boards allocated for student activities and situated in the refectory or common room.

## Raising awareness

Are all students in the school/college made aware of the trip rather than just the organising group and close friends. If more awareness is raised, new customers may be attracted to go on the trip, which will improve sales. The reputation of the trip will be enhanced because the poster campaign has made the trip very popular and now many new customers will want to go.

## Evidence-gathering activity

Think about your promotional campaign and evaluate the success of the planning by using the following checklist:

| Name of campaign | Yes | No |
| --- | --- | --- |
| Did it inform? | | |
| Did it raise awareness? | | |
| Did it make people buy the product? | | |
| Did it enhance the image of the product? | | |
| Did it improve sales? | | |
| Did it attract new customers? | | |
| Did it maintain existing customers? | | |

Make a note of the discussions which have taken place between yourself and your group. The notes will need to be kept safely and used as evidence for your portfolio.

# AIDA

The objectives of any promotional campaign can be summarised by referring to the principles of AIDA. To have maximum visual impact a promotional campaign will ideally be professionally designed. In order to be successful a poster, video or TV advertisement must be able to:

- **A** attract **attention**
- **I** maintain **interest**
- **D** create a want or **desire** for the product
- **A** stimulate **action**, e.g. the purchase of the product

We will consider examples of promotional material which have been produced by the Youth Hostel Association and Club 18–30 to see how the AIDA principle can be applied.

## Attention

- A dramatic scene is set on the front of the YHA brochure creating an image of adventure and excitement within safe limits (safety equipment is clearly in evidence).
- Both the YHA and 18–30 brochures are clearly targeted at selected user groups.
- There is no mention of cost on the YHA brochure but the organisation has a reputation for providing value-for-money accommodation and affordable facilities.
- The immediate impact of the 18–30 brochure is of fun packed beach holidays for young people. The colours are bright and lively and the model is dressed appropriately in youthful clothing.
- Affordable prices for young people in destinations which are famous for their lively nightlife.

## Interest

You will quickly lose interest in the product if you do not immediately relate to the image which is created by the brochure. The image on the front of the brochure may be reinforcing an image which has already been created through previous publicity materials. This would apply to organisations such as the YHA which is well known and has an excellent reputation.

## Desire

If the image created coincides with the individual's needs it may make the individual feel that he/she wants to participate or purchase the product.

# Action

The brochures provide information which will then enable the individual to become involved, such as booking details.

## Activity

Consider the material which you have produced for the student event.

Analyse your materials using the AIDA technique.

Does your promotional material:

1. Attract interest?

2. Maintain interest?

3. Create a desire?

4. Stimulate action?

When you are carrying out this exercise think about your target group: How does your promotional material relate to them?

## Evidence-gathering activity: Time plan

Prepare a time plan for your event in which you list:

1. The dates by which each stage of the campaign should have been achieved.

2. Who is responsible for each activity and by when should they have completed their work.

**Key skills satisfied:** *Communication* **C2.2**
*Information Technology* **IT2.3**

# Promotional campaign checklist

By following the evidence-gathering activities which are contained in this element you will have:

- Chosen a product or event on which to plan a promotional campaign.
- Market tested your ideas.
- Prepared a detailed promotional campaign.
- Kept a log of the discussions and activities which have taken place and recorded any modifications to your original plan.

You may wish to use the following headings as a checklist:

| Steps | Activity | Achieved |
|---|---|---|
| Step 1 | **Brainstorming session** – Generate ideas for a product or service which you can promote | |
| Step 2 | **Objectives** – List the objectives of the campaign | |
| Step 3 | **Target market** – Identify your target market | |
| Step 4 | **Market research** – Test your ideas on the targeted group | |
| Step 5 | **Promotional activities** – Choose appropriate activities to promote your product and justify your choice | |
| Step 6 | **Media** – Choose the most appropriate media through which to promote your product. Explain why you have chosen it | |
| Step 7 | **Time plan** – Prepare a time plan listing target dates by which each of the activities should be achieved. Indicate who is responsible for each activity and by when | |
| Step 8 | **Other factors** – Make a list of other factors which might affect the success of your campaign | |

# Run and evaluate a leisure and tourism promotional campaign

## Promotional materials for use in campaigns

Promotional materials and methods come in a wide variety of forms.

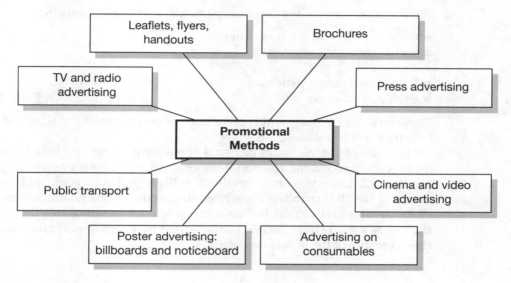

Fig. 2.15

Prepare appropriate promotional materials for use during the campaign

## TV advertising

This is a very expensive form of promoting a product or an event, costing thousands of pounds for a few seconds. The benefits though can be the high viewing figures, especially during peak viewing times when popular programmes are shown such as Coronation Street which can attract an audience of 15 million people. This form of advertising is able to maximise the exposure of the product to a very large number of people.

Advertisers can target groups depending on the time of day or year at which they advertise. An example of this is that many holiday companies heavily promote their holidays on television immediately after Christmas and New Year. This is when many people will be looking forward to their summer holidays. This will be in contrast to the cold winter weather they are possibly experiencing at the time.

## Cinema/video advertising

When you hire a video there are usually three or four trailers of recently released films. These trailers promote the forthcoming film and try to persuade you to rent the video. This same method can also be found in the cinema. You will also see products advertised in the cinema which can be purchased there, such as ice cream or chocolate.

## Direct mail shots/leaflet drops

Direct mail is a method of targeting particular market segments by:

- Geographical area (by post code).
- Socio-economic grouping.
- Age.
- Previous spending patterns.
- Existing customers.

These customer groups will receive information on products which the company feels they will be interested in.

One example of this could be that if you are a member of a local leisure club you may receive specific information if the centre is promoting a newly refurbished fitness suite. Because you are a member it is likely that your home address will be on record at the club enabling them to contact you personally. If however the leisure centre decides to distribute leaflets to the whole surrounding area this could be considered as a mail shot which is characterised by geographical area rather than the characteristics of the leisure centre users.

## Press advertising

Press advertising refers to advertising in magazines or newspapers. In newspapers this can take place at three levels: the national, regional or local press.

| National press | Daily Telegraph |
| | Daily Mirror |
| | Mail on Sunday |
| Regional press | Yorkshire Post |
| | Liverpool Echo |
| | London Evening Standard |
| Local press | Guildford Times |
| | Chester Chronicle |

The nature of an event will determine which type of newspaper the advertisement is to be featured in. For example, an advert for a village summer fete will have a much greater relevance and impact in the local newspaper. In contrast to this the launch of a national product, for example the opening of a theme park of national significance, will definitely require national and regional coverage and is also likely to appear in the local press especially regarding the recruitment of staff to work at the theme park.

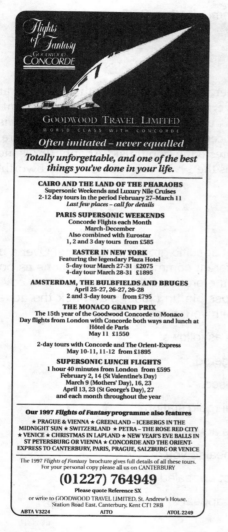

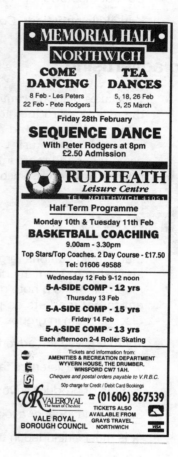

**Fig. 1.29** *Examples of newspaper advertising*

## Activity

Look in a variety of newspapers, both local and national. Identify and cut out adverts from both types for leisure and tourism products. Create two display posters, one depicting local and national leisure products and services and the other depicting local and national tourism products and services.

Cut out the newspaper titles you have used and display them on your poster.

**Key skills satisfied:** *Communication* **C2.2**

# Radio advertising

This takes place on commercial radio stations both at national and local level. Again the event or product advertised will be specific and relevant to the status of the radio station used and its audience. For example, Classic FM is more likely to promote a classical music concert or opera than Atlantic 252 where the listeners tend to be younger and more interested in pop music. Atlantic 252 is more likely to promote pop music concerts such as the 1996 Oasis concert at Knebworth.

## Activity

Many radio stations target specific groups of listeners. Over a period of a month try and listen to as many different commercial radio stations as possible. Using a tape recorder, make a note of the products they are advertising covering as many different target markets as possible. In class, play back the adverts and jingles and discuss them in groups with your tutor

Try to analyse the adverts as follows:

1. Age of the listeners targeted.

2. Type of product advertised.

3. Is it a national or a local radio station?

4. Is music included in the advert?

5. Why did the advert appeal to you?

6. Explain why the product appealed to you.

7. Why did the advert not appeal to you? Was it irritating?

# Billboards/posters/notices

Billboards are large display panels which are located in prominent positions. These are usually found in urban areas where there is a large volume of passing traffic.

They are used to display posters which will give information; for example, products or services which are on sale nationally such as Sky TV advertising forthcoming attractions.

A poster campaign is the method of advertising most likely to be selected by students when promoting one of their events. For example, a student Rag Week.

These posters can usually be inexpensively produced and easily displayed on college notice boards or in local shop windows.

A popular location for poster/billboard advertising is around the perimeter fencing of a football pitch. Where possible, to have maximum effect, these will face the television cameras so that not only will the spectators in the ground see the advert but also television viewers.

## Public transport advertising

This form of advertising can be found on the side of taxis, buses, trams and underground trains. One form of advertising might be a poster. Another could be where the vehicle has the advertisement professionally painted onto the bodywork. Sometimes this may just be on one part of the vehicle, usually the door, or alternatively the whole vehicle may be a mobile advertisement for the leisure product and would be painted in the corporate colours.

This is an effective way of circulating your message.

## Brochures

Brochures can take a variety of forms, e.g. a glossy A4 holiday brochure which is almost like a holiday book, which in some cases can include up to one hundred pages, many in full colour. The brochure shown in Fig. 2.19 is a typical example of a tour operator's brochure.

## Leaflets/handouts

Leaflets are the most common form of promotional material which is widely distributed as they can be inexpensively produced. For example, it may be possible to get a quantity of 10,000 glossy A4 leaflets folded into three for approximately £400. Because of the ease of distribution leaflets can be picked up from a variety of sources. These may be the venue itself, Tourist Information Centres, libraries, and other visitor attractions. As it is easy to fold these leaflets you will usually see them displayed either on counter tops or display racks

## Use of merchandise in promotion

Sometimes the merchandise which people want is the advertising medium.

**Brand names** – many large sports manufacturers emblazon their company name and logo prominently on their T shirts, sweat shirts, baseball caps, jeans or sports shoes.

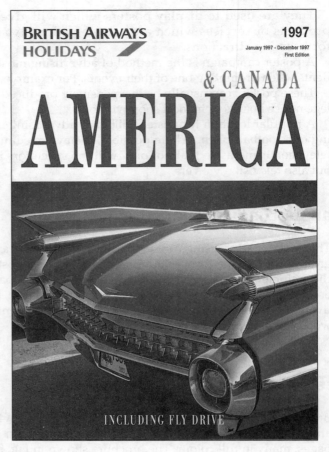

**Fig. 2.17** *British Airways – tour operator's brochure*

## Activity

Look at a range of magazines and cut out a selection of advertisements for clothing and footwear which prominently display the manufacturer's name and logo. Use the cuttings to create your own display.

**Key skills satisfied:** *Communication* **C2.1b**

## Sponsorship

In addition to the manufacturers' advertising on their own sports wear many other companies have seen advertisements on clothing as an effective way of displaying their product name. One example of this is the English Rugby Union Team who have promoted Cellnet on their training tops. A second example can be seen in the popular football shirts that have the name of a product displayed across the front; for example, Goodyear Tyres sponsors Wolverhampton Wanderers.

# Visitor attractions

Many visitor attractions seek to increase their exposure to the public by promoting their name and logo on items which can be purchased in souvenir shops. For example, rubbers, notepads, pencils and sticks of rock.

## Evidence-gathering activity

In groups consider the methods of promotion you would use to promote an end of term disco.

You will need to consider:

1. Cost of materials.

2. Cost of advertising.

3. Practicality in terms of display.

4. Skills of the group.

5. Timing of the advertisement (lead time to event).

6. Who you are hoping to attract (target audience).

7. Time available to produce the promotional material.

Keep a diary of your discussions and justify your choice of promotional material.

**Key skills satisfied:** *Communication* **C2.1a, C2.1b**

> Participate effectively in the running of the campaign

Look at the marketing plan you have prepared as part of your evidence-gathering activity. You will now have to put your plan into action for your campaign to be successful. It is important that your group works well together as a team assigning roles to individuals depending upon their particular skills. You will need to consider the resources which you have available. These resources can include the following.

## Skills

Each person should be allocated a role which best matches their personal skills. These skills may be artistic or organisational.

## Money

The amount of money, or the budget, which has been allocated will determine the whole nature of the campaign in terms of type of publicity which is used and the extent of the coverage. In our example of the student campaign the budget is likely to be very limited and therefore the money will be used very economically. It would not be feasible or appropriate to produce a glossy brochure promoting a student disco.

All the money available for the campaign must be strictly controlled as people will need to be accountable when a balance sheet is produced.

## Materials available

The amount of money allocated to the campaign will determine the type of materials to be used. In our low budget student campaign the students will have few materials to work with. In contrast, large corporations such as First Leisure, Thomas Cook and Whitbreads plc will allocate substantial amounts of money to purchase advertising materials. The difference in scale is relative though. First Leisure will carry out campaigns which are intended to reach a national audience. In contrast to this our student group is aiming its campaign at other students within the college.

## Equipment

Other equipment which is used during promotional campaigns includes:

- Communication equipment – e.g. telephones, fax machines, computer for e-mail.
- Equipment to produce the promotional materials – e.g. photocopiers, computers with desk top publishing facilities such as PageMaker and printers. This type of equipment may not be available to students because of the cost implications.

## Activity

Make a list of the other equipment which you are likely to need to carry out your promotional campaign.

Are you likely to meet any problems in using this equipment in terms of:

1. Do you have the skills required to use the equipment?

2. Do you need to obtain permission to use the equipment?

## Time available

In planning your promotional campaign you will have taken into account:

● The timing of the campaign, i.e. When should the event be publicised?
● The amount of time available between the date of which the plan was written and the date at which the promotional activity is planned to take place.

Time must be allocated within this period for each of the tasks which you have allocated at each stage of the campaign.

The timing of the campaign is crucial. In large organisations, for example the theme park Camelot, which is located at Charnock Richard near Preston, promotions may be planned for specific times of the year. Special rates may be offered to encourage visitors during specified periods – for example, school half term holidays.

During the initial planning stages of this campaign Camelot must plan when they want the promotional material to appear and then allocate the tasks within a specified time period to meet the deadline for advertising. If the advertisement appears too early in relationship to the event its impact may be lost. This may be because many people have forgotten about the advert or have thrown the newspaper away. In the eventuality of this happening the Camelot's advertising campaign will have had very limited success with the possibility that the targeted sales for that period may not be achieved.

## Information

The students must decide what information they need in order to carry out their campaign. This information could be:

● **Results of market research** – This may be as simple as asking friends if they are interested in attending the disco
● **Cost of materials** – The students will require information on the cost of materials required to carry out their campaign
● **Cost of the advertising medium** – If the students use the college notice boards this will not cost them anything, however they may decide to place a small advertisement in the local newspaper. In order to do this the information required to place the advert will include:
  – Advertising costs.
  – Copy date – the students' advert will need to reach the newspaper in sufficient time for it to be typeset.

– The students may find it useful to talk to people in the leisure and tourism industry who have previously been involved in promotional campaigns. This information will provide them with the benefit of their experience. A list of people to ask may include tutors, parents or local business people.

## Aims and objectives

In our disco plan the chief aim and the main objectives might be:

- **Aim** – To sell a specified number of tickets which will contribute to the success of the event and ensure that a financial break even point is achieved.
- **Objectives:**
  - To inform students of the forthcoming event.
  - To provide details such as 'what, when and where'.
  - To allow students sufficient time to buy tickets.
  - To provide students with sufficient opportunities to buy tickets.

To effectively participate in the promotion of the students disco the organising students need to form a working group. Their responsibilities will be areas of:

- Research.
- Planning/preparation.
- Implementation.
- Evaluation.

## Research

Market research should produce information which will give the opinion of the target group. This information will help to make judgements on the viability of the event. In the case of the student disco the working group may need to gather information either through questionnaires or word of mouth.

## Planning and preparation

- Decide on the type of promotional materials.
- Who will design them? In house by students or professionally?
- Where will the promotional material be displayed?
- Who will be responsible for displaying the materials?
- Who is responsible for the marketing budget?

## Implementation

The plan is put into action. Team members carry out their roles and responsibilities.

# Evaluation

The working group will need to look back to the original objectives and ask themselves the following questions:

- Have the objectives been achieved?
- If not, how might the plan have been improved?

As the working party become more involved in the campaign team members will need to collaborate with each other in order to swap ideas, check progress and generally to keep each other informed. A simple system of monitoring progress would be to arrange a series of regular meetings. At the meetings students will need to keep notes on the progress and details of any actions which each member of the team must take.

> Evaluate the effectiveness of the campaign

After the promotional campaign has taken place an organisation should always evaluate its effectiveness. In a large organisation the marketing manager may be required to explain the success or failure of a campaign surrounding an event.

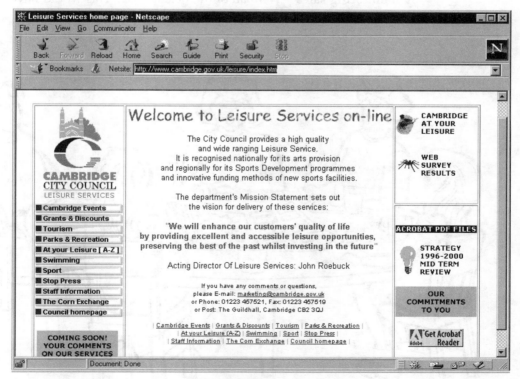

**Fig. 2.18** *Cambridge City Council web page*

Imagine a joint promotion involving, for instance, Cresta and Eurostar. Following the promotion the marketing manager would evaluate its effectiveness by comparing the number of bookings prior to the campaign with those achieved during and after the campaign. These may also be compared with comparable figures from the same period of the previous year.

If it was found that bookings were significantly higher the objective of increasing sales will have been achieved. If however there was no significant difference in the number of bookings a revised campaign would be considered to achieve the objective of increasing sales.

One promotional method which many organisations are now experimenting with is to set up information pages on the Internet, as shown in Fig. 2.18. One method of judging the success of these is by the number of responses received by e-mail.

## Evaluation of the college disco promotional campaign

You have run the campaign and the disco has taken place. So, was the event successful?

How did your promotional campaign contribute to the success of the event?

There are a number of questions which we can ask to evaluate the success of the campaign.

- By **monitoring sales** – Were all of the tickets sold? This would have been one of the main objectives of the promotional campaign.

- By **questioning** – A sample of students could be selected and asked the following questions:
  - How did you hear about the disco?
  - Did the posters give sufficient information?
  - Do you feel that you were informed about the event early enough?
  - Was it easy to buy tickets?
- After the event has taken place:
  - Did the promotional campaign reach the correct target market?

  The way in which this question could be asked is by:
  - questionnaires
  - personal interviews
  - meetings with customers, i.e. students and staff
  - through discussions within your groups

## Evidence-gathering activity

Organise a team meeting where you discuss the effectiveness of your promotional campaign. You could design a questionnaire based on similar questions to those asked about the student disco.

1. Did your campaign meet the following objectives:
   - Did the campaign inform the public?
   - Did the campaign raise public awareness?
   - Did the campaign make people want to buy the product?
   - Did the campaign enhance the image of the product?
   - Were new customers attracted?
   - Were existing customers retained?

**Remember:** It may be difficult to measure some of these objectives.

2. Personal contribution:
   - How well do you feel that you carried out your personal role in the promotional campaign?
   - How might your personal performance have been improved?

3. Team effort:
   - How well did your team work together?
   - Was there sufficient discussion amongst team members?
   - Were the allocated team roles appropriate?

Keep a note of all the meetings that you attend and keep a record of the people present at meetings, the items which were discussed and indicate which team members led the discussions.

Include with this record a list of your contributions which can be used as evidence in your portfolio.

> Make recommendations for improving future campaigns

The information gathered from the evaluation should allow you to consider any recommendations or possible changes you would like to make in future campaigns.

## Objectives

An analysis of the strengths and weaknesses of the promotional campaign should be carried out and a record (minutes) made of any comments. The minutes should then be passed on to the next organising committee. In the minutes reference should be made to all key stages of the campaign. These are:

- Objectives.
- Research.
- Planning.
- Preparation.
- Implementation.
- Evaluation.

For example, consider the following situation:

| Situation | Insufficient tickets have been sold. |
|---|---|
| Analysis | This may be because an assumption was made that each student would bring a friend to the disco. This did not happen as the majority of students came alone. |
| Recommendation | To encourage each student to bring a friend a second ticket could be offered at half price. This special offer would form a feature of the promotional campaign. |
| | Alternatively if it is assumed that each student will only buy one ticket then the pricing structure should be altered so that more is charged per ticket. |

## Evidence-gathering activity

Refer to the promotional campaign which you planned in Element 2.2.

Prepare a word-processed report which will summarise the evaluation of the campaign.

You will then need to prepare a presentation based on any recommendations highlighted in improving future promotional campaigns.

This presentation is to be presented to a group of students of the new organising committee.

**Key skills satisfied:** *Communication* **C2.1a, C2.1b, C2.2**
*Information Technology* **IT2.1, IT2.2**

# Revision questions

1. List the 4Ps of marketing.
2. What kind of information is gathered through market research?
3. What is the difference between primary and secondary data?
4. What is meant by the target market?
5. Describe ways of dividing a market into segments.

# Unit 3

# INVESTIGATE CUSTOMER SERVICE

**Explain the principles of customer service in leisure and tourism**

**Investigate the provision of information as part of customer service**

**Investigate and demonstrate sales techniques as part of customer service**

**Provide and evaluate customer service in leisure and tourism**

The aim of this unit is to introduce and explain what is meant by the term 'customer service'. We will explain the importance of providing good customer service to organisations, customers and employees and this will be illustrated through a number of case study leisure and tourism organisations.

We have also included a number of practical activities so that you can take part in role play situations and evaluate for yourself whether your customers were satisfied.

# Explain the principles of customer service in leisure and tourism

Explain what customer service is

## What is customer service?

Customers are vital to the success of any organisation. Without customers leisure and tourism organisations will fail. The money which the customers spend on the products and services of an organisation is used to pay for the wages of the staff employed there. It is important therefore to keep customers happy and satisfied by providing them with the products which they want at the right price and in the right manner. This means making the customer feel valued.

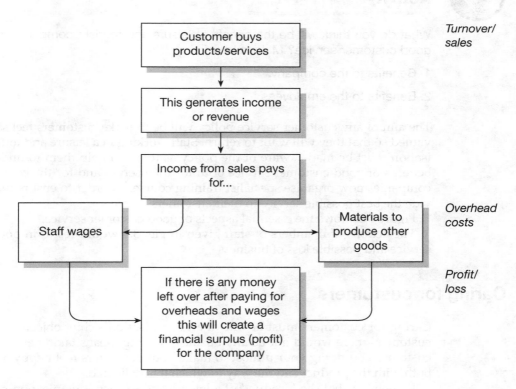

**Fig. 3.1** How sales help create profit

Satisfied customers will return to buy further products and will help the business to thrive.

## Customer service policies

Most leisure and tourism organisations will have a customer service policy which describes their strategy for looking after customers. The policy will emphasise how highly the organisation values their customers. The term the 'customer is king' is often used to describe the value which leisure and tourism organisations place on their customers.

Figure 3.2 shows *The Customer Charter* which has been issued by the Northern Ireland Tourist Board. This document outlines the standard service which visitors to a TIC in Northern Ireland can expect.

Larger leisure and tourism organisations, such as Thomas Cook and McDonald's, will have a written customer service policy whereas smaller organisations may have an implied or an unwritten understanding amongst their staff of the importance of the customer to the company's success.

## Activity

What do you think will be the benefit to leisure and tourism companies of providing good customer service? Make a list of:

1. Benefits to the company.

2. Benefits to the employees.

The aim of any customer service policy will be to make customers feel satisfied and valued so that they will want to return. Staff working in a leisure and tourism organisation must be made aware of the policy as this will help them to understand the benefits of good customer service both for themselves and for the company. Many companies now organise specialist training courses in order to ensure that staff provide the best possible service to their customers.

Figure 3.3 shows the essential aspects of good customer service.

The actions of members of staff given in Fig. 3.4 would result in poor customer service and possible loss of business.

## Caring for customers

Caring for customers must be one of an organisation's chief objectives as without customers there would not be any business. Caring means taking an interest in the customer and doing your utmost to make your customers feel happy and satisfied both with the product and the way in which it is delivered.

Remember that the 'product' of a leisure and tourism organisation may not just be a physical product such as a meal but may also be a service or experience which is provided.

## INTRODUCTION

This leaflet explains the full range of services we offer through the tourist information centre (TIC), the standards of service our customers can expect, and what you should do if we do not provide the service you expect.

The leaflet also contains a comments form which gives you the opportunity to tell us what you think of the service you received, either good or bad, and to make any suggestions which you feel would improve the services of the TIC.

## WHO ARE WE?

The TIC is one of a network of such centres in Northern Ireland and is the only one operated by the Northern Ireland Tourist Board. In 1995 the TIC dealt with 279,450 enquiries from both visitors and Northern Ireland residents.

## WHERE ARE WE?

The TIC is in central Belfast and is well signposted from the city centre, our address is:

St. Anne's Court
59 North Street
Belfast BT1 1NB

## HOW TO CONTACT US?

There are a variety of ways to use our services. Most of our customers call in to the TIC with no appointment being necessary, however you can also contact us by writing to the above address, by telephoning (01232) 231221 or fax (01232) 312424.

There is also a Freephone number (0800 404050) which can be used for our all-Ireland accommodation reservations service, a credit card is required for this service as we need to take a deposit to confirm reservations.

## WHEN CAN YOU CONTACT US?

The TIC is open Monday to Saturday from 9.00 am until 5.15 pm all year round, we also open longer hours during the summer months. Outside the TIC's normal hours of opening there is a telephone answering service and a computerised information service which can be used by personal callers.

## WHAT CAN WE DO FOR YOU?

The following range of services are available from the TIC and can be requested by any of the means detailed in the section on 'How To Contact Us'.

* Free information on tourist attractions, accommodation, transport, events, entertainment, where to eat throughout Northern Ireland.

* The TIC also provides an accommodation booking service for Northern Ireland, Republic of Ireland and most parts of Great Britain. This service is subject to a small booking fee and in most instances a deposit will also be required. This service is available to both personal callers and through the Freephone 0800 404050, a credit card is required for telephone reservations. Within Northern Ireland all accommodation is regularly inspected by the Northern Ireland Tourist Board and must meet certain minimum standards.

* The TIC also provides the following services which are available only to personal callers:

* Bureau de Change service.

* The sale of tickets eg. events, walking tours, and transport.

* The sale of a wide collection of maps, books, postcards, stamps, photographic material and a wide range of locally produced gifts and souvenirs.

## WHAT STANDARDS OF SERVICE CAN YOU EXPECT FROM US?

We have set ourselves challenging targets for the provision of these services and we promise to:

Deal with personal callers within 10 minutes, the member of staff who will always wear a name badge including details of foreign languages spoken.

Respond to 90% of all written enquiries within three working days. When it is not possible to respond within this time we will tell you when you can expect a full response. All replies will include the name of the member of staff who has handled the enquiry.

Respond to telephone calls within an average of 20 seconds, and send written replies within two working days where required, this includes messages left on our answerphone, all callers will be given the name of the member of staff who responds to their enquiry.

Respond in a friendly, positive and professional manner to all customers.

Have staff who are fluent in at least one major foreign language in addition to English.

The results of our actual performance against these targets will be displayed in the TIC and included in the Northern Ireland Tourist Board's Annual Report.

St Anne's Court
Tourist Information Centre

**Fig. 3.2** The Customer Charter

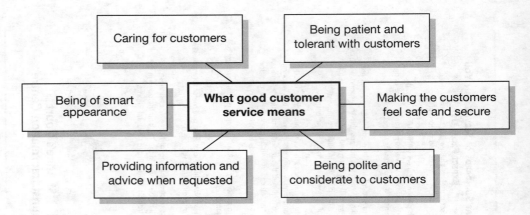

**Fig. 3.3** *Examples of good customer service*

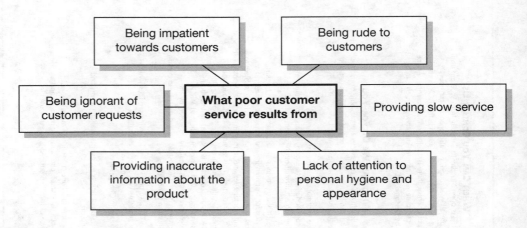

**Fig. 3.4** *Examples of poor customer service*

## Activity

Working in groups of 2 or 3 students discuss two leisure or tourism organisations which you have visited recently and make a note of the products or service which you purchased. Think about the way in which you were treated by the staff employed by these organisations. Do you feel as if the organisations which you visited treated you well and made you feel valued?

What improvements would you suggest to the standard of service which you received?

Each group should now make a presentation of their findings to the rest of the class.

**Key skills satisfied:** *Communication* **C2.1a, C2.1b, C2.2**

# Meeting customer needs

Every customer will have personal needs, wants and requests which are exclusive and individual to that customer. Therefore every customer has individual needs. Customers will therefore look to leisure and tourism organisations to meet their individual needs.

The **primary** need of the customer is to purchase the product or service which an organisation offers. Customers will also have **secondary** needs which will help influence the customer to make a decision as to whether to buy the product or not.

**Secondary needs** will include the need for:

- Advice.
- Information.
- Feeling safe.
- Feeling secure.

For example a very common need for information can be illustrated by the case of a customer, Mr Smith, telephoning a theatre box office to ask for information about performance times, availability of tickets and how much the tickets will cost.

In order to meet the needs of customers such as Mr Smith the box office receptionist will require a variety of information to be at hand. Typical information will include:

- The time the show starts and finishes.
- If the performance times vary at weekends, matinees or bank holidays.
- Whether there are any tickets available.
- The prices of tickets for different seats.
- Whether there are discounts for special groups.
- What the parking and transport arrangements are.
- How to pay for tickets.
- Arrangements for collecting tickets which have been booked over the phone.

Mr Smith needed to know whether tickets were available for a particular date and the time of the performance. The needs of Mr Smith's enquiry have been met, he received satisfactory answers to his questions and was able to book two tickets for the 7.30 pm performance of Grease on 6th of May.

On arrival at the theatre Mr Smith will need to be advised where a secure cloakroom can be found. He also asks the box office staff where is the safest place to park his car.

If the theatre staff are unable to answer Mr Smith's questions about car parking satisfactorily the following actions concerning his car may possibly occur:

- Mr Smith's car might be stolen, clamped or may get blocked in.
- He may receive a parking ticket.
- If parked in an obstructive way the car may be towed away.
- The vehicle may be damaged, vandalised or broken into.

# Achieving customer satisfaction

If Mr Smith's enquiries are dealt with swiftly, efficiently and politely the theatre staff will have gone a long way towards ensuring that their customer is satisfied. All of this activity has taken place before Mr Smith and his wife have watched the play. If they are happy with the treatment they have received from the theatre staff prior to watching the performance this will help to create an atmosphere in which the couple feel happy and relaxed and will be awaiting the play with eager anticipation.

## Activity

Call in at your local rail or bus station and ask for prices and times of the next available service to a major city such as London, Cardiff, Glasgow, Belfast, Newcastle or Birmingham.

Use the following chart to record how well your need for information was met by the staff at the station.

| Evaluation of service provided | Yes | No |
| --- | --- | --- |
| Were you given accurate times (check in the printed timetable)? | | |
| Were you provided with details of costs and any possible discounts? | | |
| Did the clerk give you details about the return journey? | | |
| Was your enquiry dealt with promptly and efficiently? | | |
| Were you dealt with in a polite manner? | | |

Explain what is achieved through effective customer service

The English Tourism Council runs a customer care training programme which is entitled 'Welcome Host'. As the title implies, the host or provider of the leisure or tourism product/service must provide a friendly, efficient and effective service in order to please its customers.

The following extract from 'Welcome Host' summarises the tourist board's philosophy on meeting customer needs:

*In an increasingly competitive and international market place, customer care is one of the best ways you can help sustain the commercial viability of your tourism business and give it a competitive edge.*

In order to improve an organisation's standard of customer care and to achieve customer satisfaction all staff must be aware of the customer care policy and why it is an essential part of the operation of the company.

In the following scenario Happy Valley, a leading visitor attraction in Bournemouth, organises a training programme to induct new members of staff in the organisation's customer care policy and to reinforce the policy to existing members of staff.

Happy Valley has devised its customer care policy to try to help the attraction achieve a number of objectives, as illustrated in Fig. 3.5.

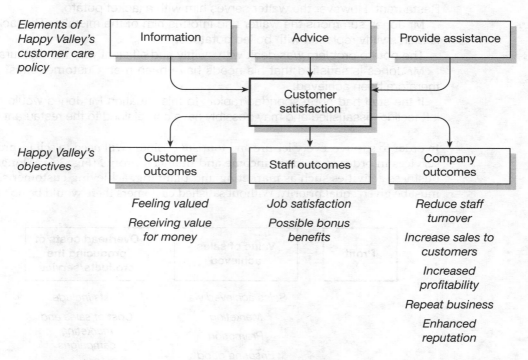

**Fig. 3.5** *How achieving customer satisfaction helps Happy Valley meet its objectives*

# Customer satisfaction

A satisfied customer is one who is happy with the product or services they have purchased and the way in which they have been dealt with by the staff providing the service.

Happy customers are those who have received the following treatment:

- Accurate information about the product/service has been provided.
- The customer feels that value for money has been provided.
- Courteous and prompt attention have been provided.
- The customer's desire for that particular product/service has been fulfilled.

Customer service may also be achieved through the provision of advice or help following a complaint or a query. After receiving this information or advice the customer is happy that his or her needs have been met.

## Customer Service Situation 1: Storm in a Teacup Restaurant

Mr Jones requests boiled potatoes with his meal in the Storm in a Teacup Restaurant. However the waiter serves him with a jacket potato.

Mr Jones summons the waiter and informs him of the mistake. The jacket potato is then swiftly replaced with boiled potatoes.

The potato problem was dealt with swiftly and efficiently by the restaurant staff.

Mr Jones is satisfied that his needs have been met. Customer satisfaction has therefore been achieved.

If the staff had not responded rapidly to this situation Mr Jones would have been left feeling dissatisfied and may possibly have complained to the restaurant manager.

In order to survive, every leisure and tourism business will need to sell its products and services in order to produce income and financial profits (Fig. 3.6). Alongside other business activities such as marketing and planning, achieving customer satisfaction must be given equal priority. Without satisfied customers there would be no business.

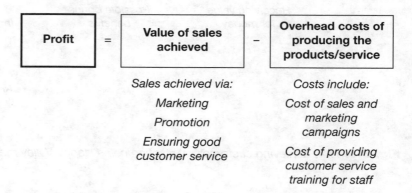

Fig. 3.6 *How good customer service helps achieve profits*

# Customer loyalty

Once a leisure or tourism organisation has made a sale to a customer it will want to encourage the customer to be loyal to the organisation so that the customer will want to return to buy further products. Good customer service can therefore produce customer loyalty which results in repeat business.

If we return again to Mr Jones who is dining in the Storm in a Teacup Restaurant we can see the importance of providing good customer service in order to retain customer loyalty.

At the time of the potato incident in the Storm in a Teacup Restaurant Mr Jones was entertaining a very important business client. Mr Jones had previously told his client about the excellent reputation of the restaurant.

When the potential potato problem was dealt with swiftly this justified Mr Jones' judgement of the restaurant.

The two businessmen subsequently agreed to meet again the following week in the same restaurant to discuss further business deals.

Good customer service was also provided at the second meeting and, as a result, two further table bookings were made, one by Mr Jones and the other by his client.

In keeping its customers satisfied the Storm in a Teacup Restaurant has achieved the following:

- Repeat business.
- Enhanced its reputation.
- An increase in sales.
- An increase in profits.

# Job satisfaction

Employees are also customers of the organisation and are known as **internal customers**. A member of staff should expect to receive from the organisation the same standard of service as **external customers**, i.e. the general public, receives. The employee may not be buying the product or service of their organisation but should expect the same level of service from their managers which should include:

- Being made to feel a valued and important part of the organisation.
- Receiving prompt attention to requests.

- Being kept informed of developments of the progress of the organisation.
- Being treated with respect.
- Receiving a level of training which meets their needs.

By treating its employees in this way the organisation will encourage employees to take a pride and interest in their work which should ultimately lead to a better standard of service for the customer.

When members of staff are made aware of the importance of good customer service they can understand why the implementation of the customer care policy by all members of staff is vital to the success of the organisation. Everyone within the organisation has a responsibility for creating a product which meets the needs of the customer whether they have direct 'face to face' contact with the customer or not.

By carrying out the principles of the organisation's customer care policy employees themselves may receive benefits such as:

- Self-satisfaction – in carrying out their job role well.
- Pride in their job and company.
- Interest in understanding their importance.
- An increase in confidence and competence which may then lead to promotion.
- Possible financial benefits.

It is vital therefore that *all* members of staff of an organisation, not only those who are 'front of house', are fully briefed in the customer care policy and that they all recognise the importance of achieving good customer service for the benefit of:

1. The customer.
2. The organisation.
3. Themselves.

## Safe and secure environment

For customers to feel happy and satisfied they must feel safe and secure within their environment. Many leisure and tourism companies try to create an image as the provider of a service which is safe and secure.

For example, the award winning advert for British Rail's Intercity service claims to 'take the strain' and shows customers relaxing in a safe, warm and comfortable environment on their journey.

Explain the importance of customer service

## Customer service

Good customer service is important to:

- The customer.
- The organisation.
- The employees.

Good customer service is important to each of these groups in different ways as each group will have a different set of objectives or needs.

## The importance of customer service to the customer

The needs of the customer will be quite different to those of the organisation and are summarised in the Customer Charter shown in Fig. 3.7.

### Activity

Consider yourself as a customer who wishes to buy a pair of trainers in a sports shop. Apart from the physical need of wanting a pair of training shoes, what other needs or expectations might you have when purchasing the shoes?

## The importance of customer service to the organisation

Providing good customer service is of vital importance to an organisation as it will help the organisation to achieve its objectives. The objectives of an organisation are usually laid out in a mission statement.

Figure 3.8 shows the Mission Statement of the Tourism & Hospitality Training Council in Northern Ireland. One of the main objectives is to improve business performance, i.e. sales and profits, of the tourism industry in Northern Ireland.

This can be achieved by *'attracting, retaining and developing highly skilled staff'* to encourage excellence in the provision of customer satisfaction.

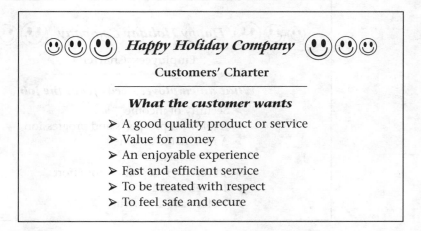

**Fig. 3.7** *Happy Holiday Company – Customers' Charter*

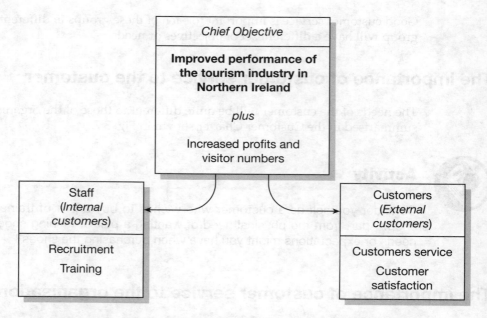

**Fig. 3.8** *Mission Statement – Tourism and Hospitality Training Council, Northern Ireland*

## The importance of customer service to staff working in the organisation

Through keeping the customer satisfied the employees of an organisation can achieve a number of personal objectives (Fig. 3.9).

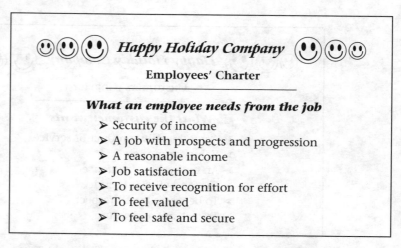

**Fig. 3.9** *Happy Holiday Company – Employees' Charter*

It is therefore in the employees' interests to keep the customer happy and satisfied; whether they have direct contact with the customer or not everyone within the organisation must recognise the importance of working together as a team in order to produce a quality product which will satisfy the needs of customers and make them want to return for more.

At the end of the day, the money which the customers pay for products and services (revenue) helps contribute toward the cost of the employees wages. Customer satisfaction is therefore directly responsible for:

- Creating jobs.
- Maintaining wage levels.
- Ensuring job security.

The benefits of good customer service are summarised in Fig. 3.10.

---

Describe and give examples of types of communication used in customer service

---

Working in leisure and tourism means that you will probably have a high level of face-to-face contact with customers. Situations in which you will have face-to-face contact vary from airport check-in desks to golf driving ranges, from youth hostels to entertainment's arenas and from bus company information desks to purpose-built sports centres.

The ways in which you communicate with your customers are wide and varied.

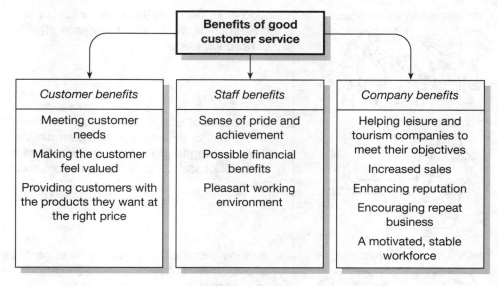

**Fig. 3.10** The benefits of good customer service

| Type of communication | Examples of types of communication |
|---|---|
| With individuals  | This is one of the most personal forms of communication as there is direct contact between yourself and the customer<br><br>*Example*: A customer paying a receptionist for the hire of a squash court in a leisure centre |
| By computer  | Computers are very useful for storing information. They can also be used as a means of communication through systems such as electronic mail (e-mail) where messages are transmitted from computer to computer |
| Written communication  | Written communications can take the form of letters, memos or posters. If fax machine facilities are not available the company may wish to send a letter confirming the details of a reservation made |
| Communicating with groups  | A good example of staff communicating with groups of customers is where a tour representative briefs a group of holidaymakers |
| Poor communication  | This is a case of where communications have broken down. The body language of the employee is unwelcoming to the customer and indicates that the member of staff does not wish to communicate with the public |
| Telephone communication  | Telephone enquiries is one of the most common methods of customers obtaining information about the product or service they are interested in<br><br>*Example*: British Rail run a central reservation service which customers can ring to find information on train times and prices |

## Activity

In the following Table we have listed examples of different types of communications between members of staff and customers.

One example has been completed for you. Try to find examples of other situations where these types of communications take place between staff and customers.

| Type of communication | Example 1 | Example 2 |
|---|---|---|
| Face-to-face | Customer ordering a meal in a restaurant | |
| Keyboard | Travel agency consultant using the CRS (central reservation system) to book a holiday for a customer | |
| Written | A coach operator sending out a mail shot to local clubs | |
| Telephone/fax | Telesales staff cold calling potential customers to encourage them to buy timeshare apartments | |
| Non-verbal | An assistant in a TIC speaks to the customer with their back facing the customer | |
| Group communication | A guide providing a tour of a museum | |

Word process your results in table format and file the table in your portfolio as key skills evidence.

**Key skills satisfied:** *Information Technology* **IT2.2, IT2.3**

## Activity

Cold calling is one method of selling which frequently uses the telephone as a means of communication. It is used by many leisure and tourism companies.

Find out what the term 'cold calling' means. Do you think cold calling encourages good customer relations?

## Methods of communicating good customer service

Good communications between the staff of an organisation and its customers can only exist where there is also a positive attitude towards customers and a high standard of customer care.

The following methods help to convey concern for your customers:

| Good customer service | Examples of situations |
| --- | --- |
| Be willing to give good customer service | Verbal communications: 'Can I help you madam?' or 'Is there anything else you would like?' |
| When asked for information do not use technical jargon | A waiter asking questions such as 'Do you require the *table d'hôte* or the *à la carte menu?*' might confuse customers and make them feel uneasy |
| If you don't know the answer or don't know how to do something, don't pretend to, find someone who does | A student on work placement in a travel agency may offer 'Yes, I can make that booking for you' (without having received the necessary training) |
| Keep your workplace as neat and tidy as possible | A neat and tidy reception area will give an impression of an efficient and effective service |
| Stay alert, look interested | If a travel clerk sits with their feet on the desk this gives the impression that they cannot be bothered to deal with the customer |
| Help customers, whenever possible take the initiative to advise your customers in the best possible manner | If you are working in a TIC be prepared to take the time to advise visitors to the area to see as many sites as possible |
| Don't keep a customer waiting unnecessarily | If you are working as a receptionist and an incoming telephone call asks for a certain extension number often no-one answers immediately. It is good practice to explain to the waiting client that you are doing your best to connect them |

| Good customer service | Examples of situations |
| --- | --- |
| Reply promptly to written requests for information | If possible acknowledge the receipt of letters by return. You could say in the letter of acknowledgement that you will deal with the request as soon as possible. Also make sure that all details such as name, address, post code are correct |
| Say thank you and smile. Try not to show signs of impatience even if a customer is being very difficult | A customer in a restaurant spends a long time choosing a meal and then changes his mind |

**Customers sometimes make providing good customer service difficult**

## Listening skills

From the above list it can be seen that it is essential to be patient with customers and develop good listening skills, even though the customer may sometimes be very difficult. By listening carefully to requests this will help you to identify quickly the needs of the customer and then hopefully to satisfy them.

Take your time when dealing with customers and don't rush. By paying attention to what your customer is saying this will:

- Make the customer feel important and valued.
- Help you to identify the customer's needs accurately.

# Feedback loop

It is important to check that the customer has understood the information you have provided him or her with. This will ensure that:

- You have identified the customer's needs correctly.
- The correct product is being provided.
- The customer is aware of the product which he or she is being provided with.

The simplest way of ensuring that both you and your customer understand each other is to ask the customer a number of questions to check their understanding. If the customer has clearly understood then the feedback loop is complete (Fig. 3.11).

## Activity

Imagine that you are working as a hotel receptionist. Based on the examples of the swimming pool party booking (Fig. 3.11) write out a script for a typical feedback loop between yourself and a customer.

Word process your script as an informal report. This can be useful evidence of key skills in your portfolio.

**Key skills satisfied:** *Information Technology* **IT2.2, IT2.3**

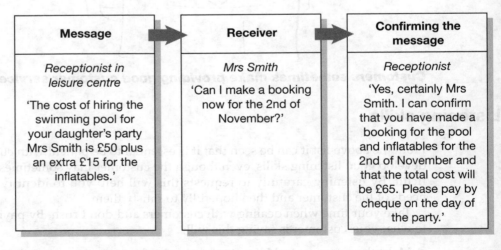

| Message | Receiver | Confirming the message |
|---|---|---|
| *Receptionist in leisure centre* 'The cost of hiring the swimming pool for your daughter's party Mrs Smith is £50 plus an extra £15 for the inflatables.' | *Mrs Smith* 'Can I make a booking now for the 2nd of November?' | *Receptionist* 'Yes, certainly Mrs Smith. I can confirm that you have made a booking for the pool and inflatables for the 2nd of November and that the total cost will be £65. Please pay by cheque on the day of the party.' |

**Fig. 3.11** *Feedback loop*

# Examples of poor customer service – how to make the customer feel awkward

| Poor customer service | Examples of situations |
|---|---|
| Making the customer feel like a nuisance | A receptionist who is reluctant to deal with a customer as they are too busy typing a letter |
| Rushing customers | Don't assume that your customer already has all the information required to make a decision |
| Trying to deal with two things at once | Give the customer your full attention. If you are dealing with a telephone enquiry don't try to deal with a second customer at the same time |
| Don't tell lies | Pretending information has been sent out when it hasn't. The customer may become suspicious and will lose faith in the organisation |
| Not taking responsibility for poor service | If your customer has had a bad experience don't try to blame others. Take responsibility yourself |
| Not bothering to suggest alternatives | If you tell your customer that all the tickets for tonight's concert have been sold and don't bother to suggest an alternative date |
| Providing a service – reluctantly | Letting the customer know that meeting their needs is not really your job – but you'll do it anyway |
| Making the customer feel uncomfortable | Poor body language makes customers feel unwelcome: avoiding eye contact; sighing; not standing still whilst dealing with customers |
| Making fun of customers | A customer who is obviously a visitor to your country and is not fluent in English will feel unwelcome if you take great delight in smirking and sniggering at their attempts to communicate with you |

## Activity

In groups of 3 to 4 students choose one of the examples of poor customer service described above. Write a short role play.

Act out your role play in front of your class and ask your fellow class members to make a list of points of poor customer service.

**Key skills satisfied:** *Communication* **C2.1b, C2.3**

Give examples of customer service in selected leisure and tourism organisations

# Customer service at Quarry Bank Mill

As a visitor attraction Quarry Bank Mill recognises the importance of providing good customer service. This fact was recognised in 1993 when the site won a commendation in the First Direct/Daily Telegraph Customer Care Competition.

Quarry Bank Mill is committed to providing a first-class service for its customers and this is reflected in its staff training policy which is explained in the *Interpretation Manual*. The manual is designed to draw together and enhance the skills of demonstrators, interpreters and guiding staff to provide a quality service.

| Services provided by QBM | Customers of QBM |
| --- | --- |
| Interpretation of the mill and its artefacts | National Trust members |
| | School parties |
| Museum | General public |
| Mill shop | Special interest groups |
| Educational service | |

*The manual will be supported by individual and group training programmes which will be run annually across the site. There will also be an element of performance evaluation appraisal. It is a commitment by the museum to create a consistent, high quality experience for all our visitors.*

Quarry Bank Mill's customer care policy is based on the code of practice laid down in the English Tourist Board's visitor charter.

Quarry Bank Mill defines customer/visitor care in the key points listed in Fig. 3.12.

```
┌─────────────────────────────────────────────────┐
│              Quarry Bank Mill                     │
│                                                   │
│            A definition of visitor care           │
│   Visitor care is...                              │
│                                                   │
│   The provision of a consistently high quality    │
│   service...                                      │
│                                                   │
│   ➢ By all National Trust staff                   │
│                                                   │
│   ➢ Which matches or exceeds visitors' expectations│
│                                                   │
│   ➢ Ensuring the best possible experience and     │
│     impressions of what the National Trust has    │
│     to offer                                      │
│                                                   │
│   ➢ For everyone's mutual benefit                 │
│                                                   │
└─────────────────────────────────────────────────┘
```

**Fig. 3.12** *Quarry Bank Mill – A definition of visitor care*

# Who benefits from visitor care at Quarry Bank Mill?

In their staff training for visitor care Quarry Bank Mill emphasises that it is not only the customer who benefits from good customer service but also the staff themselves and the National Trust (Fig. 3.13).

Visitors to any visitor attraction will expect to be provided with a service which meets their needs and in a way which shows that the facility cares for the customer

```
┌─────────────────────────────────────────────────┐
│               Quarry Bank Mill                    │
│                                                   │
│               How do we benefit?                  │
│                                                   │
│   The visitor   Enjoys the visit more             │
│                 Sees more                         │
│                 Learns more                       │
│                 Gets value for money              │
│                 Is encouraged to visit more       │
│                 May become a volunteer            │
│                                                   │
│   Quarry Bank Mill Trust  Gains and keeps members │
│                             and visitors          │
│                           Increases revenue       │
│                           Enhances reputation     │
│                           Is helped to maintain/  │
│                             develop the mill      │
│                           Gains volunteers        │
│                                                   │
│          You  Increased satisfaction in your work │
│               Visitors are friendlier             │
│               Visitors respect you                │
│               Your day is more enjoyable          │
│                                                   │
└─────────────────────────────────────────────────┘
```

**Fig. 3.13** *Quarry Bank Mill – Who benefits from good visitor care*

thus ensuring customer satisfaction. This is summarised by Quarry Bank Mill in the statement of visitor expectations given in Fig. 3.14.

## What services does Quarry Bank Mill offer to meet customer needs

As well as providing a museum and information service to the public Quarry Bank Mill also provides a range of other services (Fig. 3.15), to ensure that their customers have a pleasant experience.

## Dealing with difficult situations

Quarry Bank Mill train their staff how to deal with difficult situations and how to convert a difficult situation (Fig. 3.16) into an opportunity to provide good customer care.

The Quarry Bank Mill visitor care policy is drawn together in 'The Commandments of Visitor Care' (Fig. 3.17).

### Visitor First Scheme

Comments from visitors regarding the museum are invited on the Visitor First Scheme (Fig. 3.18). The feedback received from customers will be used to influence future amendments to the Visitor Care Policy.

---

**Quarry Bank Mill**

*Visitors expect...*

| | |
|---|---|
| To be educated, informed | To be welcomed |
| To feel secure and at ease | To feel important |
| Value for money | Information |
| To see something interesting | Efficiency |
| Polite and friendly assistance | To be thanked |
| Professionalism | |

*Visitors do not want...*

To be rushed
Too much attention
To feel unwelcome, unwanted
Too many rules and regulations

---

***Fig. 3.14*** *Quarry Bank Mill – Visitor expectations*

```
Quarry Bank Mill

What service do we offer

Practical service   Access arrangements
                    Atmosphere
                    Car parking
                    Signs
                    Comfort
                    Refreshments
                    Gifts
                    Information (e.g. brochures)
                    Membership
                    Lavatories

Personal service    Welcome
                    Smile/greeting
                    A first impression
                    Advice, help guidance
                    Security (at ease, not threatened)
                    Appearance
                    Attitude
                    Information (your knowledge of the property and the Trust)
```

Fig. 3.15  *Quarry Bank Mill – The services offered to customers*

```
Quarry Bank Mill

Every 'difficult' situation is an opportunity to
provide exceptional visitor care...

Listen
Understand
Explain
&
Don't compete!
```

Fig. 3.16  *Quarry Bank Mill – How to deal with difficult situations*

**Quarry Bank Mill**

***The Commandments of Visitor Care***

Visitors are the most important people at Quarry Bank Mill and should be treated as such

Visitors are not dependent on us, we are dependent on them

Visitors are not an interruption to our work, they are the reason for it

Visitors do us a favour when they call, we are not doing them a favour

Visitors are there to argue with or match wit with, we are there to accommodate them

Visitors bring us their needs, we are there to fulfil them

Visitors deserve our best treatment, we must make sure that they receive the best

Visitors are part of our business, not outsiders

Visitors are the life blood of Quarry Bank Mill, without them we would have no reason for existence

***Fig. 3.17*** *Quarry Bank Mill – The commandments of visitor care*

**Quarry Bank Mill**

***Visitors First Scheme***

Do **YOU** have any **COMMENTS? IDEAS? SUGGESTIONS?**

At Quarry Bank Mill we are committed to making sure that you are delighted with your visit to the Mill. We welcome and value your suggestions and thank you for taking time to help us improve

Please use this space or ask to speak to the Visitor Services Manager at the office in the Mill Yard.

---

Day.............................. Date ..............................

Are you a National Trust Member? YES NO

If *not* a National Trust Member when did you last visit? ..............................

Please fill in your name and address if you would like to be entered into our draw for a bottle of Champagne

Name ..............................

Address ..............................

..............................

**THANK YOU VERY MUCH FOR YOUR INTEREST AND HELP**

***Fig. 3.18*** *Quarry Bank Mill – Visitor First Scheme*

# Assignment

'Customer service policy'

**Key skills satisfied:** *Communication* **C2.1a, C2.1b, C2.2, C2.3**
*Information Technology* **IT2.1, IT2.2, IT2.3**

## Situation

You are working for a regional tourist board and you have been asked to contribute your ideas towards good customer service within your area. Working in teams you must present your findings to a meeting of the local tourist association. The aim is to encourage local visitor attractions to adopt a standard policy towards customer care.

## Tasks

### Part A

Each team member should be allocated one of the following methods of communicating to customers:

1. With individuals.
2. With groups.
3. Face to face.
4. Written.
5. Telephone.
6. Computer based.
7. Non-verbal.

The teams should then draw up two lists:

1. Examples of good practice in communicating with customers, including the importance of developing listening skills and the use of feedback loops.
2. Examples of bad practice in communicating with customers which should be discouraged.

The teams will then present their findings to the local tourist association.

### Part B

Each team must then choose two local organisations, one representing travel and tourism and the other representing leisure, and investigate how they follow good codes of practice for customer care.

The results of this investigation should be produced as a word-processed report.

# Investigate the provision of information as part of customer service

It is vital to the success of any leisure or tourism organisation that its employees have a wide range of knowledge which will include not only information about the facility and its services but also the significance of the facility locally, regionally and nationally.

To ensure that customer needs are met, employees may have to be able to provide a wide range of information such as:

- Knowledge of the facility:
  - admission prices
  - opening times
  - services available
  - travel directions
- Knowledge of the surrounding area:
  - where to stay
  - other facilities in the area

If customer satisfaction is to be achieved information will have to be presented:

- Clearly
- Precisely
- Accurately
- Promptly
- In an appropriate manner

To help illustrate the importance to an organisation of its employees having a wide range of knowledge we will use the example of Eureka! – The Museum for Children to highlight examples of good practice.

## Eureka! – The Museum for Children

Eureka! is a very different type of museum and the first of its kind in the UK (Fig. 3.19). Situated in Halifax, West Yorkshire, this museum has been designed to teach children up to the age of twelve about themselves and the world around them. Eureka! uses a range of interactive, 'hands on' displays and actively encourages children to role play with and touch, listen and smell the exhibits.

Eureka! has a reputation for providing excellence in customer service. Peter Clinker, the Operations Director, said: 'Customer care is crucial to the success of the museum.'

The good practice in customer care which is shown by the museum has been recognised by the leisure and tourism industry through many notable awards. The English

**Fig. 3.19** *Eureka! – The Museum for Children*

Tourist Board named Eureka! the 1993 Visitor Attraction of the Year. The Yorkshire Tourist Board gave it the Customer Care Award in 1995, and Visitor Attraction of the Year in 1993 and 1996, and in 1994/95 parents throughout the UK voted Eureka! the most Parent Friendly Museum in Tommy's Campaign Awards. The museum has also picked up awards for the provision of facilities for visitors with special needs.

Figure 3.20 lists some of the other notable achievements of Eureka!.

> Explain the value to the customer of leisure and tourism employees having a broad range of knowledge

In order to meet the needs of its customers it is vital that the staff of Eureka! are aware of the specific requirements of its customers. The museum has been designed specifically for children and accompanying adults. Therefore the information provided will be tailored to meet the needs of the main customer group.

All new members of staff at Eureka! undergo a period of induction training. This is a five-day process which comprises:

## Eureka! Awards

**1993 Visitor Attraction of the Year**
English Tourist Board, England for Excellence Award

**1993 Visitor Attraction of the Year**
Yorkshire and Humberside Tourist Board

**1993 Tourism for All**
Yorkshire and Humberside Tourist Board

**1993 Main Architecture Award**
The Royal Institute of British Architects

**1993 British Gas Adapt Award**
For best practice in access for people with disabilities

**1994 Most Parent Friendly Museum**
Tommy's Campaign Parent Friendly Awards

**1994 National Heritage Museum of the Year Award**
The most imaginative use of interactive multi-media technology

**1994 Interpret Britain Award**
The society for the Interpretation of Britain's Heritage

**1994 Yorkshire Loo of the Year**
British Tourist Authority

**1994 BT Environment Week Award**
Highly commended for establishments committed to a brighter future

**1994 Roy Castle Good Air Award**
For providing a smoke free area

**1995 Most Parent Friendly Museum**
Tommy's Campaign Parent Friendly Awards

**1995 Best Practice Award**
British Urban Regeneration Association

**1995 Customer Care Award**
Yorkshire and Humberside Tourist Board

**1995 Leisure and Tourism Loo of the Year**
British Tourist Authority

**1996 Visitor Attraction of the Year**
Yorkshire Tourist Board

***Fig. 3.20*** *Eureka! awards*

- A two-day formal course covering aspects such as company strategy and organisation, health and safety, customer care and marketing.
- Three days of work shadowing an experienced member of staff to find out how the exhibits work and to gain experience in dealing with customers.

The induction training stresses to the staff the value to the customer of:

- Anticipating and meeting customer needs.
- Providing accurate information.
- Ensuring customers have a valuable and enjoyable experience.

*Meeting customer needs*
Eureka! aims to meet the needs of their customers by 'Looking after customers, making them welcome and enhancing their experience'.

As the museum is aimed at the specific market group of children, parents, teachers and carers the kind of information needs which this group might have will include:

- Are there any refreshment facilities?
- Can children wander freely around the museum?
- What is the procedure for lost children?

*Providing accurate information*

The information which Eureka! provides to its customers must be accurate. For example, if a customer rang to enquire about opening times and was given inaccurate information resulting in the customer arriving too late to fully explore the museum the customer would naturally be dissatisfied.

All staff must be fully familiar with the customer information which is contained in the Fact File shown in Fig. 3.21.

## Activity

Make a list of some of the benefits to the customer of receiving accurate information about a facility. What impression is a customer likely to have of a facility which has provided incorrect information?

| Benefits to the customer of receiving accurate information | Problems created for customers by receiving inaccurate information |
| --- | --- |
|  |  |
|  |  |
|  |  |
|  |  |

*Saving customers time and money*

Receiving prompt and accurate information in response to a request can save customers valuable time and money. Eureka! offers special admission rates for groups and at certain times of day. For example, visitors are admitted for half price after 3 pm during term time.

### Broad range of knowledge

The staff induction process at Eureka! lasts for five days. The first two days are spent familiarising staff with the following types of information:

**Fig. 3.21** Eureka! – Fact file

**Fig. 3.22** Eureka! – Information and services

- **Organisational knowledge**
  - The products and services available at Eureka!, as shown in Fig. 3.22.
  - Admission prices plus any special rates and discounts.
  - Procedures for health and safety.
  - Emergency procedures.
  - Staff structure at the museum.
- **Knowledge about Eureka! within the leisure and tourism industry**
  - The number of visitors to Eureka!
  - The museum's achievements through maintaining high standards of customer service.
- **Understanding of the regional context of Eureka!**
  - To be aware of other facilities within the Yorkshire area.
  - To be able to provide local travel directions.
  - To be able to advise visitors of tourism information services available locally.
- **Understanding of the national context of Eureka!**
  - To understand how unique Eureka! is and what other similar museums there might be in the UK.
  - To provide travel directions to visitors from overseas.

## Activity

Choose a leisure or tourism facility which you have visited or which is close to where you live. Make a list of the specific 'organisational knowledge' which you think the staff working at that facility might need to have.

Word process this information as a memo to be circulated to relevant members of staff.

**Key skills satisfied:** *Information Technology* **IT2.2, IT2.3**

Explain what organisational knowledge leisure and tourism employees should have

A visit to any leisure or tourism facility will be enhanced if the staff treat their customers well. The staff who have face-to-face contact with the customer at Eureka! are known as 'Enablers' – this means enabling the customer to get the most from the experience of visiting the museum. Part of providing good customer care at Eureka! depends upon the Enablers having a good knowledge and understanding of the organisational aspects of the museum.

*Products available*
During the induction period the Enablers at Eureka! learn about the range of products and services available at the museum.

The products can be broken down into:

- Exhibits – Over 400 interactive exhibits are available in the four main exhibition areas (Fig. 3.23):
  - Me and my body
  - Living and working together
  - Invent, create, communicate
  - Things
- Outdoor facilities – Outside in the Eureka! park there is:
  - The Hazard Dome
  - Picnic facilities
  - The Health Trail
- Special events and workshops (Fig. 3.24).
- Catering facilities.
- Car and coach parking facilities.
- Toilets and baby changing facilities.
- Facilities for people with special needs.

The Enablers are available throughout the museum to help and advise visitors. They will actively get involved with children, assisting them to work with the exhibits.

During the busy school holiday periods the Enablers will also provide entertainment for visitors who may have to queue outside.

*Prices*
In order to deal with customer enquiries promptly and efficiently the staff at Eureka! must have a good knowledge of admission prices. They will also be aware of any special discounts which might apply.

For example, Eureka! has a 'Special Schools Service' on which it can offer a special rate for shorter visits.

*Health, safety and security*
For the safety and security of employees and customers at Eureka! it is essential that all staff understand the health and safety requirements and are fully aware of emergency procedures, such as:

- First aid.
- Fire drills.
- Security alerts.

## Invent, Create, Communicate!

Explore the world of communications in *Invent, Create, Communicate!* Try out different ways of sending messages, from simple techniques through to the hi-tech inventions of today.

Broadcast the news across the *Eureka!* airwaves in the TV Studio, help save a yacht in distress, then put yourself in the picture on the front page of a newspaper.

Try out the Music Box, full of unusual musical inventions where your every touch will make delightful sounds.

## Me and My Body

Meet Scoot the Robot. Scoot wants to know all about you and how your body works. Collect your passport to record your personal details as you journey through the exhibition.

Record your height, play digestion pinball to see how food travels through your body, watch a skeleton pedalling and find out what will happen to you as you grow and change.

At the end of your journey, enter your passport information into Scoot's computer to see just how unique and special you are.

## Things

*Things* lets you use a whole range of tools and technology to discover a lot more about many of the everyday objects we take for granted. You can explore how they are made, how they affect our lives. Use levers and wheels to change the expression on a giant mechanical head, or take on the role of detective and use different tools to decide whether something is real or fake.

Things are designed to provide what we need in our everyday lives. In *Things*, you can design your own perfect chair using a giant moveable model.

## Living and Working Together

*Living and Working Together* helps you uncover the secrets of work and everyday life in and around a Town Square and provides a setting for you to role-play in an adult's world. Be a customer or cashier in the Shop, withdraw money from a cash machine in the Bank, sort the mail in the Post Office, fill a car up with petrol in the Garage or work the machines in the Factory.

Inside the House you can dress-up in the attic, make your favourite meal in the kitchen, lift the lid on the workings of the flush toilet in the bathroom and find out how the gas, water and electricity get into the house.

***Fig. 3.23** Eureka! – Exhibits*

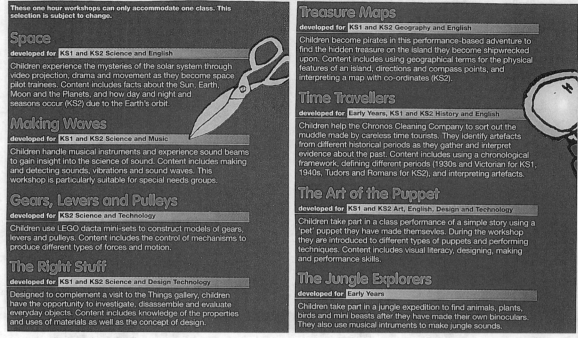

**Fig. 3.24** *Eureka! – Educational events*

As part of their induction programme the staff are trained to deal quickly and efficiently with emergency situations whilst reassuring the customers.

All employees in any leisure or tourism facility must therefore be aware that they are responsible for the health, safety and security of themselves and their customers and should be familiar with the terms of the Health and Safety at Work etc. Act 1974 (see page 277).

*Organisational structure*
The staff structure at Eureka! is shown in Fig. 3.25. It is important that every member of staff is aware of the organisational structure of the facility in which they work. If the employee needs to find out further information to satisfy a customer's needs then this might be obtained from the direct line manager or from another member of staff in a different department.

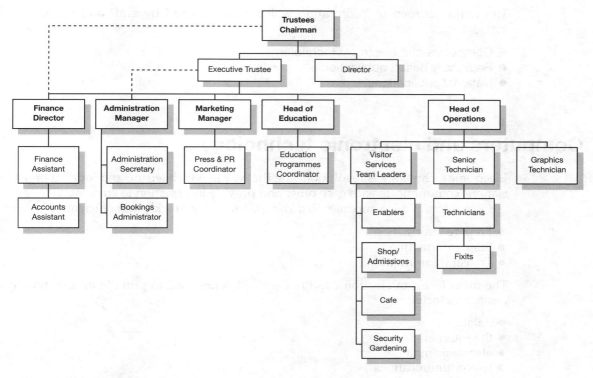

**Fig. 3.25** *Eureka! – Staff structure*

At Eureka! staff at all levels, including the managers, take responsibility for dealing with customers. By liaising with the customers this keeps the senior managers in touch with their clients and helps them to appreciate the needs of the customers.

## Activity

Working in small groups, find out the organisational structure of the school or college at which you are studying. When you have found this information lay it out as a chart, similar to the format shown for our example of Eureka!.

**Key skills satisfied:** *Information Technology* **IT2.2, IT2.3**

Describe sources of information which are used as part of customer service

In order to provide customers with accurate information the staff themselves must be aware of the main sources of information which help them to provide good customer service.

The main sources of information which may be used by staff and customers include:

- Computers and electronic technology.
- Regionally based publications.
- National publications.

# Computers and electronic technology

Electronic technology is revolutionising the way in which leisure and tourism organisations communicate with each other and provide information to customers.

Computers allow companies to do all the following quickly and efficiently:

- Prepare information.
- Store information.
- Transmit information.

The main forms of electronic technology which are used to provide information to customers include:

- databases
- the Internet
- electronic mail
- telecommunications

## Databases

A database is used to store information such as customer or product details. A database is similar to a card index filing system or catalogue/directory but instead of being recorded on paper the information is stored on a computer disk.

The records contained within an electronic database can be rapidly accessed by the computer operator and the details may be amended on screen.

It is possible to sort the data contained in the database in a number of ways, for example:

- Alphabetically by surname.
- By geographic area.
- By date of birth.
- By interests and hobbies.

A computerised database is therefore much more flexible than a paper-based card index or filing system where customer or product details may only be filed in one way.

## The Internet

The Internet is an interactive computer-based communication network which is sometimes known as the 'information superhighway' because of the speed at which information is made available.

Leisure and tourism organisations can make information available to customers via the Internet. Eureka! makes use of this type of communication system to inform customers of their facilities and of any special events (Fig. 3.26).

The advantage of the Internet is that any changes to information details can be made immediately. The disadvantage, however, is that many customers may still not have access to the Internet.

## Activity

If your school/college has an Internet facility ask your teacher if you can access the Eureka! home page. In order to do this you will need to know the Eureka! web page address which is:

**http://ourworld.compuserve.com/homepages/eureka_museum**

Assess how the Eureka! Web page can be used by potential customers.

**Key skills satisfied:** *Information Technology* **IT2.3**

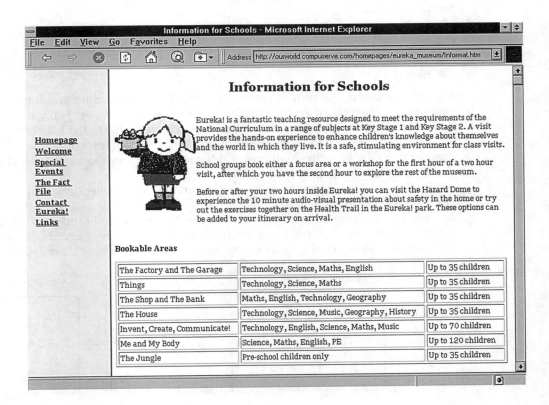

***Fig. 3.26*** *Eureka! – Web page*

# Electronic mail (e-mail)

Electronic mail – or e-mail as it is more commonly known – is a method of sending messages electronically from one computer to another using the telephone network.

To use e-mail you will need to have a modem attached to your computer and have appropriate software. The modem converts the signal from the telephone line to a digital signal which can be understood by the receiving computer (Fig. 3.27). You will also need to take out a subscription with a server or information provider such as Compuserve. The server collects the e-mail messages and sends them 'down line' to the destination computer. With the appropriate equipment messages can be sent quickly and cheaply around the world.

This is a relatively new method of communication which at the moment tends to be used only by larger leisure and tourism organisations.

Customers of Eureka! can request information from the museum by sending an e-mail message to the Eureka! electronic mail box which is:

100306.2220@compuserve.com.

# Telecommunications

Telecommunications means to communicate using the telephone network which may include:

- Telephones.
- Fax.
- Viewdata systems such as Istel.
- Electronic mail.

Telephone communication is the main method used by leisure and tourism companies to communicate directly with their customers. This is a very convenient method of verbal communication as all customers will have access to the telephone system.

Fax messages are more commonly sent between organisations. A fax machine, linked to a telephone line will transmit letters and pictures to another machine at the end of the telephone line.

Staff at Eureka! receive training in handling customer telephone enquiries as part of their induction training.

The use of computers has revolutionised the retail travel industry. Using viewdata systems such as Istel and Fastrack high street travel agents can access the information systems of major tour operators and airlines, check availability of pack-

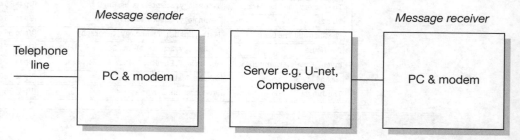

**Fig. 3.27** *How electronic mail is transmitted*

age holidays and flights and make bookings directly via the computer terminal. In a similar way business travel agencies such as Carlson Wagonlit will use systems such as Galileo, Sabre and Amadeus to make airline reservations.

## Activity

Working in groups design a questionnaire to collect information about the methods used by leisure and tourism organisations in your area to communicate with their customers. Each group should choose a different leisure and tourism facility.

As a class gather together the information you have collected and produce a pie chart or bar graph to show the most frequently used types of communication.

# Regionally based publications

Regionally based publications can provide a wealth of information about local leisure and tourism facilities.

Customers will be able to find information from the following range of sources:

| Type of publication | Examples | Type of customer information listed |
|---|---|---|
| Timetables | Leisure Lines – Regional Railways local timetables | Schedule of train times, details of special offers |
| | National Express Winter Coach Guide | Regional coach timetable giving details of departure times, destinations and costs |
| Brochures | Flyer for St Patrick's Trian, Armagh | Details of displays and special events |
| | | Location details |
| | | Opening times |
| Local authority publications | These may be specifically produced for local leisure or tourism facilities or may be a regional guide such as the brochure 'Welcome to West & South Yorkshire' which was produced by the City of Leeds Promotions and Tourism Unit and Calderdale Council | Description of the region |
| | | Details of tourist attractions in the local area |
| | | Local accommodation |

| Type of publication | Examples | Type of customer information listed |
|---|---|---|
| Telephone directories | Yellow Pages – Manchester South<br>The Thomson Local – Chester Vale Royal | Telephone directories classify facilities for leisure and tourism under standard headings and obviously provide addresses and telephone numbers |
| Newspapers | Chester Chronicle<br>Birmingham Evening Post | Advertisements for local leisure and tourism facilities, e.g. Chester Zoo<br>Special offers in restaurants and theme parks, e.g. Camelot |
| Maps | A–Z Street Map of Bradford<br>Ordnance Survey Landranger 90 series – Penrith, Keswick & Ambleside area | The A–Z series of street maps provides details street layouts and a comprehensive index<br>OS maps use symbols to describe geographical features and are useful when rambling or orienteering |
| Lists of sporting and arts venues | Booklet 'What's on in Dumfries & Galloway' | Date, time and place of local sporting, cultural and horticultural shows and events |
| Accommodation listings | Booklet 'Calderdale Accommodation Guide' | Details of both serviced and self-catering accommodation including name, address and telephone number of establishment, grading, facilities and prices |

## Activity

Working in pairs create a grid like the example shown above and list details of publications from leisure and tourism facilities which are close to your school/college. Make a note of the information which is contained in the publications.

Try to collect examples of the publications as they can be stored as evidence in your portfolio.

# National publications

The UK's top leisure and tourism attractions are listed in national directories which are available to people across the country in the national network of Tourist

Information Centres (TICs). Such information may also be found at the attractions themselves.

These publications are also available to overseas visitors and may be distributed by the British Tourist Authority in their overseas offices.

| Type of publication | Example | Type of customer information listed |
|---|---|---|
| Newspapers | Mail on Sunday<br>Daily Telegraph | Sporting events<br>Pull out holiday supplements<br>TV viewing guides<br>Advertisements and press releases for visitor attractions<br>Currency exchange rates for holidaymakers<br>World weather conditions, e.g. snow conditions for skiers |
| Magazines | Holiday Which? | Holiday advice and hints for travelling<br>Best value holidays<br>Reviews of destinations |
| Government publications | British Tourist Authority (BTA) Digest of Tourist Statistics | Government publications provide information about specific sectors of the leisure and tourism industry. For example the Digest of Statistics provides facts and figures on domestic, inbound and outbound tourism to the UK |
| Trade journals | Travel Trade Gazette<br>Leisure Week | News of the performance of tour operators, travel agents and airlines and any new government regulations<br>Reports on new destinations<br>Employment opportunities in travel<br>Trends in leisure provision<br>Employment opportunities in the leisure industry<br>Invitations to tender for leisure projects |
| National association publications | YHA Accommodation Guide | Such publications are produced for national interest groups such as the Youth Hostels Association (YHA). This members guide provides information on the location of hostels, facilities available, costs and travel directions |

| Type of publication | Example | Type of customer information listed |
|---|---|---|
| Timetables | Flight Travel Guides | Details of scheduled flights by major airlines to domestic and overseas airports |
| Sector listings | AA Bed & Breakfast Guide | Guides for specific sectors or types of facilities/venues associated with leisure and tourism. The guides mentioned include details of hotel, guest house or camp site name, address, telephone number, facilities available, details of grading, costs |
| | RAC Inspected Hotels Guide | |
| | AA Camping & Caravanning Guide | |
| Brochures | Buckingham Palace | These are the brochures of nationally known leisure and tourism facilities containing information such as details of exhibits, opening times, other facilities available, travel directions, costs |
| | Eureka! | |
| | Cotswold Camping | Brochures are sometimes produced by large retail chains such as Cotswold Camping which provide information on products which customers can buy and on trends in the outdoor leisure industry |
| Guide books/maps | Michelin Tourist Guides | Tourist guide books will give information on a particular area such as Baedeker's Guide to London which contains details of sightseeing, hotels, shops, maps and facts and figures |
| | Baedeker's Guides | |
| | Where to Fish Guide | |
| | Pictorial Guide to the Lakeland Fells | Activity guides provide information on pursuits such as walking and fishing and include details of the best routes or sites, hints and additional information such as access rights. The series of guide books written by Alfred Wainwright detail many famous walks in the Lake District. The walks are illustrated by sketches and comments by the author giving an overall picture of what to expect when walking. Such activity guide books may well be used in conjunction with maps from the OS Landranger and Pathfinder series |
| | Ordnance Survey (OS) maps – Landranger and Pathfinder series | |

 **Activity**

Visit your nearest Tourist Information Centre. Look at the range of information that is available for customers. Identify which information would be used throughout the UK and list the details using the same type of table as above.

In this section we will show how the staff at Eureka! identify the information needs of their customers and ensure that they provide clear information to meet those needs.

A visual aid used by Eureka! to assist all visitors to the museum is the Satoshi figures which convey information about directions and instructions on how to use the exhibits. As you can see from the Satoshi figures shown in Fig. 3.28 These characters hold an instant appeal to the main client group of the museum – children.

The main types of visitors to Eureka! will include:

- Very few non-English speaking.
- People from different cultural backgrounds.
- Visitors of different ages.
- Families with children between 3 and 12 years who live within a 2-hour drive.
- People who are visiting friends and relatives (VFR).
- Visitors with specific needs.
- Primary school groups from schools within a 2-hour drive.
- Other groups, such as Brownies.

**Fig. 3.28** *Eureka! – Satoshi figures*

## Activity

Look at the Satoshi figures shown in Fig. 3.28. Which of the above customer types do you think will identify with these characters?

# Communication skills

When they are being interviewed for a job at Eureka! potential 'Enablers' must prove that they have good communication skills. This is essential to enable them to communicate with the wide range of customers which the museum attracts.

The 'Enablers' must demonstrate the following skills:

- The ability to use simple and clear language in order to make themselves understood by children of varying ages.
- Provide information which is accurate and clear.
- Show an understanding of the structure of the organisation.
- Show an understanding of the function and operation of the exhibits.
- Be sensitive to and aware of the specific needs of certain customers.
- Ideally to be multi-lingual or to be able to communicate using sign language.
- Show patience and tolerance when dealing with customers, especially those from different cultural backgrounds where communication may be difficult.

| Customer type | Typical customer need | How Eureka! meets customer information needs |
|---|---|---|
| Non-English speaking visitors | To understand instructions for the exhibits and direction signs | Dual headset guides explain the exhibits in English and Urdu |
| | | Some of the staff are multi-lingual |
| | | The Satoshi figures help to convey visual messages |
| | | The Enablers will talk slowly and clearly and will stop to check that the customer has understood the information they have been given |
| Visitors from different cultural backgrounds | Visitors should feel comfortable with the way in which the information is presented, i.e. not be offended | The Enablers are trained to understand the needs of people from different cultural backgrounds |
| | | The Enablers will respect the wishes of such visitors |
| | | The staff are trained to speak clearly and use simple language where appropriate |

| Customer type | Typical customer need | How Eureka! meets customer information needs |
|---|---|---|
| People of different ages | Customers need to have information provided to them at varying degrees of complexity depending upon their age. The exhibits are aimed at children between the ages of 3 to 12 who will be accompanied by their parents, guardian or teacher | The Enablers may use diagrams, maps or leaflets to help explain the instructions<br><br>The Satoshi figures will convey information in a way which is appealing to young children<br><br>The Enablers will use simple language which is appropriate to the age of the visitor<br><br>The Eureka! exhibits are bright, easy to read and appealing to children |
| Business visitors | Teachers who are accompanying school parties and wish to identify activities which are relevant to the various levels of the National Curriculum | A nominated enabler is available to assist teachers for the first hour of the school visit<br><br>Eureka! produces teacher specific material such as the 'Education Resource Pack'<br><br>The 'Curriculum Choices' leaflet informs teachers of which activities are appropriate to the various key stages of the National Curriculum |
| Visiting friends and relatives | The needs of people who are visiting their friends and relatives in the Halifax area | Eureka! will provide entertainment for the whole family<br><br>Staff can provide information about other attractions in the area<br><br>A range of visitor information is available in the local TIC |
| People with specific needs | This may include people who have:<br><br>Visual impairment<br>Audio impairment<br>People with mobility problems | Dual headset guides describe the exhibits and their purpose<br><br>The Enablers will write down instructions for people who have poor hearing or communicate using sign language<br><br>Access to the museum and exhibits is enhanced by ramps, lifts and wide gangways |

## Activity

As a pupil/student you are a customer of your school/college. What are the particular information needs of the customers of your organisation?

Think about the different type of people who are customers of your school. Make a list of the needs of the customers and how these are met by the school.

# Other information needs

Other information needs which customers of Eureka! might have include:

- What happens if we lose the children?
- How to act if there is a fire alarm.
- How to behave in the event of a security alert.

## Lost children

In the event of children becoming separated from their parents at Eureka! the Enablers will assist in the search for the missing child. If, however, it is the parent who has gone missing the lost child will be cared for by an Enabler whilst a tannoy message is relayed asking for the parents of the child to report to the information desk.

On average the length of time between a lost child alert being raised at Eureka! and the adult and child being reunited is usually less than four minutes.

## Emergency procedures

If there is a fire or security alert at Eureka! an intermittent bell is sounded. The Enablers are trained to instruct customers to leave the museum, indicating the nearest exit point. Customers are then advised by Enablers to retire to a safe distance away from the building.

A loud hailer message will tell the customers when it is considered safe to re-enter the museum and they are asked to form an orderly queue at the main entrance. All of the museum staff, including the managers, are involved in this process.

In the case of an emergency situation the Enablers are instructed to remain calm and to provide clear and simple instructions to the customers.

## Assignment

'Is customer service at British Rail on the right track?'

Key skills satisfied: *Communication* **C2.1a, C2.1b, C2.2, C2.3**
*Information Technology* **IT2.1, IT2.2, IT2.3**
*Application of Number* **N2.1, N2.2, N2.3**

## Situation

You are a GNVQ Leisure and Tourism student on work placement at your local mainline railway station. You have been asked by Station Master Leeding to conduct a passenger survey over the period of one week. The purpose of the survey is to evaluate the quality of the information which is provided to passengers and to highlight whether any additional information services are required.

## Tasks

Design a questionnaire which asks people passing through the station their reasons for using rail travel and whether they are satisfied with the information which they are provided with. Your questionnaire should be word processed.

A typical questionnaire might look like Fig. 3.29.

At the end of your placement you will be required to make a visual display to the Station Master Leeding which will include:

1. Details of what information is available to customers at the station.
2. What additional information customers have said they would like.
3. A summary of customer opinion about the quality of information provided at the station.

| British Rail Passenger Survey | | | | | |
|---|---|---|---|---|---|
| Name of station: | Student name: | | Date: | | |
| 1. What is the main purpose of your journey? | Leisure | | Business/work | | |
| | Education | | Shopping | | |
| 2. How often do you use this station? | Daily | | Weekly | | |
| | Monthly | | Less | | |
| 3. What is the cost of your journey? | Less than £2.00 | | Between £2–£5 | | |
| | Between £5–£10 | | More than £10 | | |
| 4. Are you satisfied with the information which is provided by this railway station? | Yes | | No | | |
| 5. What other information do you feel should be provided to customers? | | | | | |

**Fig. 3.29** *Passenger questionnaire*

Use the data you have collected about the purpose of the visit and the frequency of use of the station to produce a series of bar graphs and pie charts.

Use these statistics to help you form a number of conclusions, for example:

- Do the majority of travellers think there is sufficient information?
- Are people on shopping expeditions looking for a certain type of information?
- Are business travellers more satisfied or less satisfied about the information provided than school children using the same service?

# Investigate and demonstrate sales techniques as part of customer service

Any organisation needs to sell their products or services in order to stay in business. To maximise sales leisure and tourism organisations will want to ensure that their customers receive the best possible service in order to:

- Ensure customer satisfaction.
- Ensure the customer returns.

Happy satisfied customers will ensure that repeat sales are made and that leisure and tourism organisations meet their financial objectives.

*Remember!*
*Happy customers = Repeat business*

Explain the importance of selling as part of customer service

## What is a satisfied customer?

A satisfied customer is one who:

- Has had their needs met.
- Feels they have received value for money.
- Wants to return for more.

## How sales techniques can be used to meet customer needs

The following example (Fig 3.30) follows through the case of a customer, Jane Percival, who wishes to improve her level of fitness and lose weight. Jane sees an advert for Inches, a ladies' gym, and visits the gym to see whether they can meet her needs.

Jane feels she has received a personal service from Inches Fitness Club as they have listened carefully to her needs and provided her with a means of achieving her goal. The sale of this service was achieved by the professional way in which the instructor dealt with her request.

| Customer needs | Meeting customer needs |
|---|---|
| Jane's reasons for wanting to join a gym are as follows:<br><br>To improve her fitness level<br>For body toning and to improve her physique<br>To lose weight<br>Image enhancement<br>To socialise | The instructor at Inches Fitness Club welcomes Jane and informs her that it is company policy that all new members receive induction training. This is an important part of the sales process as it helps to ensure that:<br><br>Customers use the equipment safely<br>The needs of the customer are identified and met |
| **Customer needs are met** | **Meeting customer needs – providing a service** |
| After the induction session Jane feels confident that joining Inches Fitness Club will help her to fulfil her need. The initial product looks good and Jane feel reassured that she is joining a reputable club which employs well qualified instructors. A sale is therefore made as Jane pays her subscription to the club. Jane has therefore fulfilled her initial need – which is to join a gym and to have devised a programme for improving her level of fitness and losing weight. Of course it will take a while for her to achieve her goal. | *The induction process*<br><br>The instructor discusses with Jane her reasons for wanting to join Inches Fitness Club and checks her general state of health. The instructor then takes Jane around each piece of equipment in the fitness suite and explains the following:<br><br>How to use the equipment safely<br>The benefits of using the equipment<br><br>The instructor will then:<br><br>Provide an accurate demonstration<br>Provide a supervised trial exercise routine |

***Fig. 3.30*** *Meeting customer needs*

The instructor:

- Listened carefully to Jane's needs.
- Made Jane feel as if she was a valued customer.
- Provided encouragement to make Jane feel she could achieve her goal.

In this way a product is sold to a client which meets the needs of the customer whilst at the same time providing benefits to both the customer (Jane) and the organisation (Inches Fitness Club; Fig. 3.31).

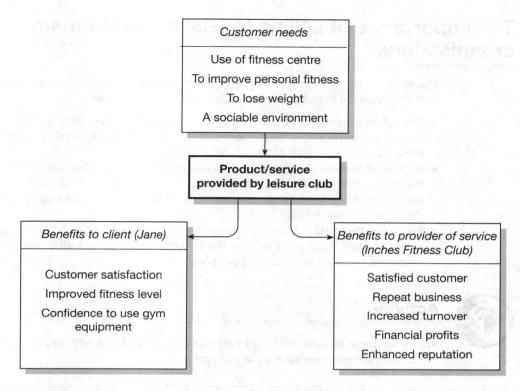

**Fig. 3.31** *Benefits to client and provider of meeting customer needs*

## Activity

Write down some of the leisure or tourism products or services which you have used recently.

What personal benefits did you receive from using these products? What do you think might have been the benefits to the organisations which sold you the products?

List your results in the following table:

| | Product/service purchased | Provider of the product/service | Benefits to the customer | Benefits to the provider |
|---|---|---|---|---|
| 1. | | | | |
| 2. | | | | |
| 3. | | | | |

# The importance of selling to leisure and tourism organisations

The importance of selling products and services and achieving customer satisfaction is in the financial benefits this will bring to the organisation

- **Repeat business** – If Jane is happy with the service she receives from the fitness club she will probably renew her subscription for the following year. Good customer service therefore creates happy, loyal customers.
- **Increased business** – Jane might be encouraged to use other services provided by the club for which she may have to pay extra charges such as aerobics sessions or beauty therapy. Good customer service therefore generates extra business from the same customer base.
- **Financial benefits** – Through providing good customer service and satisfying the needs of customers such as Jane the Inches Fitness Club will increase its level of sales and possibly increase its profit level.

## Activity

Visit your local leisure club and find out details of any membership schemes and induction programmes which the club runs.

> Describe and give examples of sales situations in leisure and tourism organisations

Leisure and tourism is a very diverse industry and therefore the range of situations in which a leisure or tourism product/service can be purchased is equally varied.

# Travel and tourism products

Travel and tourism products such as package holidays, airline flights, rail tickets and foreign currency can be bought from a high street travel agency such as Thomas Cook or Going Places. Travel agents provide a retail service by selling you the products of tour operators such as Thomson Holidays or Cosmos.

The travel agency therefore sells you two main products or services:

- The package holiday – which has been organised by the tour operator.
- Advice and assistance in booking the holiday.

It is also possible to buy holidays directly from tour operators such as Eurocamp and Portland. To buy a holiday provided by one of these tour operators you would probably see an advert in a newspaper or on the television and then write to or ring the tour operator directly to obtain a brochure and a booking form.

# Trips and excursions

Trips and excursions are often provided by national coach operators such as Stagecoach who also advertise in local newspapers. Such trips can be booked directly by either completing the coupon in the newspaper or by ringing the trip organiser.

Trips might also be sold by a travel agent as part of a package holiday. For example, tourists travelling to Florida will often pre-book tickets to visit some of the main attractions, such as the Magic Kingdom and the EPCOT Center, whilst there. The benefit to the customer is that it will prevent them from having to queue for entrance tickets at the various venues and the benefits to the travel agency and tour operator is that they will have achieved extra sales and commission.

# Retail outlets

Many leisure and tourism facilities will have additional retail outlets on site. For examples, leisure centres often have a small shop which sells useful items such as swimming costumes, water wings and goggles. A stately home such as Chatsworth House has a souvenir shop in which visitors can purchase postcards, tea towels and other souvenirs to remind them of their visit or to give as gifts to their friends and relatives.

Retail outlets such as these provide a useful source of extra income to the leisure or tourism facility.

## Activity

Write a list of some of the leisure and tourism facilities you have visited.

What is the main product or service provided by that facility? What other additional products or services could you buy whilst at that site?

# Bars, restaurants and cafés

There are thousands of bars, cafés and restaurants within the UK ranging from small village teashops to national fast food chains such as Burger King.

Whatever the size or scale of the venue each of these catering outlets will be trying to provide their customers with a service which

- Serves high quality food and drink.
- Gives a fast efficient service.
- Provides value for money.
- Lives up to the customers' expectations.

## Activity

Make a list of bars (if you are over 18), restaurants and cafés which you visit on a regular basis.

What are your needs when visiting these catering outlets? How are your needs met?

## Selling memberships

There are many different types of leisure and tourism organisations to which you can become a member.

If you are interested in history and old buildings and monuments then you may wish to become a member of the National Trust (Fig. 3.32).

### Application for membership

TO: THE NATIONAL TRUST, FREEPOST MB1438, BROMLEY, KENT BR1 3BR

*Twelve-month membership*

☐ **Individual:** £26 and, for each additional member living at the same address, £18. One card for each member.

☐ **Family group:** £48 for two parents or partners and their children under 18, living at the same address. Please give names and dates of birth of all children. One card covers the family.

☐ **Under 23:** £12 please give date of birth

☐ **Education group membership:** £14–60 See Special Information for National Trust Members, and tel. 0181 315 1111 for further details.

*Life membership*

☐ **Individual:** £625 (£405 if aged 60 or over and retired). One card admits the named member and a guest.

☐ **Joint:** £740 for lifetime partners (£490 if either partner is aged 60 or over and retired). Two cards, each admitting the named member.

☐ **Family joint:** £850 two cards, each admitting the named parent or partner and their children under 18 living at the same address. Please give names and dates of birth of all children.

Rates valid until 31 March 1997.

| SOURCE D71 | | | | DATE | |
|---|---|---|---|---|---|
| FULL ADDRESS | | | | | |
| | | | | POSTCODE | |
| TITLE | INITIALS | SURNAME | | DATE OF BIRTH | VALUE £ |
| | | | | | |
| | | | | | |
| | | | | | |
| | | | | | |

AMOUNT ATTACHED:
CHEQUE/POSTAL ORDER £
Delete as appropriate

Please allow 28 days for receipt of your membership card and pack

Credit/debit card payments can be made by telephoning 0181 315 1111 (office hours)

Immediate membership can be obtained by joining at a National Trust property, shop or countryside information point

We promise that any information you give will be used for National Trust purposes only. We will write to you about our work and will occasionally include details of products by third parties developed in association with the Trust. We would also like to send you separate details of such products but should you prefer not to receive these separate mailings, please tick this box. ☐
The National Trust is an independent registered charity (no. 205846)

### *How you can support the National Trust*

# JOIN AND ENJOY YOUR LOCAL MEMBERS' ASSOCIATIONS AND CENTRES

Join your local Association and share your interest in the Trust with like-minded members from your area: over 100,000 members already have.

**What is a National Trust Association or Centre?**
It is a local club run by members, for members.

**Where can you find one?**
There are 190 all over England, Wales and Northern Ireland.

**What do they offer?**
Coach outings, lectures, parties, rambles, tours and holidays in Britain and abroad – and friendship.

They also raised over £650,000 last year for the National Trust as well as providing practical help at National Trust properties and offices.

### *How can you join?*

There is an annually-updated leaflet showing the location of every Association throughout 'the country. This gives a contact name, address and telephone number for each Association.

**All you need to do**
is call the Membership Department at PO Box 39, Bromley, Kent BR1 3XL
tel. 0181 315 1111
or
contact Tom Burr, Associations Liaison Manager at Eastleigh Court, Bishopstrow, Warminster, Wiltshire BA12 9HW (tel. (01985) 843600)

**Fig. 3.32** *National Trust membership application form*

On the other hand, if your main interest is sport you may wish to join a football sup-porters' club such as the Manchester United Supporters' Club (Fig. 3.33).

Information about memberships is available from a range of different sources. You may see advertisements in special interest magazines or you may pick up some information whilst visiting the facility itself. Memberships are sold on the basis of the benefits you will gain from becoming a member.

For example, the benefits of becoming a member of the Manchester United Football Supporters' Club are:

- Members receive priority when booking tickets.
- Personal accident cover.
- Official year book and personal membership card.
- Discount on MUFC merchandise.
- Travel benefits.

The main benefits to the organisation which sells the membership are:

- Regular annual subscriptions provide an additional source of income.
- Helps to retain the loyalty of customers.
- Additional products are often sold to members.

---

Dear Supporter,

I wish to thank you for your request to become an official member of Manchester United. I am pleased to report that such is the progress of the reconstruction of the North Stand of our stadium, that we are now in a position to invite applications for Premier League home matches from all members, including first time applicants such as yourself.

It is highly beneficial to become a member, not only for the ticket priority over non-members, but also for the comprehensive package of benefits available to you which are all listed overleaf.

Before completing the form you are asked to read the 'Terms and Conditions' of membership carefully.

The subscription fees for the 1995-96 season, which includes postage and packing are as follows:

| | **ADULTS** | **JUNIORS** (born after 15th August 1979) |
|---|---|---|
| Great Britain | £12.00 | £6.00 |
| Eire & Europe | £15.00 | £9.00 |
| Rest of the World | £20.00 | £15.00 |

* All payments **must** be made in sterling.
* Cheques, postal orders and bank drafts should be made payable to 'Manchester United'.
* If paying by cheque, please write your full address on the reverse. Cash can only be accepted from personal callers.

You should allow at least 14 days from the receipt of your application for delivery of your package, although foreign applicants may have to allow slightly longer due to any postal delays.

Thanks for the interest you have shown and I look forward to welcoming you as a members of Manchester United Football Club.

Barry Moorhouse
Membership Secretary

**allsports**
OFFICIAL SPONSORS OF THE MANCHESTER UNITED MEMBERSHIP SCHEME
**Membership Secretary - Barry Moorhouse**
Telephone **0161 872 5208** Facsimile **0161 877 9711**
The Manchester United Football Club plc, Sir Matt Busby Way, Old Trafford, Manchester, M16 0RA
Chairman & Chief Executive: C.M. Edwards, Directors: J.M. Edelson, Sir R. Charlton CBE, E.M. Watkins, R.L. Olive, R.P. Launders.

**Fig. 3.33** *Manchester United FC Supporters' Club application form*

## Activity

Are you a member of any leisure or tourism organisation? If the answer is 'Yes', write down the reasons why you joined and the benefits of being a member.

If the answer is 'No', look through a number of specialist magazines for advertisements for subscriptions. What benefits are listed in the advertisements?

> Describe sales techniques required of employees in the leisure and tourism industry

If you work in the leisure and tourism industry you will have a high degree of face-to-face and personal contact with customers. It is therefore essential that anyone working in the industry has good communication and listening skills.

As there are so many different selling opportunities within leisure and tourism the techniques used by staff can vary enormously. Whatever situation a product or service is sold in it is always important to:

- Create a positive first impression.
- Gain and retain the customer's attention.
- Have the ability to open a conversation.
- Identify the customer's needs using a range of 'open' and 'closed' questions.
- Handle complaints efficiently and effectively.
- Develop good telephone techniques.
- Keep good records of sales, transactions, bookings, complaints.

Let us consider a range of selling situations and the sales techniques which might be used within them.

| Selling situations | Selling opportunities | Typical sales techniques |
|---|---|---|
| Retail outlets | Fairground candyfloss stall | Gain attention – be extrovert, loud, brash |
| | | Create a 'fun' image |
| Travel agencies | Travel consultant – counter sales | Know how to open a conversation |
| | | Use a range of open and closed questions to identify customer needs |
| | | Create an image of a friendly, efficient service |
| Bars | Counter sales | This will vary depending upon the type of bar: |
| | | Hotel/city centre bars will try to portray a professional, efficient image for business clients |
| | | Local bars (pubs) will try to establish a friendly, homely atmosphere for regular clients |
| Accommodation | Hotel reception desk | Create a professional image |
| | | Majority of reservations will centre around a variety of communication methods: telephone, fax, e-mail |

| Selling situations | Selling opportunities | Typical sales techniques |
|---|---|---|
| Memberships | Health clubs, video clubs, gourmet clubs | Need to establish a strong relationship with customers as they are purchasing an expensive product over a period of time |
| Selling trips | Coach operators, tour operators, group organisers | May advertise in local newspapers or in travel agency windows |
| Selling excursions | For instance the British Lions 1997 tour of South Africa | Important to identify and target enthusiasts. The tour can be segmented so that the customer chooses just the part they are interested in |
| Direct selling | Timeshare apartments | The initial contact is usually made by mailshot or telephone sales offering a range of enticements to attend a sales event |

The techniques of selling start the moment your customer arrives at your facility. In order to be successful in selling your product you must be able to make the customer immediately feel at ease, comfortable and confident that you are able to provide, or will try to provide, a service which meets their needs.

Let us consider a situation where a husband and wife, Mr and Mrs James, are celebrating their silver wedding anniversary. Mr James has arranged a special night out at a London theatre.

**CASE STUDY**

## A Night at the Theatre

After spending an enjoyable day looking at the sights of London Mr and Mrs James return to their hotel to prepare for their special, anniversary night out.

On arrival at the theatre their taxi door is opened by the doorman who direct the couple into the theatre where they will collect their pre-booked tickets.

The box office receptionist welcomes the couple and acknowledges that they have made a prior booking by telephone (**maintaining records**)

*A positive first impression has been created.*

The receptionist greets Mr and Mrs James with: 'Good evening, how may I help you?'

This is a good example of **starting a conversation** with the use of an **open question** which invites the customer to express his needs. Compare this with the situation if Mr James was asked a **closed question**: 'Can I help you?' to which he can only reply 'Yes' or 'No'. If Mr James' answer was 'No', then the conversation may not have proceeded any further.

*The conversation is opened*

The use of the open question by the receptionist prompted Mr James to relate the story that he had booked the tickets by telephone and that he was now here to collect them personally. The receptionist then comments that the couple have arrived early and in which case would they like to have a drink in the bar before the performance. The couple are then directed to the theatre bar.

On arrival in the bar the bar attendant greets the couple with an **open question**: 'Good evening, what would you like to drink?' This question invites Mr James to make a purchase. If the question had been 'Would you like a drink?', his reply might have been 'No' and a potential sale could have been lost.

The bar attendant then invites a further sale by explaining to the couple that it is possible to pre-order drinks for the interval. She invites Mr James to place his order with the open question: 'What drinks would you like me to have ready for you during the interval?'

The bar attendant then directs Mr and Mrs James to the entrance of the auditorium where an usher guides them to their seats. The usher advises the couple that they will need a 20 pence piece for their opera glasses and that change is available if they need it.

Mr and Mrs James have had a series of pleasant experiences prior to the show and are now in a happy and relaxed mood, eagerly awaiting the production.

In our theatre example the management of the theatre has trained the staff to provide a welcoming atmosphere for their guests so as to create a positive first impression. The main product of the theatre is the show but as the guests have been well treated immediately upon their arrival at the theatre they are then likely to make further purchases of secondary items such as drinks, confectionery and programmes.

## Activity

Imagine that you are an assistant in the TIC in your local town. Draw up a list of open and closed questions which you might ask the customers.

The first couple of questions have been completed for you.

|   | Open questions | Closed questions |
|---|---|---|
| 1. | Good morning, how may I help you? | Good morning, can I help you? |
| 2. | Where are you staying? | Are you staying locally? |
| 3. | | |
| 4. | | |
| 5. | | |

# Handling complaints

Complaints will always be made by customers. You can't please everybody all the time – although you must try!

The manner in which complaints are dealt with is very important. If complaints are handled badly the customer is unlikely to return to purchase further products and services. However if a complaint is handled swiftly and efficiently then customer satisfaction might still be achieved.

Some important things to remember when handling a complaint are:

- To listen attentively.
- Always thank the customer.
- Only apologise in general terms – don't grovel.
- To provide support for the customer.
- Always ask questions.
- Try to find a solution.
- Agree a solution.
- Follow your solution through – make sure you deliver what you promise.
- And in the future, try to anticipate complaints before they arise.

## Activity

Have you ever complained about a product you have purchased?

Create a storyboard which tells the detail and manner of your complaint. It should also record the way in which the complaint was handled by the member of staff.

Word process this storyboard and illustrate it using graphics from your word-processing package. Explain how the use of information technology has helped you to clearly present, your storyboard.

**Key skills satisfied:** *Communication* **C2.3**
*Information Technology* **IT2.3**

# Maintaining records

It is important that records of all dealings with customers and transactions in a leisure and tourism organisation are maintained. This will include details of:

- Sales.
- Bookings.
- Memberships.
- Complaints.

Having this information at your fingertips, whether on a computer or a paper-based system, will enable you to provide better customer service.

For example, when Mr James purchased his theatre tickets he provided details of his home address. The theatre kept this information on file and after the event made a point of contacting Mr James to ask him to complete a customer service questionnaire. At the same time the theatre had inserted a list of future productions in the envelope.

> Demonstrate effective sales techniques selling selected leisure and tourism products and services

To help appreciate some of the techniques involved in selling leisure and tourism products and services it is useful to act out selling situations in the form of role plays. By putting yourself in the role of either the customer or the provider of the product/service it helps you to appreciate the importance of different selling techniques.

## Activity

Working with a small group of students, choose one of the following role play situations. Using the details you have been given write a script for the role play to demonstrate how different selling techniques can be used to meet the needs of the customer.

# Role plays

Whilst you are taking part in or observing the role plays it is useful to make a note of your own performance and that of other group members. An observation form would be useful to record comments and to make recommendations for improvements.

[*Tutor's Note*: As these are situations which students may encounter on work experience it might be worth either videoing or tape recording the role plays. The students involved will then have the opportunity to assess their use of selling techniques in the various situations.]

## Creating positive first impression – The TIC Assistant

You will have learned from the case study of Mr and Mrs James on pages 227–8 that it is important to create an inviting atmosphere in which the customer feels comfortable in order to achieve customer satisfaction. Positive first impressions are created by:

- Welcoming customers.
- Being polite and of smart appearance.
- Quickly assessing customer needs by asking a series of open questions.

**Customer:** You are an American visitor to the historic city of Canterbury and you wish to find out more details on sites of historical interest in the local area. (You may wish to alter the town or city to meet your local circumstances.)

**Employee:** You are an assistant in the TIC in Canterbury. Your role is to create a positive first impression, welcome the tourist and quickly identify the needs of the tourist.

In order to carry out this role play you will need to research some of the more important visitor attractions in the Canterbury area.

## Handling complaints – Bare wires

When taking part in this role play refer back to the table on page 186 which lists some important points on how to handle customer complaints and how to provide good customer service.

**Customer:** You are staying in a hotel in Spain and you have just found some dangerous wiring in your bedroom. You find your tour representative and make a complaint.

**Employee:** You are an overseas representative working for Airtours plc.

Your role is to act in a confident manner and to be able to convince and reassure the tourist that you will arrange for the hotel staff to solve the problem as quickly as possible.

## Maintaining records – Leisure centre assistant

This role play will emphasise the importance of keeping accurate records of bookings made. The leisure centre assistant will need to refer to a bookings sheet from the previous week.

**Customer:** You have booked a squash court at your local leisure centre. You arrive ready to play at 8.00 pm only to be told by the assistant that your court, which you had booked by phone last week, was actually booked for 7.00 pm. You are understandably upset.

**Employee:** You are employed as a leisure centre assistant and one of your responsibilities is to take telephone bookings.

Your role is to show the customer the bookings sheet and to confirm the details of the original booking. You will then need to offer the customer an alternative time     or date.

## Assignment: Element 3.3

**'Effective sales situations'**

**Key skills satisfied:** *Communication* **C2.1a, C2.1b, C2.2, C2.3**
*Information Technology* **IT2.1, IT2.2, IT2.3**

### Situation

You are working for a regional tourist board as part of a team of consultants. Your team has been asked to consider a number of sales situations as a number of customer complaints about local visitor attractions has been received recently.

### Tasks

#### Part A

Firstly your team must produce a formal report which cover the following topics:

1. Why selling is important to achieve customer satisfaction.
2. A description of the different types of selling situations which exist in leisure and tourism.
3. A description of the types of selling techniques which are used in the leisure and tourism industry.

The report should be word processed.

#### Part B

Your team must now set up a series of role play situations in which you can demonstrate to members of the tourist board the effectiveness of different selling situations for creating good customer service.

Your role plays must be based around the following techniques:

- Creating positive first impressions.
- Starting a conversation.
- Using open and closed questions.
- Handling complaints.
- Telephone sales.
- Maintaining records.

#### Part C

The team should also devise a role play observation sheet which members of the tourist board can complete whilst watching your team perform the role plays. The form should include space for general comments and recommendations for improvements.

# Provide and evaluate customer service in leisure and tourism

In this element you will be given the opportunity to provide customer service in a series of simulated role play situations. If you have a work placement this could provide you with an ideal opportunity to practise the customer care skills you have learned about on real customers.

## Identify customer needs for selected situations

The diverse nature of the leisure and tourism industry means that people who work in the industry will encounter a wide range of types of customers in a vast range of situations, from pubs to stately homes and from seaside resorts to museums.

The needs and specific requirements of customers of leisure and tourism organisations will therefore vary considerably.

All leisure and tourism organisations, however, will work to the same basic criteria for dealing with their customers. These will include:

- Caring for their customers.
- Meeting customer needs for:
  - help
  - assistance
  - information
- Achieving customer satisfaction.

## Identify the types of information required by customers in selected situations

Customers need to know certain basic facts about a product or service, such as cost and availability, before they will buy it. Information on how to use the product or service may also be critical to the customer's enjoyment or satisfaction received.

Some of the different types of product and user information are shown below:

| Product information | User information |
| --- | --- |
| Cost of product/service | Instructions on how to use product |
| Subscription rates | Membership details |
| Opening times | |

In order to achieve customer satisfaction, staff working in a facility must have a good knowledge of the product or service they are selling or providing so as to meet the information needs of the customer.

# Meeting information needs at Travelodge

Travelodge has a network of over 160 locations in the UK and Europe. Most of the lodges are located close to motorways or main travel routes and are ideally located for business people and holidaymakers alike (Fig. 3.34).

The lodges are very competitively priced and provide a consistently high standard of accommodation.

Travelodge reservations staff can be contacted on the Roomline central reservations number of 0800-850950. Their telesales staff are specially trained to quickly identify customer needs.

The following dialogue is typical of how a member of the Roomline reservations team will deal with a customer enquiry:

## Customer Service Situation:
## Travelodge – selling accommodation

Business woman Joyce Bluebottle wishes to book accommodation for an overnight stay. She needs to book a reasonably priced room for one night and decides to ring Roomline central reservations to see if there are any vacancies at Travelodges near Taunton in Devon.

Joyce dials 0800-850950

*Reservations*: 'Good evening, Roomline. Where would you like to stay?'

*Joyce*: 'I have got a business meeting in Taunton next Tuesday. Do you have a Travelodge there?'

*Reservations*: 'Our nearest lodges are at Ilminster and Tiverton. Where will you be travelling from?'

*Joyce*: 'Southampton.'

*Reservations*: 'In that case Ilminster will be the most convenient. Would you like to book a room at the Ilminster lodge?

*Joyce*: 'Yes, please.'

*Reservations*: 'Which nights would you like to stay?'

*Joyce*: 'For one night on Tuesday 22nd November please.'

*Reservations*: 'OK that is one room for one night. Would you like smoking or non-smoking?'

*Joyce*: 'Non-smoking.'

*Reservations*: 'I will check availability for you now. Yes, a room is available. How many people will be sharing the room?'

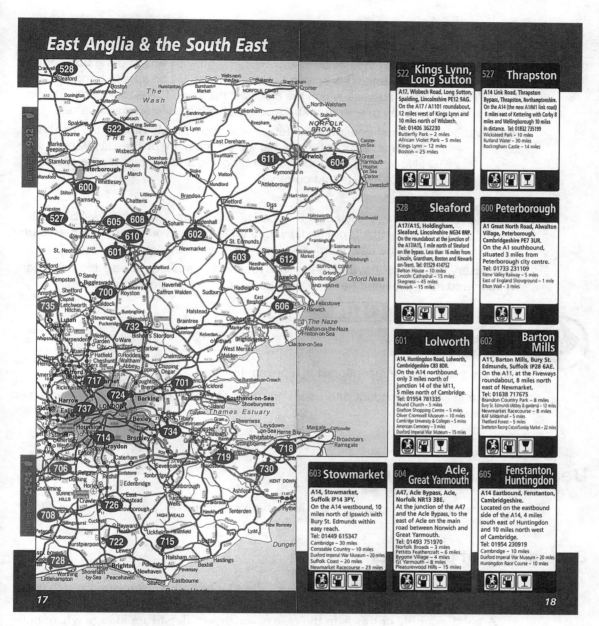

**Fig. 3.34** *Travelodges in East Anglia and the South East*

*Joyce:*   'One, just myself.'

*Reservations:*   'With which major credit card do you wish to make a reservation?'

*Joyce:*   'Access.'

[The receptionist will now take Joyce's credit card details including the card's expiry date.]

| *Reservations*: | 'The name on your Access card please and first initial.' |
| *Joyce*: | 'Bluebottle, as in the insect, and the initial is J.' |

[The receptionist will then confirm Joyce's postcode. By entering the postcode details onto the reservations screen the receptionist will be able to bring up details of Joyce's address which the clerk will then ask Joyce to confirm. This is for security reasons to ensure that Joyce is not using a stolen credit card.]

| *Reservations*: | 'I'll just confirm your details with you now Ms Bluebottle. You have booked a room for one person on the night of Tuesday 22nd November. The room is non-smoking and the rate for the room will be £42.95. Is that correct?' |
| *Joyce*: | 'Yes.' |
| *Reservations*: | 'Is there anything else I can help you with? The room will be available after 3 pm and if you need to cancel you can do so up to 6 pm on the day of arrival without charge. Thank you for calling.' |

The reservations staff have carefully analysed Joyce's needs for advice and information and have provided her with a product which meets her requirements.

## Activity

You are working as a receptionist in a private health club.

Make a list of the product and user information which customers are likely to ask you for.

# Dealing with problems

Whatever products or services you are selling problems will always occur.

## Explanation of problems

When problems happen customers usually like to be kept informed of what the problem is.

A good example of this is in the case of an airport departure lounge where holidaymakers are awaiting the flight to their destination. They become understandably annoyed if their flight is delayed, especially if they also have young children travelling with them who are likely to become irritable and impatient. This situation can be made worse where no explanation for the delay is provided. In such situations the best policy for the airline is to be frank and realistic with the passengers as to why their flight is delayed and when they can realistically hope to take off.

## Activity

Think of any times when you have been waiting for either a bus, train or plane and there has been a delay. How were you informed of the delay, if at all?

## Solutions to problems

If and when problems occur it is important to try to suggest an alternative to the customer. For example, if a customer in a restaurant orders a certain item from the menu only to discover that there is none left then the waiter should suggest an alternative.

Another example could be a customer wishing to book a concert ticket for a certain night only to discover that all tickets for that performance have been sold. The box office receptionist should then suggest to the customer that they attend a performance on an alternative evening.

## Activity

You are working in a gift shop and a certain popular souvenir has sold out. A customer asks for the item.

What action might you take to solve this problem and still achieve customer satisfaction? What action might cause the customer to be dissatisfied?

To help present this information clearly it is useful to have a stock record sheet, which will show when stocks are running low and need reordering. Design a stock record sheet on which to record the necessary information.

**Key skills satisfied:** *Application of Number* **N2.1, N2.2, N2.3**

## Unrelated/ancillary information

As well as needing information about the leisure or tourism facility itself, customers may need to know a range of other information. For example, if the customer does not normally use them he may need to know the local bus times. Customers may also want to know about what other facilities or services there are in the local area.

## Activity

You are working as a hotel receptionist. A customer enquires about a booking but also asks you about visitor attractions in the local area. You are a new member of staff and you do not have the knowledge and are not sure where to find it immediately.

Describe how you would ensure that the customer request was satisfied.

# Types of customer

The needs of the customer are individual and will depend upon a variety of factors such as:

- Age
- Gender
- Sporting ability
- Income
- Special needs
- Mobility
- Interests
- Ethnic origin

The needs of customers will also vary depending upon whether you are dealing with **individuals** or **groups**.

The information needs of different types of customers will therefore vary. Figure 3.35 indicates some of the information needs that are specific to different types of users.

Every customer has their own specific needs but it is usual to classify customers into different groups depending upon these characteristics. Staff must be well informed themselves in order to deal with the different needs of the wide range of customers they are likely to come into contact with.

## Activity

How would you classify yourself as a customer?

Your class is considering visiting a theme park. What information would you need to have before you could make a decision?

# Information needs in selected situations

We will now consider how the needs of customers can be met in three different situations:

- An outdoor activity centre
- A private sector playscheme
- Airport departure lounge

## Situation 1: Outdoor activity centre

If we think about the different types of customers who might use an outdoor activity centre we can break these down into a number of activity types, for example:

- School educational visit.
- A group of ramblers.
- An inner city youth club.

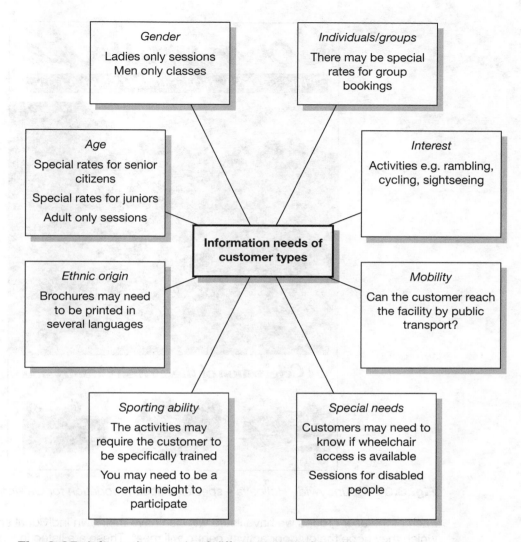

**Fig. 3.35** *Information needs of different types of customer*

Each of these three user types will have common needs or requirements as customers. The basic customer care requirements of an outdoor activity centre will include:

- Staff must be friendly, polite and efficient.
- High standards of health and hygiene must be maintained.
- The health and safety of customers and staff must be maintained.
- Any organised or supervised activities must be led by staff with appropriate qualifications.
- Value for money is essential.
- That the accommodation is clean, warm and dry.
- Customer expectations must be fulfilled.
- All equipment must be appropriate and well maintained.

**Fig. 3.36** *Countrywide Holidays – specialist accommodation for walking holidays*

Each of the user groups we have listed will also have their own individual set of needs which they hope the outdoor activity centre will meet. These are listed in Fig. 3.37.

All three groups therefore have different needs as users but there will be a common set of factors which will influence the activities which each group takes part in. There is therefore a common need for the following type of information:

● Up to date and regular information on weather conditions.
● Any areas of potential hazards.
● Details of sites of local interest.
● Advice on how to use the centre equipment.
● The qualifications of the staff who are leading activities.
● Details of local services such as bus routes and times, chemists, cafés, pubs and garages.

This information is vital if customers are to carry out activities with safety. An element of customer satisfaction is therefore being provided with a product or service which is delivered with their safety and security in mind.

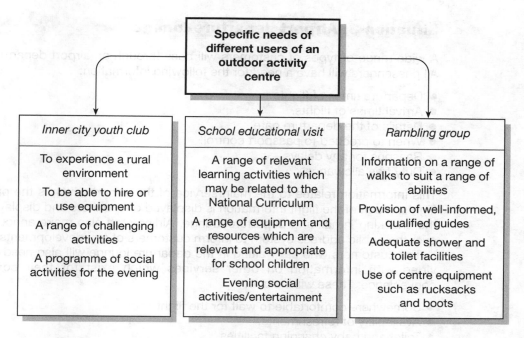

**Fig. 3.37** *Specific needs of different client groups*

## Activity

Imagine you are a holidaymaker staying in a tent on a campsite.

Make a list of what you think your information needs might be.

## Situation 2: Private sector playscheme

A private sector playscheme will need to meet the personal needs of children and parents. Parents will also have a need for information to give them the confidence that their children are in safe hands.

The needs of the children taking part in the scheme will be to be entertained with a range of toys and activities in a warm and safe environment. From the parents' point of view their immediate need is for their children to be entertained whilst they carry out other activities which are difficult to do when you have children with you, such as going to work or doing the shopping.

The parents' need for information will have to be satisfied before leaving their off-spring at the playscheme. The information which parents require will include:

- The cost of the service.
- Opening times.
- Age at which children can be left.
- Details of activities.
- Details of staff qualifications.
- Parking arrangements.
- Telephone number.

## Situation 3: Airport departure lounge

A wide range of types of customers will pass through an airport departure lounge. All passengers will have a need for the following information:

- Departure times of flights.
- Arrival times of flights.
- Details of the departure gate.
- When to proceed to passport control.
- Reasons for any delays.
- Duty free allowances.

This information relates to the main service of the airport which is the provision of flights. Much of the flight information is displayed on monitors and display boards in the checking in hall and departure lounge. Airline staff also make announcements over the public address system to inform customers of any developments.

The customers who are waiting in the departure lounge will also need to be provided with information on other services which exist for their comfort and convenience. These will include:

- Somewhere comfortable to wait for the flight.
- Availability of refreshments.
- Toilet and baby changing facilities.
- Shopping and currency exchange facilities.
- Facilities for passengers with limited mobility.

By developing a reputation for providing good customer service airports hope to attract new business. For example, Fig. 3.38 shows a survey which was conducted at Birmingham International Airport to investigate customer satisfaction with the retail and catering facilities available at the airport.

> Demonstrate effective customer service in selected situations

When you are dealing with customers you must ensure that you are:

- Showing that you care for the customer.
- Identifying and meeting customer needs.
- Achieving customer satisfaction.

# Caring for customers

Showing that you care for customers means taking an interest in your customers and making them feel valued. You can achieve this by greeting the customers in a friendly manner. Try to smile at customers, this will help to make them feel welcome. If you know a customer's name try to use it, this will also help to make the customer feel at ease.

# BIRMINGHAM INTERNATIONAL AIRPORT Ltd

**Commercial Audit Survey    Main Terminal**    Serial

Interviewer    Date:

**Sex**    Male..........1
Female.......2

We are conducting a consumer survey to identify your opinions, attitudes, habits and general satisfaction with the retail and catering facilities within the airport

Could you spare me a few moments of your time to answer a few questions?

**G1. What is your reason for visiting the Airport today?**

i) Meeter / Greeter
ii) Weeper / Wailer
iii) Visitor
iv) Employee

v) Domestic Business Pass
vi) Domestic Leisure Pass
vii) Intl Business Pass
vi) Intl Leisure Pass

**G2. Frequent Flyer**

Domestic

International

**G3. What is your Flight Number**

**G4. Have you used any of the following today**

| | | |
|---|---|---|
| **Catering Facilities** | **Shopping Facilities** | **General Services/ Facilities** |
| i) Yes | i) Yes | i) Yes |
| ii) No | ii) No | ii) No |

**G5. Have you been satisfied with the current range of**

| | | |
|---|---|---|
| **Catering Facilities** | **Shopping Facilities** | **General Services/ Facilities** |
| i) Yes | i) Yes | i) Yes |
| ii) No | ii) No | ii) No |

**G6. How does the following compare to other Airports you have used?**

|  | Better Than 1 | Same As 2 | Worse Than 3 | N/A 0 |
|---|---|---|---|---|
| Quality of Catering Facilities | | | | |
| Quality of Shopping Facilities | | | | |
| Quality of General Service Facilities | | | | |
| Range/Choice of Catering Facilities | | | | |
| Range/Choice of Shopping Facilities | | | | |
| Range/Choice of General Service Facilities | | | | |
| Value for Money of Catering Facilities | | | | |
| Value for Money of Shopping Facilities | | | | |
| Value for Money of General Service Facilities | | | | |

**G7. Age**

i) 18 or under
ii) 19-25
iii) 26-30
iv) 31-35
v) 36-40
vi) 41-50
vii) 51-64
viii) 65+

**G8. Group**

i) Child
ii) Teenager
iii) Pre Family
iv) New Family
v) Maturing Family
vi) Established Family
vii) Post Family
viii) Older Couple
ix) Older Singles

Comaudit96 0896 (Pink Main)

---

**C1. You said that you have used the catering facilities today, which did you use?**

i) Cafe Bar
ii) Cafe Select
iii) Visitor Centre Buffet
iv) Garfunkels
v) Bayleys Ice Cream
vi) The Granary
vii) Airside Buffet
viii) Airside Bar
ix) Shakespeare Pub
x) Domestic Lounge Bar / Buffet

**C2. What was your main reason for using the catering facilities?**

i) Wanted something to eat / drink
ii) liked the products offered
iii) Delayed flight
iv) Other:

**C3. What did you purchase?**

i) Drink
ii) Biscuits / Cakes
iii) Sandwiches / Baguettes
iv) Other snack
v) Salad
vi) Pizza
vii) Pasta
viii) Full Hot Meal
ix) Other

**C4. How much did you spend?**

i) £00.00-£ 2.50
ii) £ 2.51 - £ 5.00
iii) £ 5.01 - £ 7.50
iv) £ 7.51 - £10.00
v) £10.01 -£15.00
vi) £15.01 -£20.00
vii) £20.00+

**C5. Thinking back to your previous visit(s) to the airport did you use any of the catering facilities? If yes which ?**

i) Cafe Bar
ii) Cafe Select
iii) Visitor Centre Buffet
iv) "Restaurant"
v) Bayleys Ice Cream
vi) The Granary
vii) Airside Buffet
viii) Airside Bar
ix) Shakespeare Pub
x) Domestic Lounge Bar / Buffet

**C6. On this / these occasion(s) what was your main reason for using the catering facilities?**

i) Wanted something to eat / drink
ii) liked the products offered
iii) Delayed flight
iv) Other:

**C7. Were you satisfied with the range of catering outlets?**

| | Today | Previously |
|---|---|---|
| i) Yes | | |
| ii) No | | |
| iii) Don't know | | |

Why not?

**C8. Did you feel that you received value for money?**

| | Today | Previously |
|---|---|---|
| i) Yes | | |
| ii) No | | |
| iii) Don't know | | |

Why not?

**C9. Did you find the product to be of good quality?**

| | Today | Previously |
|---|---|---|
| i) Yes | | |
| ii) No | | |
| iii) Don't know | | |

Why not?

Comaudit96 0896 (Pink Main)    **continued**

---

***Fig. 3.38*** *Customer survey form, Birmingham International Airport*

You will need to develop your communication skills if you work in the leisure or tourism industry. Make the effort to talk to the customers, but don't forget to listen as well. Listening to customers will help you to identify their needs.

McDonalds Restaurants show that they care for their customers by providing them with the opportunity to comment on the service they have received by using customer service forms such as the one shown in Fig. 3.39.

## Activity

Write a letter to any large local leisure or tourism organisation and ask if they can send you a copy of their customer comments form.

## Meeting customer needs

Listen carefully to your customers. This will help you to establish their needs for help, assistance and information.

If you are working as a consultant in a travel agency you could try to establish the needs of your customers by asking a series of open questions. If however you ask a closed question such as 'Can I help you?' this can only be answered by 'Yes' or 'No'. If the customer's reply is 'No' then it is difficult for you to take the conversation further and you will not be able to establish the needs of the customer.

Using open questions however will help the travel consultant to establish the specific needs of the customer and will help to create good customer rapport.

The travel consultant will observe the customer browsing through the brochures on the racks. The brochures which the customer glances at will give the consultant a good idea of the type of holiday the customer is looking for.

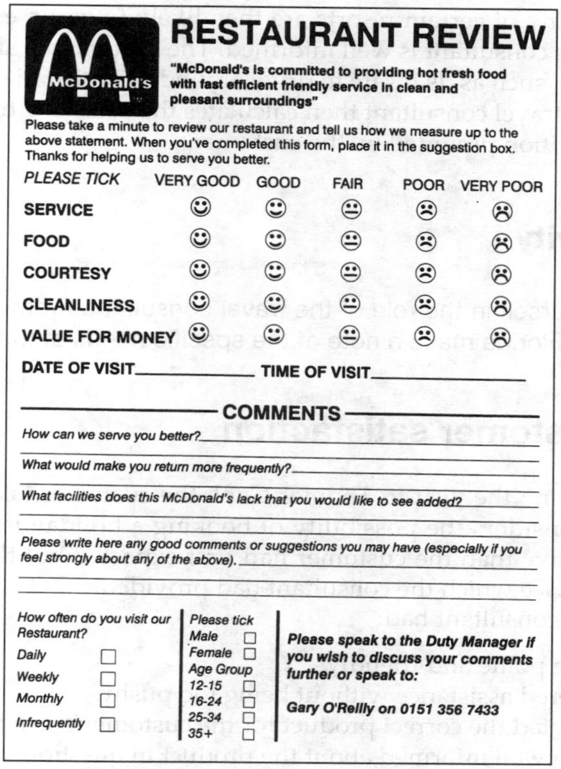

McDonald's

**RESTAURANT REVIEW**

**"McDonald's is committed to providing hot fresh food with fast efficient friendly service in clean and pleasant surroundings"**

Please take a minute to review our restaurant and tell us how we measure up to the above statement. When you've completed this form, place it in the suggestion box. Thanks for helping us to serve you better.

| *PLEASE TICK* | VERY GOOD | GOOD | FAIR | POOR | VERY POOR |
|---|---|---|---|---|---|
| **SERVICE** | ☺ | ☺ | 😐 | ☹ | ☹ |
| **FOOD** | ☺ | ☺ | 😐 | ☹ | ☹ |
| **COURTESY** | ☺ | ☺ | 😐 | ☹ | ☹ |
| **CLEANLINESS** | ☺ | ☺ | 😐 | ☹ | ☹ |
| **VALUE FOR MONEY** | ☺ | ☺ | 😐 | ☹ | ☹ |

**DATE OF VISIT**__________ **TIME OF VISIT**__________

**COMMENTS**

*How can we serve you better?*__________

*What would make you return more frequently?*__________

*What facilities does this McDonald's lack that you would like to see added?*__________

*Please write here any good comments or suggestions you may have (especially if you feel strongly about any of the above).*__________

*How often do you visit our Restaurant?*
*Daily* ☐
*Weekly* ☐
*Monthly* ☐
*Infrequently* ☐

*Please tick*
*Male* ☐
*Female* ☐
*Age Group*
*12-15* ☐
*16-24* ☐
*25-34* ☐
*35+* ☐

***Please speak to the Duty Manager if you wish to discuss your comments further or speak to:***

***Gary O'Reilly on 0151 356 7433***

***Fig. 3.39*** *McDonald's Restaurants' Customer comments form*

## Meeting customer needs at Thomas Cook

The consultant in Thomas Cook notices that the customer is looking at brochures such as Airtours and British Airways Florida giving an indication that the customer is interested in a holiday in Florida.

*Travel consultant*: 'We can offer a range of discounts on certain tour operators for Florida holidays at the moment. Are you looking for a fly-drive package or room only?'

*Customer*: 'I'm not sure really. I've never been to Florida before. What would you recommend?'

*Travel consultant*: 'I went to Florida last year and I would certainly recommend the fly-drive option and we can offer some really low rates for car insurance. It's cheaper to buy it here rather than waiting until you arrive in Florida. Are you taking any children with you?'

*Customer*: 'Yes, I've got two daughters. They really want to visit the Magic Kingdom...'

As the conversation continues the travel consultant is continually identifying the needs of the customer. The more relaxed the customer feels with the consultant the more she will reveal about herself and her individual needs. Questions about the suitability of certain resorts are then likely to occur, especially if the customer feels that the consultant is well informed. The customer is also likely to ask about security aspects, such as 'Is it safe to drive around Miami at night?'

The travel consultant then calculates the price of a holiday in Florida based on the information provided by the customer.

## Activity

Put yourself in the role of the travel consultant. From the discussion about the holiday in Florida make a note of the specific needs of the customer.

## Achieving customer satisfaction

Following the visit to Thomas Cook the customer takes the travel brochures home and considers the possibility of booking a holiday in Florida. It is a little bit more expensive than the customer had first expected but the customer was happy about the advice which the consultant had provided.

The consultant had:

- Been polite and friendly.
- Offered assistance without being too pushy.
- Selected the correct product for the customer's needs.
- Been well informed about the product in question.
- Reassured the customer about aspects of safety and security.
- Achieved additional sales which were not originally expected.

The customer felt comfortable about the product which was on offer and decided to return to Thomas Cook to book a two-week holiday in Florida.

## Activity

Write a script for a role play where a customer in a travel agency does not receive satisfaction.

> Maintain accurate records for selected situations

## Records

An efficient and well-organised company will keep detailed records of customers and the transactions which take place, such as:

- Details of customers.
- Records of sales.

- Records of bookings made.
- Records of cash received.

By keeping all transactions well documented this will help the organisation to provide a better standard of customer service.

For example, a customer books a badminton court at a leisure centre by phone. When the customer arrives the badminton court has already been let to another customer who just called in by chance. The receptionist had not bothered to make a note of the telephone booking and as a result the court was double booked. Customer satisfaction was not therefore maintained in this instance.

## Customer details

The membership application form shown in Fig. 3.32 (page 224) shows one of the methods used by leisure and tourism organisations to gather details about their customers.

Customer information can be used in a number of ways to help achieve further customer satisfaction:

- By identifying customer needs.
- To use in mail shots to inform customers of other products which they may wish to purchase.

Leisure centres usually keep detailed records of customers. The records may be kept on cards which are filed in an index system or as a computerised database.

A typical customer record form or card might look like Fig. 3.40.

## Littlebridge House Hotel
### Customer Details Form

| Name: *Jane Wright* | Date of booking: *10 August 1997* |
|---|---|
| Address: *40 The Mews*<br>*Tarporley*<br>*Cheshire Wa5 6Ty* | Special requirements: *Ground floor*<br>*Vegetarian* |
| Tel No.: *01736 556008* | Payment method: *Cheque* |
| Type of accomodation booked:<br>*Twin with ensuite* | Advert seen in:<br>*Where to stay in the Lake District* |
| No. of nights: *2 nights* | Add to mailing list *yes* |

**Fig. 3.40** *Typical customer record card*

# Sales details

Details of sales are recorded on receipts or invoices which may be passed to the customer for his/her personal records. Receipts are important, as if a customer has any cause for complaint they may return the product with proof of purchase.

For example it is usual to present a customer in a restaurant with an itemised bill which the customer may wish to check before paying.

Sales receipts confirm the details of the product or service which the customer is buying and help to achieve customer satisfaction as the customer will know exactly what is being provided and how much it will cost.

The Airtours receipt shown in Fig. 3.41 indicates the following details:

- The supplier of the product.
- Customer details.
- Flight details.
- Details of accommodation.
- Car hire details.
- The total cost of the holiday.
- The date by which final payment is due.

If the customer is satisfied with all of the details shown in the Airtours invoice then the invoice will be settled.

## Activity

Save some receipts for leisure or tourism products you have purchased.

Make a note of the following details:

1. Supplier of the product.

2. Name of the customer.

3. Product/service purchased.

4. Cost.

# Booking information

It is essential that leisure and tourism organisations keep full and accurate details of all bookings which have been made. Bookings may be made:

- By post.
- By telephone or fax.
- Verbally.

When bookings are received they will be recorded in a bookings diary or will be entered into a computerised software program.

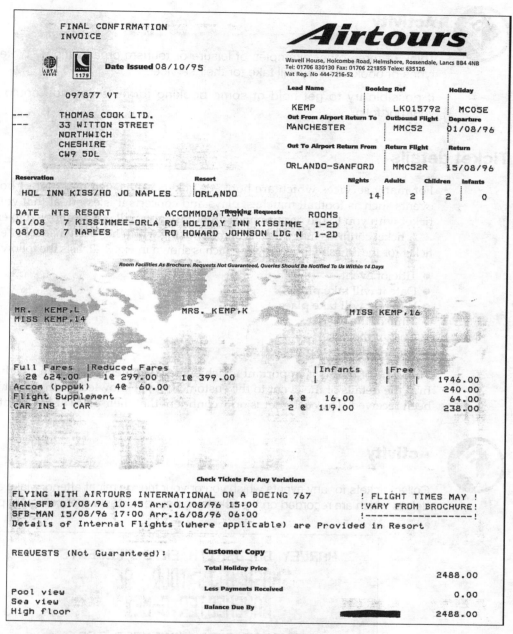

```
FINAL CONFIRMATION
INVOICE                          Airtours

                                 Wavell House, Holcombe Road, Helmshore, Rossendale, Lancs BB4 4NB
                                 Tel: 01706 830130 Fax: 01706 221855 Telex: 635126
      Date issued 08/10/95       Vat Reg. No 444-7216-52
1179
                                 Lead Name        Booking Ref      Holiday
   097877 VT
                                 KEMP             LK015792         MC05E
   THOMAS COOK LTD.               Out From Airport Return To  Outbound Flight  Departure
   33 WITTON STREET               MANCHESTER         MMC52       01/08/96
   NORTHWICH
   CHESHIRE                       Out To Airport Return From   Return Flight   Return
   CW9 5DL
                                 ORLANDO-SANFORD    MMC52R       15/08/96

Reservation                      Resort
                                                 Nights  Adults  Children  Infants
   HOL INN KISS/HO JO NAPLES      ORLANDO          14      2        2        0

DATE  NTS RESORT          ACCOMMODATION Booking Requests  ROOMS
01/08  7  KISSIMMEE-ORLA  RO HOLIDAY INN KISSIMME   1-2D
08/08  7  NAPLES          RO HOWARD JOHNSON LDG N    1-2D

        Room Facilities As Brochure. Requests Not Guaranteed, Queries Should Be Notified To Us Within 14 Days


   MR. KEMP,L              MRS. KEMP,K                  MISS KEMP,16
   MISS KEMP,14


   Full Fares  |Reduced Fares                    |Infants  |Free
     2@ 624.00 |  1@ 299.00     1@ 399.00        |         |          1946.00
   Accom (pppwk)    4@ 60.00                                           240.00
   Flight Supplement                    4 @  16.00                      64.00
   CAR INS 1 CAR                        2 @ 119.00                     238.00


                        Check Tickets For Any Variations

FLYING WITH AIRTOURS INTERNATIONAL ON A BOEING 767    ! FLIGHT TIMES MAY !
MAN-SFB 01/08/96 10:45 Arr.01/08/96 15:00             !VARY FROM BROCHURE!
SFB-MAN 15/08/96 17:00 Arr.16/08/96 06:00             !------------------!
Details of Internal Flights (where applicable) are Provided in Resort


REQUESTS (Not Guaranteed):      Customer Copy
                                Total Holiday Price
                                                              2488.00
Pool view                       Less Payments Received
Sea view                                                         0.00
High floor                      Balance Due By
                                                              2488.00
```

**Fig. 3.41** *Airtours invoice for a holiday in Florida*

The types of bookings which might be made will include:

- Travel agencies     Details of holidays booked, tickets sold.
- Leisure centre     Bookings for the sports hall, squash and badminton courts.
- Restaurant     Details of meals and special functions booked.

## Activity

Think of three other examples of leisure or tourism organisations. Write down the types of bookings they will take for their services.

If possible try to get hold of some booking forms which you could include in your portfolio.

## Ticket details

For many services which are booked, tickets are issued as proof of booking. For events such as football matches, plays and concerts it is essential that you take your ticket with you to the performance otherwise you will not be allowed to enter.

A ticket confirms many details of the booking which has been made. For example, the ticket for the Smash Hits Tour '96, which is shown in Fig. 3.42, lists the following details:

- Title of event.
- Date it will take place.
- Where it will take place.
- Time of the event.
- Cost of the ticket.
- Seating details.

The issue of tickets is important in achieving customer satisfaction as it helps to confirm the details of the event to the customer and acknowledges that their request has been received. The customer is now confident that their place at the event is assured.

## Activity

Collect tickets for any events which you or your friends might attend. Make a note of the details which are recorded on the tickets and store this as evidence in your portfolio.

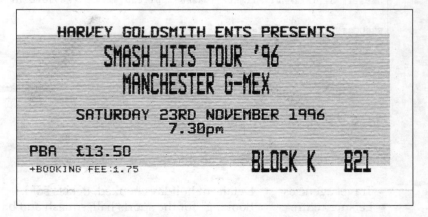

**Fig. 3.42** *Ticket for Smash Hits Tour '96*

# Cash details

Any business must keep a record of its daily cash takings. The amount of money which is taken over the counter during a day for goods sold is known as the turnover. Money may also be taken in the form of cheques or credit card transactions.

Leisure and tourism companies need to monitor their turnover. They must turnover a certain amount of cash, for which a target figure is usually set, in order to stay in business and to meet their overhead or outgoing costs.

The amount of money which has been received during the day will be recorded on a ledger sheet and may then be entered into a computerised accounting system or into the manual book-keeping system.

## Activity

One way of monitoring the amount of money which passes through a business in terms of cash received and money paid out for goods and services is to keep a record using a cash flow spreadsheet.

The following example shows the type of items which might be shown on a typical spreadsheet.

| Sea Shell Souvenir Shop – Weekly Cash Sales Analysis | | | | | | | | |
|---|---|---|---|---|---|---|---|---|
| | Mon | Tues | Wed | Thurs | Fri | Sat | Sun | Weekly total |
| Shell ornaments | 23.45 | 16.09 | 12.60 | 12.98 | 19.34 | 45.78 | 79.78 | |
| Sticks of rock | 10.56 | 23.67 | 8.96 | 3.50 | 1.26 | 30.06 | 36.89 | |
| Confectionery | 14.67 | 10.05 | 1.25 | 1.67 | 12.56 | 16.97 | 24.76 | |
| Books | 10.85 | 00.00 | 00.00 | 16.00 | 34.75 | 36.95 | 42.95 | |
| T-towels | 5.20 | 4.60 | 1.45 | 7.35 | 2.50 | 2.50 | 1.45 | |
| Total daily takings | | | | | | | | |

1. You might find it useful to reproduce the weekly cash sales analysis as a spreadsheet using appropriate software.

2. Calculate the daily cash takings for each day of the week using the spreadsheet formulae.

3. Calculate the weekly cash takings for each type of good using the spreadsheet formulae.

4. What are the average daily takings?

5. Does the spending pattern over the week show a trend? On which days would you expect sales to be at their highest?

For task 6 and 7 use the graphing capabilities of the spreadsheet software.

6. Draw a graph to show which is the best selling souvenir at the Shell Souvenir Shop.

7. Draw a graph to show which is the least popular item on sale at the shop.

**Key skills satisfied:** *Application of Number* **N2.1, N2.2, N2.3**

> Evaluate own performance in the provision of customer service in selected situations

When you are dealing with customers on a daily basis you might find it useful sometimes to step back and consider whether you are truly meeting the needs of customers and providing them with the best possible service.

To evaluate how well you are providing customer service you will need to decide what constitutes good customer service and use this as your criteria to evaluate your own performance.

## Activity

Working in groups, brainstorm ideas as to what makes good customer service.

Use these ideas to compile a self-evaluation form which you can complete either after taking part in role play simulations or after dealing with customers in the workplace.

Word process the self-evaluation form and file the completed form as evidence in your portfolio.

## Self-evaluate your performance in giving customer service

If you already have a part-time job or are about to undertake a period of work placement in the leisure or tourism industry, then you could evaluate your performance with customers using the self-evaluation form.

If you do not have access to a workplace you will need to take part in a number of simulated situations or role plays under the supervision of your tutor. Ask your tutor to film the role play using a video camera so that the film can be played back to the class.

| Customer service |
| :---: |
| *Self-evaluation form* |

| Student name: | Date: |
| --- | --- |

| Situation: |
| --- |

| Details of customers: |
| --- |

| How did I provide good customer care? |
| --- |

| What were the needs of the customer? |
| --- |

| Did any customers have specific needs? |
| --- |

| What products or services did I offer to meet the customer's needs? |
| --- |

| What record did I keep of the transaction? |
| --- |

| What would I do differently next time? |
| --- |

| Tutor Comments: |
| --- |

**Fig. 3.43** *Student self-evaluation form*

The video evidence will help when you complete your self-evaluation form (Fig. 3.43).

You will need to provide customer service to a range of different customers in differing situations. The needs of the customer in each situation will vary between the following:

- Help
- Advice
- Information
- Product
- Safety
- Security

Summarise own evaluation findings

The purpose of self-evaluation is to look back at your performance and think of ways in which you could improve the service you provided to the customer. It is important to summarise your feelings on how you performed and draw up a number of key points to remember when you are dealing with customers in the workplace.

From the self-evaluation form shown on page 253, draw up a list of points for improvement against the criteria given within Fig. 3.44.

## Assignment

**'Evaluating customer service skills'**

*Situation*

You need to demonstrate to your tutor that you can provide good customer service.

| Summary of self-evaluation |
|---|
| 1. Caring for customers<br>*Remember to always greet the customer and smile* |
| 2. Identifying customers needs<br>*Try to ask a wider range of open questions to find out more about what the customer wants* |
| 3. Dealing with customers specific needs<br>*I need to find out more about how to deal with people who do not speak English* |
| 4. Keeping records<br>*Try to write down more details of each customer I deal with as I might need to refer back to my notes* |

**Fig. 3.44** *Summary of own evaluation findings*

This needs to be carried out either whilst you are on work placement or by taking part in role play exercises which will be set up by your tutor.

You will be assessed in three different situations which will provide a range of different customers with differing needs.

*Tasks*

1. Design a self-evaluation form on which you can record your comments, similar to the form shown on page 253.
2. Each time you provide customer service complete a self-evaluation form and ask your tutor to write a comment on the form.
3. Read your own self-evaluation forms and look at your tutor's comments. From this draw up a list in which you summarise the ways in which you could improve the way in which you deliver customer service. Figure 3.44 on page 254 suggests how you might summarise your self evaluation.

Your tutor will also be completing a separate evaluation form. The tutor will be assessing you against the following criteria:

1. Did you demonstrate customer care?
2. Did you accurately identify the needs of the customer?
3. Did you keep a record of either the transaction or the discussion with the customer?

**Key skills satisfied:** *Communication* **C2.2**
*Information Technology* **IT2.1, IT2.2**

# Revision questions

1. List four reasons why good customer service will help your business.

2. Make a list of the results of poor customer service.

3. How many different customer types might you have to deal with if you are working as a Receptionist in a Tourist Information Centre?

4. Name at least six 'trade' magazines connected with the leisure and tourism industry.

5. What is the difference between an open and a closed question?

6. Give an example of a closed question.

7. Give an example of an open question.

8. Why is it important to keep a record of your customers?

9. What type of information may be kept in customer records?

10. Describe what is meant by 'direct selling'.

# Unit 4

# CONTRIBUTING TO THE
# RUNNING OF AN EVENT

**Plan an event with others**

**Undertake a role in a team event**

**Evaluate the team event**

The aim of this unit is to give you an overview of the wide range of events which take place in the field of leisure and tourism. You will need to plan and contribute to the running of an event of your choice. This will help to provide you with an insight into the practical aspects of managing and staging events. At the end of this unit you will need to evaluate how the event went and your contribution towards the planning of the event.

## What is an event?

When we describe an activity as an event we are describing a project or an attraction which does not occur on a daily basis.

Events are organised on a variety of geographical scales:

| International event | National event | Local/regional event |
| --- | --- | --- |
| Olympic Games | Wimbledon Tennis championships | Local fun run |
| Cannes Film Festival | Great North Run | Local arts festival |
| World Cup Football | Ideal Home Exhibition | Village fete |

Sometimes national events are also organised on a regional or local basis, for example Children in Need fund-raising activities. When the Children in Need event takes place in late November the regional BBC stations show the activities which are taking place within the BBC broadcasting regions nationwide. The main Children in Need presenters and personalities co-ordinate these regional programmes from the BBC national headquarters at Broadcasting House in London.

The list of events shown above covers a variety of activities involving many different numbers of people, ranging from millions of spectators world-wide for the Olympic Games to possibly thirty or forty participants in a charity fun run.

## Activity

Over a period of one week look through a range of local and regional newspapers for events which are taking place. Look also at the television pages for events which are to be broadcast.

Make a list of the events you have identified and categorise these into:

- Local/regional events.
- National events.
- International events.

A range of newspapers should be available in your college/school library or your local lending library. Ask your tutor to help you identify suitable newspapers which may be available.

# Plan an event with others

The people who organise events may be paid employees working for an event management company or may be unpaid volunteers helping to organise a local charity or community event.

The planning and organisation of many events organised by volunteers may fall outside a normal working day and it is quite likely that the organisers of an event will have to work unsociable hours, for instance:

- After their normal working day.
- At weekends.
- In the evenings.

However in the case of a professional event management company much of the planning will probably take place during a normal working day. The event itself however may well be staged out of normal working hours to maximise the number of visitors who may wish to attend, for example a weekend village fete.

There is a diverse range of types of events and, as a result, the aims and objectives of events may vary widely, for example:

| Objectives | Opportunities | Examples of events |
|---|---|---|
| Financial objectives | Local charity organising fund-raising activities; large corporation trying to maximise profits | Car boot sale; a hotel chain promoting weddings at their hotels |
| Social objectives | Creating opportunities for people to enjoy themselves; creating opportunities for people to participate | Cricket club disco; participate in a swimming gala |
| Environmental objectives | To raise awareness of environmental issues | Local tree-planting ceremony |

## Activity

Try to think of further examples of events for each of the three main categories listed above.

Describe the planning process for an event

The organisers of an event will need to plan and co-ordinate their activities carefully in order to achieve a successful outcome. Events are rarely organised by one person but by a team of individuals or specialist teams working together for large events. The team must have a structure with clearly defined roles and responsibilities so that everyone knows what they are supposed to be doing and are working towards a common goal.

The team will need to work together closely to plan the event and will need to consider each stage of the planning process. A planning meeting should be arranged at which your team sits down and discusses and agrees the points outlined in the planning process. A record of the minutes of the meeting should be kept and stored as evidence in your portfolio.

## The planning process

| Objectives | What is the event hoping to achieve?<br>To raise money for charity?<br>To involve people in the community? |
|---|---|
| Ideas | What is the event?<br>Who is it aimed at (customers)?<br>What activities will be involved?<br>When will the event take place?<br>Where will the event be staged? |
| Resources | Physical – What materials will be required? Is the venue suitable?<br>Human – What skills does the team have?<br>Financial – How much money is available to spend on the event? |
| Constraints | Are there financial constraints?<br>Are there physical constraints?<br>Is a suitable venue available?<br>Does the team have appropriate skills? |
| Contingencies | What might go wrong on the day?<br>How will the team cope with problems? |
| Roles | Who will be the team leader?<br>Who is responsible for what? |

## Activity

Think about an event which you might have been to recently. This may have been a sporting event, a cultural event or simply entertainment.

What do you think the objectives of that event might have been?

> Explain the possible objectives of an event and agree with the team the objectives of the planned event

# Objectives

An objective is a goal which you want to achieve. Typical event objectives are shown in Fig. 4.1.

The objectives of the team event must be 'SMART':

- **S**   **Specific** and easy to understand.
- **M**   **Measurable** targets must be set, e.g. target sales or customer numbers.
- **A**   **Achievable:** the objectives must be capable of being achieved.
- **R**   **Realistic:** the team must be capable of achieving the objectives with the resources which are available.
- **T**   **Time:** the objectives must be capable of being achieved within the time scale allowed.

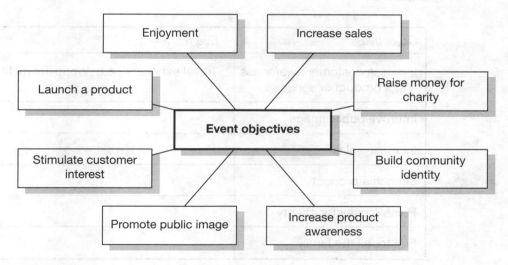

**Fig. 4.1** *Typical event objectives*

When we consider the range of objectives which might exist (Fig. 4.1) we can then think of a variety of events which can be organised to meet these objectives.

## Activity

What typical events can you think of which might be used to meet the following objectives?

| Objectives | Event |
|---|---|
| Increase customer awareness in a product or service | Travel exhibition, e.g. World Travel Market |
| Improve public image | |
| Increase sales | |
| Launch a product | |
| Raise money for charity | |
| Fun for all the family | |

Select with the team an event from a range of options which will meet the agreed objectives

When considering what event to run you will need to take a number of factors into account, for example:

- The aims and objectives of the event.
- The nature and content of the event.
- The resources required.
- The availability and cost of resources.

When you embark on this process you will be carrying out a feasibility study. The information gathered will be used to decide whether it is worth running the event or not. Therefore you must consider whether the event is feasible.

# Selecting an event

When selecting an event the team will consider a range of options which meet the needs of their objectives (see Fig. 4.2).

## Activity

In teams, carry out a brainstorming session to generate ideas for events which your class might be able to plan and run.

One member of the group should write a list of the suggestions on a whiteboard or on a flip chart.

The class should now select one event from the list of options which have been suggested and carry out a feasibility study as described for the event below.

**Key skills satisfied:** *Communication* **C2.1a, C2.2**

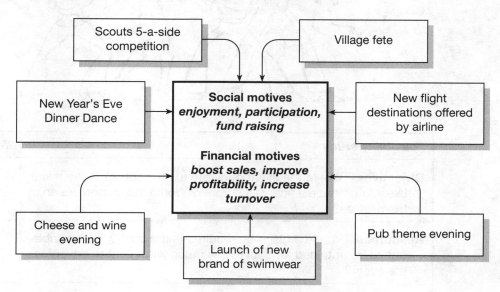

***Fig. 4.2*** *Typical events which might meet social and financial objectives*

# Feasibility study

Your team has been set the task of increasing sales in your local pub during the traditionally quiet period after Christmas and New Year.

| | |
|---|---|
| *Event* | Themed evening organised by a bar, for example a sixties hippy night |
| *Objectives* | To raise money |
| | To attract new customers |
| | To create a social atmosphere for the clients |

The team will now need to ask itself a number of typical questions to determine whether the event is feasible:

- **Event:** Sixties Hippy Night
- **Proposed date:** 10th January
- **Venue:** Bulls Head

| *Feasibility study* | Yes | No |
|---|---|---|
| **Objectives** – Would the event generate extra income? Is the event likely to produce a financial surplus? Would the customers enjoy themselves? | | |
| **Resources** – Would a disco be required (extra cost)? Can suitable outfits be obtained for staff? How much will it cost to advertise the event? | | |
| **Timing** – Is there a suitable date available? | | |

If the answer to each of these questions is 'yes' then the organisers should have a realistic chance of running a successful event. If there are several negative responses then the team should consider:

1. Staging the event in a modified format.
   *or*
2. Not staging the event at all.

> Calculate with the team what resources will be needed for the event

# Resources

A resource is a material, skill or commodity which can be used to help achieve the staging of the event.

Typical resources which might be used in event management can be broken down into three main categories:

| | | |
|---|---|---|
| *Human* | Staff skills | e.g. expertise, artistic skills, organisational skills |
| *Physical* | Materials | e.g. paper, pens, glue |
| | Fixtures and fittings | e.g. furniture, screens, exhibition stands |
| | Transport | e.g. local coach service |
| | Time | i.e. the time you have available and the way in which it is allocated |
| | Physical space | i.e the amount of space which you have at your disposal; this may be a hall, an arena or maybe a field |
| | Equipment | e.g badminton racquets, shuttlecocks |
| *Financial* | Money | i.e. the amount of money you have available to spend on staging the event |

When you are organising your event you must consider what resources you will require to stage it (Fig. 4.3). Any team will have a limited financial budget and therefore it must consider very carefully whether it can afford to purchase the resources necessary to run the event. The resources which will have to be paid for will include the purchase of materials and equipment and the payment of staff salaries.

## Activity

The Parent Teachers Association (PTA) of the local primary school has asked your class to help them plan a car boot sale. The objective of the car boot sale is to raise money to purchase computers for the school.

Make a list of the resources which you think you might need to run this event.

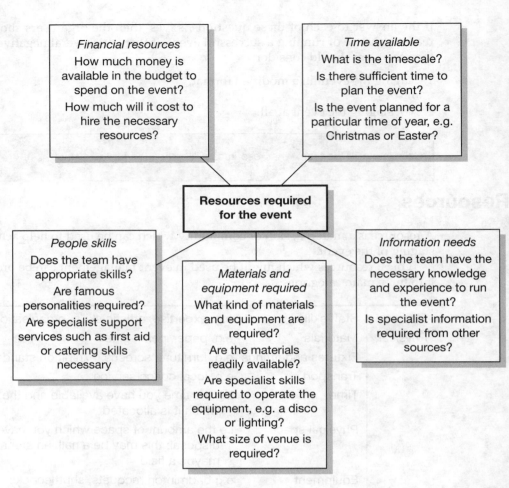

Financial resources
How much money is available in the budget to spend on the event?
How much will it cost to hire the necessary resources?

Time available
What is the timescale?
Is there sufficient time to plan the event?
Is the event planned for a particular time of year, e.g. Christmas or Easter?

**Resources required for the event**

People skills
Does the team have appropriate skills?
Are famous personalities required?
Are specialist support services such as first aid or catering skills necessary

Materials and equipment required
What kind of materials and equipment are required?
Are the materials readily available?
Are specialist skills required to operate the equipment, e.g. a disco or lighting?
What size of venue is required?

Information needs
Does the team have the necessary knowledge and experience to run the event?
Is specialist information required from other sources?

**Fig. 4.3** Resources required to run an event

Identify with the team constraints likely to affect the event

When planning an event the team must be aware of possible constraints and must take these into account when preparing the event plan. For example, the management of a hotel would be embarrassed if 200 guests turned up for a dinner dance and unfortunately there were no serving or bar staff to cater for the guests because the staff had not been asked to or could not work that evening.

If we consider the constraints that may be imposed on the planning of an event the organisers must consider many different factors:

| Event organisers' considerations | Constraints |
|---|---|
| Staff skills | Do the staff have the appropriate skills to carry out the event? |
| | Are the staff sufficiently experienced? |
| | Are specialised skills required? |
| Staff availability | Staff may not be available at the right time |
| | If the event takes place during unsociable hours extra wage costs may be incurred and it may be difficult for staff to get home after working |
| Staff responsibilities and commitments | The staff may have other responsibilities such as children which they may need to collect from school or the children may be off school because they are sick |
| Opening times | Local licensing regulations may need to be consulted |
| Facility capacity | Is the venue large enough for the anticipated number of guests or customers? |
| Customer transport times | Is transport available for customers without cars? |
| | Will public transport get the customers to the event on time? |
| Health, safety and security | Fire regulations will determine the maximum number of customers allowed into the venue |
| Equipment | Is sufficient and appropriate equipment available? |
| | How much will it cost to hire the necessary equipment? |

## Staff skills

An example of an annual event at Mid Shire College demonstrates how staff considerations may exert constraints on the running of an event as follows:

The students at Mid Shire College who have achieved their GNVQ Intermediate Leisure & Tourism qualification have been invited to a presentation dinner in the college restaurant where the meal will be prepared and served by the college catering students. In order for this event to be run successfully the restaurant manager will need to consider the staff requirements mentioned in Fig. 4.4

## Facility considerations

When planning an event the organisers must consider the suitability of a facility or venue in terms of:

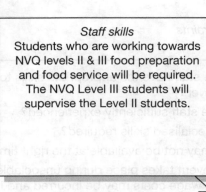

<table>
<tr>
<td>

**Staff skills**
Students who are working towards NVQ levels II & III food preparation and food service will be required. The NVQ Level III students will supervise the Level II students.

</td>
<td>

**Staff availability**
The event was planned for a mid-week date (Tuesday) because this maximised the availability of students and staff. If the event had taken place on Tuesday/Friday or at the weekend staff/student availability may have been affected due to personal social arrangements and part-time employment commitments.

</td>
</tr>
<tr>
<td colspan="2" align="center">

**Student's Presentation Dinner**

</td>
</tr>
<tr>
<td>

**Cost of staff**
In this case the dinner presented an opportunity for real work experience which is an integral part of the NVQ Catering course. However if this event was to take place at the weekend, staff costs calculated on an hourly basis would need to be costed into the price of the meal. It is college policy for all students who have to work after 10 pm to be provided with a taxi home and to not be timetabled for classes for the following morning until after 10.30 am.

</td>
<td>

**Staff responsibilities and commitments**
In the case of this event where the staff mainly comprises students aged 16–19 there are few family commitments to be taken into account. In the case of an event where staff are employed the availability of staff may be dependent on their social responsibilities and domestic commitments.

</td>
</tr>
</table>

**Fig. 4.4** *Staff resources required for Student's Presentation Dinner*

- Facility opening times.
- Facility capacity.
- Is the venue appropriate?
- Can the venue provide suitable facilities?
- The location of the venue.

## Facility opening times

The type of event which is being considered may have serious implications for the opening and closing times of the venue. For example, at a trade exhibition such as the World Travel Market or the Motor Show the venue will need to be open to the public from at least 10 am to 9 pm. However in order to stage such events the organisers will need to have access to the exhibition halls several days before the exhibition is opened to the public in order to build sets and assemble the exhibits.

## Activity

With help from your tutor prepare a report on the World Travel Market. Your report should be based on the following points:

1. What type of an event is the World Travel Market?

2. Where is it staged?

3. What time of year is it held?

4. How long does this event last?

5. How many visitors are expected?

6. How many companies exhibit at this event?

CASE STUDY

## Manchester Evening News Arena

Nynex Arena in Manchester was opened in 1995. It is Europe's largest multi-purpose indoor arena and is host to a range of entertainment such as sporting events and concerts. The Arena has now changed its name to the Manchester Evening News Arena, (MEN) Arena.

*Facility capacity*
The Arena has 3,000 square metres of floor space and can seat up to 21,000 people.

It employs approximately 37 full-time members of staff, six within the sales and marketing team. The number of people involved in the staging of specific events is considerably more than this however. The Arena employs a range of full-time and part-time staff who are hired for specific events.

The following figures show how the number of staff required to stage an event varies dramatically depending upon the type of event:

- Basketball matches: approx. 60 staff.
- Ice hockey matches: approx. 100 staff.
- Major concerts: approx. 400 staff.

*Location and accessibility of the venue*
The MEN Arena is centrally located within the UK and has excellent road and rail connections. The Arena is located adjacent to Manchester Victoria's Intercity and Metrolink Station.

### Events at MEN Arena

The type of events which take place at MEN Arena can be broken down into the three main categories shown in Fig. 4.7.

In its first year of operation (1995) MEN Arena hosted over 140 events. 170 events were targeted for 1996.

# NYNEX arena Manchester

## Facts, firsts and figures...

- Manchester is where Emmeline Pankhurst founded the Womens Social & Political Union in 1903.

- **The Arena is part of a 14 acre development site.**

- Manchester is the home of Britain's largest regional newspaper.

- **The Arena roof trusses which create the large clear span roof weigh 116 tons each.**

- Manchester is where Ernest Rutherford first split the atom.

- **The Arena utilised 161 miles of cabling and 88 miles of pipework and ducts during construction.**

- Manchester operated the World's first passenger train service.

- **The Arena substructure & superstructure contain approx 10,000 cubic metres of reinforced concrete.**

- Manchester has one of the largest university campuses in Europe.

- **The Arena seating bowl cantilevers out over the railway tracks below.**

- Manchester is the home of Europe's first television theme park.

- **The Arena roof contains some 2,400 tonnes of structural steelwork.**

- Manchester is the centre of the area responsible for manufacturing almost 50% of Britain's goods.

- **The Arena structure is isolated acoustically from the station environment, thus preventing sound transmission.**

- Manchester was where the World's first working radar transmitters were built.

- **The Arena design allows for the provision of a permanent ice floor and is served by a dedicated ice making plant.**

- Manchester is the home of the Professional Footballers Association.

- **The Arena bowl internal volume is 340,000 m³.**

- Manchester's Granada TV gave The Beatles, The Hollies and The Rolling Stones their first TV appearances.

- **The Arena project was awarded the largest ever central government grant - approx £35.5m.**

- Manchester is the home of Britain's first full time orchestra.

- **The Arena project has a vast workforce, 75% of which are from the North West.**

- Manchester is the home of Britain's largest medical school.

## An enlightening experience

OGDEN
ENTERTAINMENT
SERVICES

**Fig. 4.5** *Nynex Arena, Manchester*

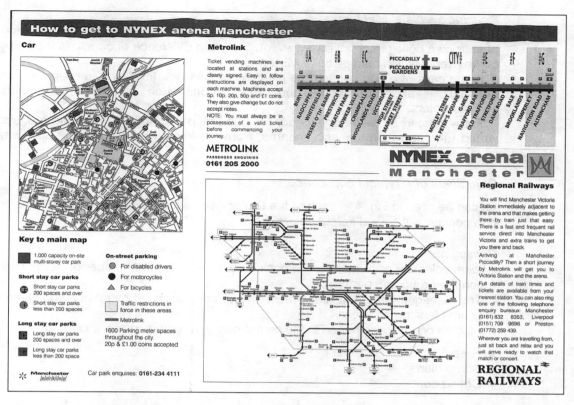

**Fig. 4.6** *How to get to the MEN Arena*

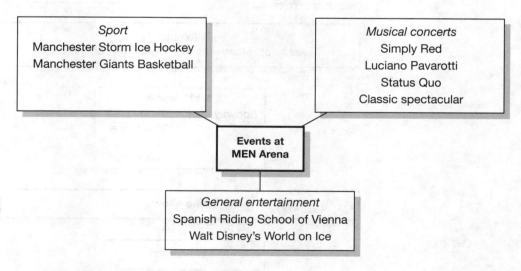

**Fig. 4.7** *Typical events at the MEN Arena*

*Planning events at MEN Arena*

Planning an event at MEN Arena is very much different in principle to the planning of your own college/school based event. The main difference of course is the scale of the events which take place at MEN Arena.

In the case of a pop concert the planning process will involve many negotiations between a variety of people and organisations such as record companies and promoters.

For a concert by an internationally famous group (Fig. 4.8) the planning process would take approximately six months; from the initial idea to the final product, which is the show.

### Objectives of a typical pop concert

As can be seen in Fig. 4.9, each of the teams involved in the organisation of a major pop concert will have different objectives.

*Constraints*

If ticket sales are poor there is the possibility of reducing the number of nights over which the group can perform.

The management of the Arena must always consider what might go wrong when they are planning an event.

All staff on duty are trained in the centre policy for emergencies, including:

● Fires.
● Bomb alerts.
● Crowd control.

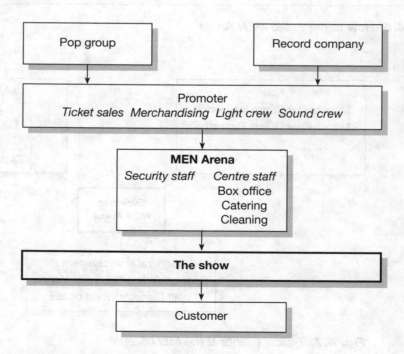

**Fig. 4.8** *Staff involved in staging a major pop concert*

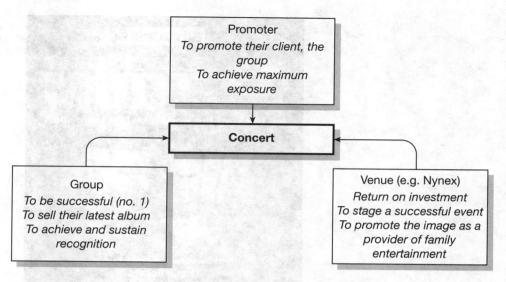

**Fig. 4.9** *Differing objectives of team*

The security staff at MEN Arena will liaise closely with the emergency services so that in the event of disruption swift remedial action will be taken.

*Team structure*
If we refer to Fig. 4.8 we can see the various teams who work together to produce the final product, which is the concert. There are also groups of people operating within the teams, such as sound and light crews, all of whom have their responsibilities to set up their respective electrical systems.

All of the teams involved will have one collective objective which is to see a successful concert being staged. Each individual team however will have a different primary objective in fulfilling its role.

● **Lighting crew** – To provide effective lighting as discussed with the group and the venue prior to the event.
● **Catering team** – Must ensure that they are ready and able to serve a large number of customers in a short period of time with the right type of food and drink. The team must ensure that all hygiene regulations are met.

# Manchester Storm Ice Hockey Team

If we use the example of the Manchester Storm Ice Hockey Team we can see a different organisational and planning structure. All the management decisions regarding the Manchester Storm are made by the management team of MEN Arena. All playing, coaching and tactical decisions of the team are made by an ice hockey coach who is employed by MEN Arena. This is a very different organisational structure (see Fig. 4.11) to the one shown for the Simply Red concert.

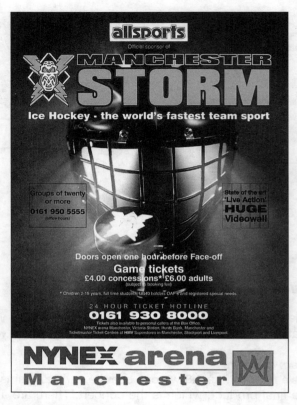

**Fig. 4.10** *Manchester Storm ice hockey team*

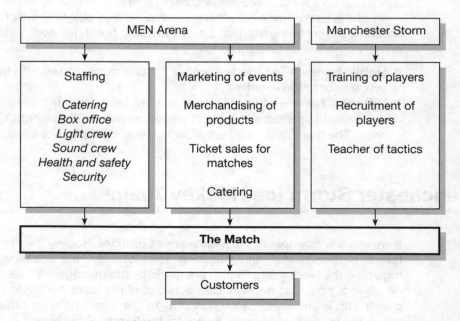

**Fig. 4.11** *Teams involved in planning an ice hockey match*

The Manchester Storm matches occur more frequently and usually before a smaller audience than major pop concerts. In the 1996/97 season alone there were 31 matches scheduled. Consequently the team involved is smaller as the end product is less complex.

## Customer accessibility and transport times

Event organisers will need to consider how accessible the venue is to its customers in terms of:

- How the customers will reach the event.
- How long the customers' travelling time will be.
- Where customers travelling by car will park.
- Any anticipated disruptions to travel such as road works and adverse weather.

## Event facilities

The National Exhibition Centre in Birmingham and MEN Arena in Manchester are two of the UK's top event facilities. The NEC is a purpose built exhibition/event centre which is located on an out of town site whereas the Nynex Arena centre is located adjacent to Victoria Station in central Manchester. In order to be successful as event venues they must both be very accessible to the public.

| NEC, Birmingham | MEN Arena, Manchester |
|---|---|
| Acres of open air car parking | Limited under cover car parking facilities within close proximity |
| Courtesy buses connect car park to exhibition halls | City centre bus service interconnects with British Rail stations such as Piccadilly, Oxford Road, Deansgate and Victoria |
| Excellent rail link from British Rail New Street Station to Birmingham International Station, en route to London Euston Station | The Manchester Metro link connects Altrincham in the south to Bury in the north via Manchester city centre and stops at Victoria Station adjacent to the Nynex Arena |
| Close proximity to the motorway network | Taxi service |

## Equipment

The nature of the event being staged will determine the type of equipment and size of venue required.

For example, a dinner dance for 200 people would require 20 tables, if each table was to seat 10 people. There will also need to be cutlery available for all types of menus.

A typical equipment list for two different types of dinner dance would comprise:

| Valentine's Night Dinner Dance x100 | New Year's Eve Dinner Dance x100 |
| --- | --- |
| 50 tables for 2 people | 10 tables for 10 people |
| 50 menus set on table | 20 menus set on table |
| 50 table candle lamps | 10 table candle lamps |
| 50 table flower displays | 10 table flower displays |
| 100 main course knives | 100 main course knives |
| 100 main course forks | 100 main course forks |
| 100 dessert spoons | 100 dessert spoons |
| 100 dessert forks | 100 dessert forks |
| 100 main course plates | 100 main course plates |
| 100 main course side plates | 100 main course side plates |
| 100 wine glasses | 100 wine glasses |
| 100 dessert dishes | 100 dessert dishes |
| Entertainment: smoochy disco | Entertainment: lively disco, bagpipes |
| Dance floor | Dance floor |

# Health, safety and security

One of the primary consideration for organisers of events is undoubtedly health and safety. There have been many examples of events within the leisure and tourism industry which have ended tragically.

Examples of such tragedies include:

- **Lyme Bay canoeing tragedy** – Four students who were on an outdoor activity holiday were tragically drowned after losing control of their craft whilst attempting to canoe across Lyme Bay in Dorset.
- **Bradford Football Club fire** – A discarded cigarette set fire to accumulated litter underneath a wooden stand. The result was an horrific fire with a number of fatalities.
- **Hillsborough Stadium disaster** – Too many football supporters congregated behind the goal at the Leppings Lane end of the ground. The resultant crush caused the death of 93 supporters.

As a result of these tragic accidents legislation has been progressively improved and modified to help identify and pinpoint as many potential eventualities and accidents as possible.

The following legislation exists to try to prevent such tragedies:

- Activity Centre (Young Persons' Safety) Act 1995.
- Health & Safety at Work, etc. Act, 1974.
- Safety of Sports Crowds and Stadia Act, 1988.
- Fire Acts, 1971.

These acts cover the safety not only of customers but also of employees and visitors to such event venues.

# Health & Safety at Work, etc. Act, 1974

If we look at the aspects covered under this act we can see that the subject of health and safety is the responsibility of everyone within an organisation. Management must make sure that all staff are inducted in aspects of health and safety as they relate to that particular facility.

The induction should make employees aware of their responsibilities to ensure that the workplace is safe for fellow employees and customers. If we consider Fig. 4.12 we can see the areas that all visitors and employees have to be aware of.

If we consider the example of the dinner dance mentioned on page 276 we can highlight some of the major health and safety considerations:

- Adequate illuminated/visible emergency signage.
- Are emergency routes and exits clearly indicated, e.g. fire exit signs?
- Adequate emergency exits.
- Details of fire assembly points.
- Nominated safety officer on duty.
- Location of correctly stocked first aid boxes.
- Gangways and exits kept clear of obstacles.
- Nominated smoke doors correctly maintained with self closer and intumescent strips.

# Safety in the kitchen

- Floors must be kept clean to avoid slips and falls.
- All equipment must be correctly maintained to avoid accidents from:
  - faulty wiring
  - gas leaks
  - faulty cut off on stoves
  - dangerous machines, e.g. meat slicer must have adequate guard
- Staff handling food must have attained a basic food hygiene certificate.
- Adequate cloths for the carrying of hot dishes (to avoid spillage).
- Staff involved in the service of food are aware of the routes which they must take to and from the banqueting hall so as to avoid collisions and accidents.
- Appropriate headgear must be worn in food preparation areas.
- Staff with cuts or abrasions must have them adequately dressed.

The health and safety considerations will depend upon the nature of the event. The following example illustrates the safety considerations which must be made for a five-a-side football match in a sports hall.

# The law relating to health and safety at work

## SUMMARY

- The Health and Safety at Work, etc. Act applies to most workers

- Everybody – employers and employees – is responsible for safety

- The employer has to:
  Provide safe equipment
  Provide safe systems of work
  Provide a safe and healthy workplace for employees and visitors
  Train and supervise workers and produce safety rules and instructions
  Consult with safety representatives

- Employees have to:
  Look after themselves
  Look after each other
  Look after members of the public and visitors
  Respect safety equipment and follow safety rules

- Manufacturers of equipment and substances for use at work have to:
  Produce safe goods that have been tested
  Provide instructions for their safe use.

**Fig. 4.12** *Summary of the Health and Safety at Work, etc. Act*

- Participants must be aware of the location of the nearest qualified first aider and the location of the first aid box.
- Any equipment used, e.g. goalposts, must be of a fit and proper nature (not damaged) and must be correctly assembled.
- Participants must wear the correct sports clothing, e.g. training shoes not football boots.
- Any spillages must be cleaned up to avoid slippery floors.
- There must be no dangerous protrusions from the wall, e.g. handles, brackets (wherever possible these must be flush fitting).
- If spectators are allowed in the sports hall to watch they must be kept away from the playing area and be constantly aware of the action taking place.

## Activity

Arrange to meet with a member of the sport staff at your college/school. If possible try to learn how to assemble a trampoline.

Identify the health and safety considerations concerned with assembling and putting away such apparatus.

## Activity

The Fire Acts 1971 were mentioned earlier. Using the text books available in your school/college library find out what the main points of the acts are. Discuss how they have been implemented in relation to your school/college.

# Security considerations

When we are considering the security of an event this will cover a variety of aspects:

- **Security** of people and their possessions. At a concert customers need somewhere safe to leave their coats.
- **Famous people**, e.g. pop stars, will require extra personal security to protect them from over eager fans.
- **Cash control** in an hotel – Rigorous cash control measures need to be in operation, for example at the end of each shift the amount of money in the tills must balance with the recorded amount of money. This will help to prevent theft by staff. When cash is being transferred around the building the management must ensure that no member of staff does this on their own. This is for their own personal safety.
- **Equipment** – when equipment is not in use in a leisure centre (for example, mats or cleaning materials) it must be stored in a secure lockable area.
- **Information** – information relating to the details of an event or its customers may be vital to its success. For example, at a prestigious golf tournament competitors may not wish to have their personal details openly available. This might include the customer's address or telephone number.

- **External security** – if we consider the external security of an event venue this may include car park floodlighting, security guides, CCTV cameras and adequate fencing.

## Activity

Choose a venue in your locality where events are staged.

Under the following headings explain how security is maintained at the venue:

1. Security of people.
2. Security of cash.
3. Security of equipment.
4. Security of information.
5. External security.

> Agree with the team contingency actions in case of emergencies and anticipated disruptions

In the event of an emergency most venues have a predetermined plan to cope with eventualities such as fires and bomb scares.

Staff will need to be aware of these procedures and must know how to act in an emergency and how to handle the customers.

Other likely disruptions to an event are poor weather conditions, e.g. rain, fog, frost or snow. Sometimes it is difficult to inform people that for example a football match, which is subject to weather conditions, has been postponed. Spectators could be informed by a variety of methods, e.g. TV, local/national radio, notices at the ground or word of mouth.

In the case of the 1996 Liverpool versus Everton derby match at Anfield, which was postponed one hour before kick off due to heavy rain, many spectators were told of the cancellation via local and national radio.

## Activity

Find the names of the safety officers at your school/college. Where can they be found in times of emergency?

Use this information to create a series of safety posters which can be displayed in the corridors of your school or college.

**Key skills satisfied:** *Communication* **C2.2**

> Agree and allocate roles for team members

Within a team there must be an acknowledged structure with well defined roles and responsibilities.

# Team structures

A team member's role will indicate the job which they have to carry out and for which they are responsible. In order for the event to run smoothly there must be effective channels of communication. The team members must talk to each other on a regular basis and keep each other and their team leader informed.

# Lines of authority

An organisational chart (see Fig. 4.13) can be used to show the lines of authority and the channels of communication. This will show team members who their direct line manager is and who their fellow team members are. Each team member will need to interrelate with other team members so that everyone is aware of the plan and each team member will need to report back to the team manager who will have total overall control.

# Channels of communication

We have highlighted some positions most relevant to the organisation of a wedding at the Four Seasons Hotel and shown the lines of authority.

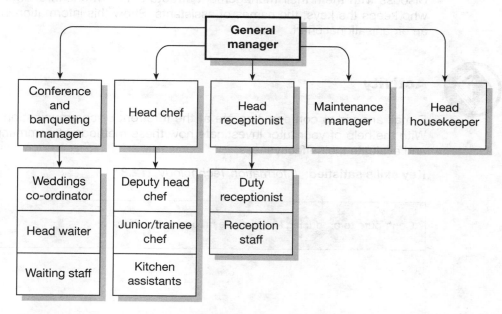

**Fig. 4.13** *Channels of communication at the Four Seasons Hotel*

# Reporting structures

In the case of a large organisation, weekly or monthly calendars of events will be produced. The schedule of events should be reported to all staff:

- The date of the event.
- Start and finish times.
- Nature of the event.
- Names and addresses of contacts.
- Staff members and their roles.
- Specialist equipment required.

The team will need to meet on a regular basis to discuss progress of the plan for the event. It may not always be necessary for the whole team to meet. Members may also communicate using a variety of other methods including:

- Telephone.
- Fax.
- E-mail.
- Word of mouth.
- Memos.
- Minutes of meetings.
- Video conferencing.

## Activity

Try to arrange an appointment with the leaders of a youth club in your local area. Discuss with them their management structure, i.e. who is in charge at the club, who keeps the keys, the names of assistants. Show this information in the form of an organisational chart.

## Activity

E-mail and video conferencing are at the forefront of communication technology. With the help of your tutor investigate how these methods of communication work and evaluate their effectiveness.

**Key skills satisfied:** *Information Technology* **IT2.3**

Contribute to producing a realistic team plan with others

# Assignment

'Children In Need charity activity'

**Key skills satisfied:** *Communication* **C2.1a, C2.1b, C2.2, C2.3**
*Information Technology* **IT2.1, IT2.2, IT2.3**

### Situation

Your tutor/teacher has asked you to plan an event to coincide with the BBC Children In Need Appeal. Your main objective will be to plan an activity which will raise money for children's charities.

### Tasks

To complete this assignment you will need to produce a brief report describing the process you used to decide and plan the event.

You may plan your activity around the following headings:

- Team members.
- Team leader.
- Title of event.
- Objectives of event.
- Resources required.
- Resources available.
- Are there any resources you need to hire/borrow?
- Allocation of team members to tasks.
- Possible constraints.
- What might go wrong.
- Contingency plans.

Your team should arrange a meeting to discuss and agree the above points which could be used as an agenda, similar to the one illustrated in Fig. 4.14.

One of the team members could be allocated the role of recording the details of the discussions and taking minutes (a record) of what has been discussed and agreed by the team members. The minutes of the meeting could be word processed and circulated to all team members and filed as evidence in your portfolio.

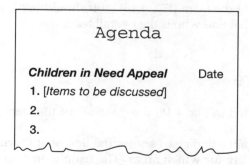

Agenda

***Children in Need Appeal***     Date
1. [*Items to be discussed*]
2.
3.

**Fig. 4.14** *Sample agenda for team planning meeting*

# Undertake a role in a team event

In this section you will be carrying out the plan which you set up with your team in the previous element. As part of the team plan you will have been allocated a role which carries with it duties and responsibilities.

Whilst carrying out your role you will understand how important planning and teamwork is in ensuring the smooth running of the event.

It is important that you keep a record or log of how you carried out your role. You should also make a note of any changes which were made to the plan and any disruptions which occurred.

Contribute to the team event according to the agreed role

Within your personal log you will need to list the title of your event and the agreed objectives of the team (Fig. 4.15). You should make it clear in the log who is responsible for what and who is the overall team leader.

## Team structure

As illustrated in Fig. 4.16, the structure of the team could be shown as an organisation chart.

The organisation chart shows the line of authority within the team and who has responsibility for which areas. The team members will report to their team leader matters such as:

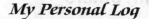

## My Personal Log

| | |
|---|---|
| **Name:** | Ross Watts |
| **Team members:** | RW, CJD, SP, NW, PHD, SMcQ, IL, CL |
| **Team Leader:** | IL |
| **Title of event:** | Children in Need – The Extortion Racket |
| **Description of event:** | To demand an excessive parking fee from college staff using the car park for the day. Team to wear fancy dress. |
| **Date of event:** | 25th November |
| **Objectives:** | To raise money for children's charities, in a light hearted way.<br>To carry out the event safely.<br>To work effectively as a team.<br>To raise awareness of the charities.<br>To handle money safely. |

**Fig. 4.15** *The objectives of the team event*

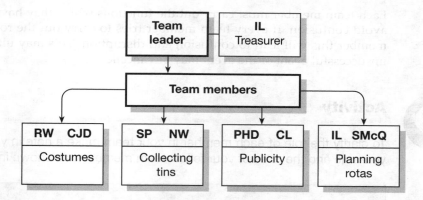

**Fig. 4.16** *Roles and responsibilities of team members*

- Problems with obtaining materials.
- Team absences.
- Conflict within the team.

The team leader will have the responsibility of trying to resolve any of these problems, to keep the team informed of any changes to the agreed schedule and to encourage the team to work together towards their common objective, which is to raise money for the BBC Children In Need appeal. A contingency plan will have to be prepared so that if certain team members are unavailable either during the planning process or on the actual day of the event, other team members will be able to take over their roles and responsibilities.

## Interrelationship with others

The team members must interrelate with each other if the planned event is to be run successfully. This will involve:

- Holding regular team meetings.
- Responding to instructions given by the team leader.
- Keeping each other informed of any changes.
- Keeping each other informed of any potential disruptions.

## Functions of team members

The organisational chart shows the agreed functions or responsibilities of each of the team members. The key functions include:

- Promotion and publicity.
- Equipment and resources.
- Finance.

Each team member must carry out the functions which they have been allocated to avoid confusion. If every team member tries to carry out the role of another team member this will lead to confusion and disruption. This may ultimately lead to an unsuccessful event or the event may be cancelled.

### Activity

To clarify the role of each member in your team make a note in your personal log of your role and the roles of your fellow team members, as shown in Fig. 4.17.

> Use available resources effectively

# Resources

In carrying out your role in the team event you will have to carefully consider what resources you have available and how you can use them effectively. The resources which you will need to consider will include some of the following:

---

### *My Personal Log*

**My role:** To arrange fancy dress costumes for my team who will dress as Snow White and the Seven Dwarfs plus the Wicked Witch.

---

***Fig. 4.17*** *Your role in the team event*

- Finance.
- Time.
- People and their skills.
- Facility and equipment.
- Information.

## Activity

Can you identify any other resources which may be required when running an event?

# Finance

Any organisation which runs events will be allocated a budget with which to purchase all the necessary materials, equipment and staff required to stage the event. The person who is in charge of handling the budget and collecting in any money which is made from the event is known as the treasurer.

Whether the event makes a financial surplus may depend upon the objectives of the event. Whatever the event is, however, the organising team will need to ensure that the cost of staging the event does not exceed the expected income from customers.

The main cost of running the students' Children In Need event will be in providing the costumes for the team to wear.

# Time

When planning an event sufficient time must be allowed in order to ensure that all the necessary resources, such as equipment and materials, will be available at the right time and that the targeted customers are given adequate notice of the forthcoming event.

# People

A team must look at the skills of its existing members and analyse whether it has the skills necessary to run the chosen event. Sometimes it is necessary to bring in people with specialist skills, e.g. costume design or promotional expertise, to help ensure the success of the event.

The team must also check whether the people it needs to run the event are available on the day for which the event is planned to take place.

# Materials and equipment

Sometimes it is necessary to hire equipment specially for an event or it may be appropriate to make or build the equipment using the skills of the team. If the organising team does not have the necessary equipment and materials these may need to be hired. The treasurer must then check that there is enough money available in the budget to pay for them. This also applies if the team needs to buy materials to make their own equipment.

Included here will need to be the cost of printing any publicity materials which are required to promote the event.

## Information

The team will need information to help plan its event. For example:

- Are there other similar events happening at the same time?
- Are there any likely disruptions to the event?

Team members will need to keep each other informed about the progress of the event plan and will also need to inform people external to the team. External people will include:

- The general public – who will be encouraged through the publicity material to become customers of the event.
- The emergency services – in case of accidents.

To contribute to the success of the students' Children In Need event Ross will need to plan what resources he needs to carry out his role effectively (see Fig. 4.18).

## Activity

In your log make a note of the resources which you will need to help you carry out your role in the team.

---

### *My Personal Log*

**Resources** – What I need to do:

1. Can we hire the fancy dress costumes from the local fancy dress hire company? (*Materials*)
   Find out how much it will cost
   Will my team members pay for their own costumes? (*Finance*)

2. Phone the local amateur dramatic society to see if they can lend us the costumes – this will save a lot of money. (*Finance*)

3. Ask if any of the team members can make the costumes. (*Staff skills*)

4. Make a decision about the costumes by 15th October – this will then give us enough time to either hire the costumes or to buy the material to make them. (*Time*)

5. Discuss the costume situation with the team at the next meeting – 3rd October. (*Information*)

---

***Fig. 4.18*** *Resources required for the team event*

Consider each of the following resources:

1. Time.

2. Finance.

3. People skills and availability.

4. Equipment and materials.

5. Information.

**Key skills satisfied:** *Communication* **C2.2**

---

Contribute to the team event with due regard to health, safety and security

---

Every organisation has a responsibility towards its employees and its customers to provide a facility which is safe and secure. In the case of event management the organisers must ensure that the activities of the event and the venue in which it takes place do not endanger the safety of the participants or spectators.

# Health and safety

When planning an event the team must try to identify possible hazards and consider what action might be taken to prevent accidents occurring.

The team must consider the following points regarding health and safety:

- The safety of the team whilst preparing for the event.
- The safety of the team and customers during the event.
- The safety of the team whilst clearing up after the event.

Event organisers must be aware of their responsibilities as laid down in the Health and Safety at Work, etc. Act, which is discussed in greater detail on page 277. Ensuring a safe environment is the responsibility of all members of the event team but often one team member is assigned with special responsibility.

In his Personal Log (see Fig. 4.19) Ross has made a note of the potential health and safety hazards of the Children In Need event which his team is planning.

# Security

## Security of the facility

The facilities in which events take place vary tremendously in size from large arenas such as the Nynex Arena in Manchester and Wembley Arena in London to small village halls or even fields. The security of the facility is very important in order to:

## My Personal Log

**Health and safety**

20th October – We held a meeting to discuss any potential hazards of our event.

We shall be stopping cars as they enter the car park to collect money. This will create a hazard to us and to others. We have decided to inform all members of staff about the event so that they will know what to expect.

CL is going to contact the local police station and ask for advice.

Although this is a fun type of event we realise that we have got to act quite sensibly otherwise there might be a nasty accident.

***Fig. 4.19*** *Potential health and safety hazards*

- Protect customers' personal safety.
- Safeguard customer possessions such as cars, coats and bags.
- Provide access for emergency services.
- Protect any materials and equipment which are being used in the event.
- Protect the customers from unwelcome, rowdy visitors.
- Protect event participants from over eager fans.
- Protect the security of cash.
- Safeguard the confidentiality of information.

The venue for the students' Children In Need event is the college car park. Any equipment which is used must therefore be kept secure within the college. The tutors who are overseeing the event must be aware that other students may try to join in the event and should therefore be vigilant to ensure that order is maintained. The college car park may also have a closed circuit TV surveillance system monitoring the car park.

The students must also consider how the money which is collected by the student team is kept secure (Fig. 4.20).

## Security of information

Customer details are the private property of organisations and must be kept confidential. This is to ensure the privacy of the customer. Furthermore, customer information is a valuable marketing tool which might be useful to other competing organisations.

Event organisers must ensure the confidentiality of customers who book with them.

Some aspects of the event may also need to be kept secure. For example at pop concerts the whereabouts of the group's hotel is often kept secret to prevent fans waiting outside and mobbing the stars.

## My Personal Log

**Security**

We need to make sure that our costumes are kept safely in the college. We can ask our tutor to lock them in the staff room overnight together with the collecting tins.

Ian is going to find out what we should do with the money after we have collected it.

Our tutor has suggested that we arrange to put the money in the college safe and that we should ask for a receipt.

**Fig. 4.20** *Security of resources and people*

## Activity

Make notes in your log about how you are going to maintain the health and safety of your team and your customers before, during and after the event.

Are there any security measures which you need to take?

Co-operate effectively with others during the team event

One of the aims of any team planning process will be that during the actual event each team member is well informed and knows exactly what his/her role is. For the event to run smoothly the team members must co-ordinate and co-operate with each other in order to achieve the common objective, a successful event. The team members must be flexible, assist each other and be professional in their approach. Co-operation during the actual event should be the end result of a series of planning meetings and discussions and will only occur where channels of communication are clear and effective.

The team leader will have the extra responsibility of encouraging the team members to co-operate with each other and may be required to intervene if problems develop between team members.

## Activity

Can you identify where there might be problems with co-operation within your team?

How well did you co-operate with your team mates during the event?

**Key skills satisfied:** *Communication* C2.1

Explain any changes to the agreed role

An effective team is one which reacts quickly to any changes to the schedule. The roles of team members are always liable to change

For example, if one of the team members is ill the others will have to take on that person's role as well as their own. A team which is flexible in its approach and well informed will be able to react quickly and take on the additional responsibilities which occur. The team leader will be responsible for implementing these changes.

Furthermore, the event may not go as planned. If it is the first time that this type of event has been run then situations may arise which were not expected. For example, if one of the team members is injured during the event one of the other members may then have to take on that person's responsibility.

In Fig. 4.21, Ross explains in his log how his role changed during the Children In Need event.

## Activity

When you are holding a planning meeting with your team make sure that you discuss what actions you might take if one of the team members is unable to attend on the day of the event and how this might affect the role of each team member. Make a record of the phone numbers of each member of the team so that you can contact each other quickly in case of an emergency.

Make a list of other possible reasons why your role in the team might need to alter.

The more prepared you are for possible changes to your role the more efficiently the event will run.

> React promptly to any disruptions to the event and inform others of any changes which might affect them

---

### My Personal Log

**Did my role change in any way?**

The day before the event was due to take place our Team Leader, Ian, was taken into hospital. He had broken his foot whilst playing football.

Our team got together to discuss who would take over his role. Our discussion was recorded and kept as evidence for our portfolios.

Ian was going to be responsible for collecting all the money together and making sure it was paid into the college safe after the event. The team decided that I should deal with the money as we had discussed this at a previous meeting.

This didn't really affect my role during the actual event. I was still able to dress up as Snow White and collect money at the car park gates. It did mean that I had extra work to do after the event though.

---

**Fig. 4.21** *Reacting to changes*

# Disruptions

A well-prepared team should be able to cope with most disruptions to their schedule and should consider at their team meetings what potential disruptions might occur. The type of possible disruption may depend upon the nature of the event.

## Anticipated disruptions

It may be possible to anticipate adverse weather conditions such as fog and snow by keeping an eye on the weather forecast. It should be possible to predict a few days in advance if the weather is going to cause a disruption to an event.

The weather conditions may affect the event in different ways:

- **Outdoor events** – e.g. sports matches or village fetes are difficult to hold if it is snowing.
- **Indoor events** – e.g. exhibitions, concerts, galas, may be affected if the weather makes travelling conditions difficult.

The event may also be disrupted if it appears that there will be fewer than expected participants or spectators at the event. This can be determined accurately if the event is ticket only. If the financial success of the event is dependent upon ticket sales it may be necessary to cancel the event should ticket sales be poor and below expectations.

## Emergencies

Events are sometimes dramatically cancelled at the last minute due to emergency situations such as accidents and fires which cannot of course be predicted. An event team will have considered actions to be taken in the case of emergencies and will also have informed the emergency services such as the police, ambulance service and fire brigade about the event.

## Deviations from the team plan

An event team may find it necessary to deviate from its original plan due to a variety of circumstances. These might include:

- **Changes in roles of team members** perhaps due to sickness.
- **Equipment and materials:** the team might discover at the last minute that the equipment they require is no longer available.
- **Anticipated disruptions** such as poor weather conditions may mean that the event has to be held on an alternative date.
- **Emergency situations** such as accidents may make it impossible to hold the event in any circumstances.

# Informing others of any changes

If it is necessary to make any changes to the plan it is vital that those participating in the event, either as organisers or spectators, are informed as promptly as possible.

- **Informing the team** – In the case of the event team, adequate notice will allow the team time to reorganise their roles and possibly take on extra responsibilities to ensure the smooth running of the event. This can be made easier by each member of the team having a list of contact phone numbers and addresses.
- **Informing the customer** – In the case of the customers or spectators of the event, promptly informing them of any changes to the proposed schedule will help to prevent possible angry scenes and will help to maintain customer satisfaction. An event management company will seriously damage its reputation and public image if it fails to keep its customers informed of any changes which affect them.

Customers may be informed of changes through a variety of media:

- Local radio stations.
- Newspapers.
- Telephone networks.
- Customer databases, i.e. names and addresses.

In the example of the students' Children In Need event the team have had to deviate from their plan slightly. Ross has made a note of the anticipated disruption in his personal log (Fig. 4.22).

> Keep a log of own contribution to the event

Each of the students who were involved in the Children In Need event kept their own personal record of their contribution to the planning and running of the event, similar to the extracts from Ross's log.

It is important to keep a record such as this because it will enable you to look back at the event and evaluate how you personally performed as a member of your team. It will also help you to identify what else you could have done to have improved your team's performance.

You could use a diary as a log book and make an entry each day recording the details of the meetings which were held and actions which were taken. The entries which you have made in your diary will then help you to write the report which is requested in the assignment for Element 4.2.

---

### *My Personal Log*

**Disruption/changes to our event**

We had originally planned to hold our event all day. However the College Principal Jack Spencer has said that he would prefer the activity to only take place between 8.30 and 9.30 am. He has also said that any donations must be purely voluntary and that we mustn't get over enthusiastic when asking staff for money.

This means that we might collect less money than we had hoped – but we will be collecting at the busiest time of day anyway.

---

**Fig. 4.22** *Anticipated changes to the planned event*

Ask your tutor to read through your log with you. Your tutor may wish to discuss your contribution to the running of the event with you and will provide you with valuable feedback on your performance.

## Assignment

**'Personal log'**

**Key skills satisfied:** *Communication* **C2.1a, C2.2, C2.3**
*Information Technology* **IT2.1, IT2.2, IT2.3**

*Tasks*

It is important that you keep a detailed log of your contribution to the running of your team's event. Using the information contained within your log, write a brief report covering the following headings:

1. Your role within the team.
2. Your responsibilities.
3. A record of the resources which were used to carry out the event.
4. How you helped to maintain the health, safety and security of your team and your customers.
5. Explain how you worked and co-operated with your fellow team members.
6. Did your role change in any way?
7. Did you have to deal with any disruptions to the event?
8. How you helped inform your team and your customers of any changes to the event.

Your report should be word processed.

A copy of your report and your personal log must be filed as evidence in your portfolio.

# Evaluate the team event

Now that you have carried out your event it is important to look back and ask your-self a few questions:

- How did it go?
- Was the event successful?
- Was the event an overall success?
- Which areas were particularly successful?
- Did we achieve our objectives?
- How could the event have been improved?

These questions can form the basis of an evaluation exercise. You will need to draw up a list of performance criteria and judge how well you met these indicators. By analysing the team's performance and assessing your role in contributing to the success of your event you should be able to draw up a list of recommendations for improvement.

In other words you will have learned through experience what works and what doesn't with regard to organising and running an event. The lessons you have learned can then be used to improve your performance in planning events in the future.

Agree with the team the criteria for evaluating the event

After the event has taken place your team should arrange a meeting at which you will discuss how the event went and how well you think your team performed.

You will need to be constructive in analysing your performance. Don't just focus on the things that went wrong, also consider what went well during the event.

The team should first of all draw up a list of criteria or points against which to analyse its performance. The evaluation criteria will provide a focus for the team discussion and could be used to form an agenda for the meeting.

The criteria may be based on achieving figures, e.g. number of tickets sold, the number of participants. This type of criteria is easy to measure because it is factual.

The performance of the event may also be judged on whether the spectators or customers enjoyed the event. It is very difficult to say whether the customers have enjoyed the event. Enjoyment cannot be measured statistically. The team would need to use their own perceptions of whether the event was enjoyable and would probably also rely on comments and feedback from their tutor and customers in order to make this judgement.

The team will need to refer back to their original plan and analyse what it was they set out to achieve through the process of planning and running the event and to what extent they achieved these objectives.

Typical criteria which the team will need to evaluate are:

- Were the objectives met?
- Were the correct resources identified and found to be appropriate?
- Was the health, safety and security of the team and the event's customers maintained?
- How well did the team co-operate?
- Did the team fulfil their respective roles?
- How well did the team handle any disruptions to their schedule?

# Were the objectives of the event met?

One of the main objectives of the event may have been to raise a certain amount of money. This is a measurable objective. The team organising the Children In Need event set themselves a target of raising £500 for children's charities. The team actually raised £840.36. The students of Mid Shire College therefore exceeded their target, as reported in the Mid Shire Chronicle (Fig. 4.23).

One of the main objectives of the students' event has therefore been successfully achieved, i.e. to raise over £500 for children's charities.

If the objectives which your team has set itself are very specific, such as the one above, they are then very easy to measure.

Some objectives are very hard to measure though. If for example one of your objectives was to entertain people or to provide an enjoyable experience, how would you measure this?

**Mid Shire Chronicle**

Students At Mid Shire College raise over £800 for Children In Need.

Leisure and Tourism students at Mid Shire College have raised over £800 for the BBC Children In Need fund in a fun fund-raising event. Dressed as Snow White and her seven dwarfs, and not forgetting the wicked witch, the comic characters planned and carried out their own extortion racket...

**Fig. 4.23** *Press release about students' event*

## Activity

Working with your team members design a questionnaire to find out whether your customers enjoyed the event you ran.

Consider carefully the questions you would ask to find out this information.

For example, your event may be to plan an end of term trip to Alton Towers. One of the main objectives of such an event would be for the students to enjoy themselves. What criteria would you use to determine whether the students had enjoyed themselves?

# Were the correct resources identified?

The team must ask itself whether the resources which they identified and used were appropriate for the event. They may have found that they did not use all of the equipment they had provided, or at the last minute the team may have had to purchase or hire additional equipment and materials. The team must also discuss whether the skills of the team members were used in the best way.

# Was health, safety and security maintained?

If there were any accidents or mishaps during the event involving either the team or its customers, these should be discussed and ideas suggested as to how dangerous situations can be avoided in the future.

Our Children In Need team should also ask itself whether the money collected was safely transported to the college finance office and kept secure in the safe.

# How well did the team co-operate?

You will need to consider how well the team co-operated. Was the line of authority effective. Were there clear channels of communication so that all team members were kept informed? Did the customers know what was happening and when? Was there any conflict between team members? If so, how do you think this could be avoided in future events?

# Did the team carry out their respective roles?

The team should discuss how appropriate were the roles which were created within the team and whether each team member carried out their allocated responsibilities. Was the team flexible enough to cope with and compensate for team members who were unable to attend on the day of the event or who were reluctant to pull their weight during the event.

How well did the team cope with disruptions to their schedule?

How were any disruptions to the event dealt with? Were disruptions handled smoothly so as not to spoil the event for others? Were the disruptions anticipated or were they emergencies? If the disruptions were anticipated what short-term decisions were made to ensure that the event ran smoothly? If there was an emergency situation, such as a fire or an accident, had the emergency services been adequately informed that the event was taking place?

## Activity

Arrange a meeting of your student team. Make a list of the criteria which you will use to evaluate your event.

> Devise with the team an evaluation form and complete it individually during evaluation

When your team has decided which criteria it will use to evaluate the success of your event, it is useful to list them in a form.

The evaluation form can then be used as the basis of a team meeting. The team should discuss each of the criteria in turn, making a note of comments made on the form.

Each team member should have a copy of the evaluation form on which they should indicate whether they feel the criteria have been achieved and also including any comments and opinions.

Ross Watts and his team have put together a form (Fig. 4.24) on which they will evaluate their team's performance in planning and running the Children In Need event.

**Evaluation form**

Title of event: **The Extortion Racket**  Date of event: **25th November**
Student name: **Ross Watts**  Team members: **RW, SP, IL, CL, PHD, NW, CJD, SMcQ**

| Evaluation criteria | Comments | Yes | No | Partly |
|---|---|---|---|---|
| **Team performance** | | | | |
| Were the objectives met? | Yes, we raised £840.36, our target was £500. | ✓ | | |
| Were adequate resources available? | I borrowed the costumes from the local drama group – this saved us a lot of money. | ✓ | | |
| Were the health and safety guidelines followed? | Yes, resulting in no recorded incidents. There were no accidents on the day. | ✓ | | |
| Were the security measures successful? | One of the collecting cans disappeared. We need to be more careful about safeguarding the money. | | ✓ | |
| Did all the team members co-operate? | Some of the team were late arriving on the day – this led to an argument. We sorted it out in the end though and everyone joined in. | | | ✓ |
| Did the team handle disruptions well? | It poured with rain but the event still went ahead. Chris managed to borrow some umbrellas which helped to keep us dry. | ✓ | | |
| Did each team member carry out their role? | Ian was taken to hospital so I had to carry out his role as well. | | | ✓ |
| **Individual performance** | | | | |
| Did I carry out my agreed role? | Yes, I was pleased with the way I carried out my duties. | ✓ | | |
| Did I use the resources well? | All the equipment and materials were used as intended. | ✓ | | |
| Did I maintain health, safety and security? | I lost one of the collecting cans. | | ✓ | |
| Did I handle disruptions well? | I asked Chris to find some umbrellas. | ✓ | | |
| **Data used to evaluate performance** | | | | |
| Money raised against target. | Our target was £500, we raised £840.36. | | | |
| Feedback from my tutor. | See separate feedback forms | | | |
| Feedback from my team mates. | | | | |
| **Recommendations for improvements** | | | | |
| What would I do differently next time | I would make sure that all the team members knew what time the event was starting at and ask them to arrive half an hour earlier. I would also ask one of the tutors to help me look after the collecting tins. | | | |

**Fig. 4.24** *Team evaluation form*

## Activity

When you have decided on the criteria you will be using to evaluate your team's performance and your own individual performance, draw up an evaluation form similar to the one used by Ross Watts and his team.

One member of the team could word process the evaluation form and distribute it to other team members.

The team could complete their individual evaluation forms at a team meeting using the forms to make a record of any comments made.

> Gather evaluation feedback from the appropriate sources and record it on the form

Another way of measuring the success of your event campaign is to gather feedback or opinions as to how the event went. Feedback can be obtained from a variety of sources:

- The customer (customer opinion).
- Fellow team members (peer assessment).
- Your own opinions (self-assessment).
- Your supervisor (assessor feedback).
- Evaluation data.

# Feedback

## Self-assessment

It may be hard for you to judge yourself how the event went as you will tend to focus on your own performance and you will probably be highly critical of yourself, or alternatively you may think you performed better than you did. It is difficult therefore to be objective and to form an accurate opinion of your own performance.

## Customer opinion

Customer opinion will probably have the most powerful influence on how you plan future events. If the customer is not happy he will not return and a potential sale might be lost. It is important therefore to gather customer opinion and to use this constructively to identify the strengths and weaknesses of your event.

Customer opinion may be gathered by:

- Asking the customer to fill in a customer comments form after the event.
- Gauging the reactions of customers during the event – did they appear to enjoy the event?
- Carry out a survey after the event to find out what the customers thought of it.

## Peer assessment

When you hold a meeting after the event, each team member will express opinions about how the event went and will also feed back information on the team's performance. Team members should try to be constructive in their criticism and should identify what was good about the event as well as what went wrong.

## Assessor

Your assessor or tutor should provide feedback on both your individual performance and the performance of your team. Your assessor should be able to provide you with an objective view and balanced impression of your own performance.

For your college/school event your assessor should provide both team and individual performance feedback and should also observe and comment on how the team self-assesses its performance.

Ask your tutor to provide you with written feedback which you can store as evidence in your portfolio.

## Activity

Arrange an appointment with your tutor so that you can receive individual feedback. Make a note of the feedback on the evaluation form which your team has devised.

Ask the tutor to attend your team's evaluation meeting so that feedback can be provided on the performance of the team. Make a note of the team's feedback on the evaluation form.

> Exchange evaluation feedback with the team constructively and positively

It is very important that when feedback is provided either by your assessor or by your own team members (peers) that this is done constructively so as to:

- Enhance the confidence of team members and individuals to encourage them to want to organise events in the future.
- Ensure that the lessons learned in planning and carrying out the event are used to improve the performance of future events.

When giving feedback the assessor should initially provide positive feedback by saying what the strengths of the team's plan were, followed by feedback on any areas where there is room for improvement. In summarising the assessor should try to conclude with positive comments so as not to undermine the confidence of the students.

Feedback must be fair but realistic so that the person receiving feedback can identify real possibilities for improving their performance and build on instances of good practice.

The team should be given the opportunity to respond to the feedback, which should be discussed and can be used to identify a number of alternative methods of organising future events.

It is important to learn from mistakes which have been made and to use this experience constructively towards improving future performance.

## Activity

At the evaluation meeting make a note of the comments which are made. Record the feedback on the evaluation form. From this make a list of ideas for future improvements.

> Summarise the overall findings of the team's evaluation

Following the feedback discussions the team should make a list of the strengths and weaknesses of their plan and the way in which they carried out the event.

The information which has been recorded in the evaluation form can be used to write a brief summary of the team's performance.

The summary should be:

- Brief.
- Concise.
- Focused on the positive aspects of the team's performance.

The whole team will need to discuss how the summary is written to make sure that all team members agree and that the report is truly representative of the opinions of the full team.

> Make and record suggestions for improvements to the way in which similar events are staged in future

The end product of the evaluation process which your team has been through is to identify examples of good practice from the planning process and actual running of the event and to balance this against some of the weaknesses which became apparent.

As a result it should be possible to put together a list of recommendations as to how future events might be handled and consequently improved.

## Activity

At a team evaluation meeting discuss what improvements might be made to future events. Base your recommendations around the following headings:

1. Your own individual performance.
2. The team's performance.
3. The use of resources.
4. Maintaining health, safety and security.
5. Improvements in team co-operation.
6. How to handle disruptions.

**Key skills satisfied:** *Communication* **C2.1, C2.2, C2.3**
*Information Technology* **IT2.1, IT2.2, IT2.3**

# Recommendations

Ross Watts made a note on his evaluation form of the recommendations which his team agreed upon:

---

### *My Personal Log*

**Recommendations for improvements**

**My personal performance**
I should have started planning my role earlier – I left it a bit late to contact the drama group. It was lucky that they had suitable costumes available. Maybe I could have asked more people to donate money.

**Team performance**
Meet on a more regular basis to discuss progress. Take more notes at the team meetings so we know what all team members are responsible for. Learn more about each others roles in case we have to take over another role (like I had to).

**Use of resources**
I think we used our resources well – can't recommend any improvements here.

**Maintaining health, safety and security**
Make sure that no money or valuables are left unattended (collection tin was stolen). Ensure that we have first aid boxes with us and that they are full. Ask if any member of staff at the college has a first aid certificate and whether they would help us if there was an accident.

**Improving team co-operation**
More meetings at the planning stage might have prevented some of the arguments which our team had.

**Handling disruptions**
The weather is usually bad in November. Plan an indoor event next time.

---

***Fig. 4.25*** *Recommendations for improving the team's performance*

# Assignment

'Evaluation meeting'

**Key skills satisfied:** *Communication* **C2.1a, C2.2, C2.3**
*Information Technology* **IT2.1, IT2.2, IT2.3**

*Tasks*

Now that you and your team have run an event you should organise a meeting at which you will evaluate how successful the event was and what recommendations can be made for future improvements.

1. As a group decide on the criteria which you will use to measure the success of your event.
2. Design a form which includes the relevant evaluation criteria. It would be useful to word process this form.
3. One of the criteria which you will use to judge success and to make suggestions for future improvements is feedback, so make sure that you include section in the form for:
   – self-assessment
   – group feedback
   – assessor feedback
4. One member of your team should make a record of what is said at the meeting. This will be recorded as 'minutes of the meeting'. The minutes should be word processed and a copy circulated to all team members. The minutes can then be stored as evidence in your portfolio.
5. The evaluation form should also be completed at the meeting and stored in your portfolio when complete.
6. At the end of the meeting your team must draw up a list of suggested improvements which could be incorporated into any future events which you run. This list should also be word processed and added to the minutes of the meeting.

# Revision questions

1. What is meant by an objective?

2. List the main parts of the planning process.

3. Describe what is meant by human resources.

4. Why is it important to consider health and safety?

5. List three Acts of Parliament which contribute to maintaining health, safety and hygiene at an event.

# Index